Postwar Cycles in
Manufacturers' Inventories

NATIONAL BUREAU OF ECONOMIC RESEARCH
Studies in Business Cycles

Postwar Cycles
in
Manufacturers'
Inventories

By Thomas M. Stanback, Jr.

NATIONAL BUREAU OF ECONOMIC RESEARCH
1962

LIBRARY OF CONGRESS CATALOG
CARD NUMBER 62-12891

EXTRACT

From materials prepared for the Joint Economic
Committee, Congress of the United States, Eighty-
seventh Congress, First Session, Pursuant to Sec.
5 (a), Part 1, "Postwar Fluctuations in Business
Inventories."

NOT PRINTED AT GOVERNMENT EXPENSE

RELATION OF THE DIRECTORS
TO THE WORK AND PUBLICATIONS
OF THE NATIONAL BUREAU OF ECONOMIC RESEARCH

1. The object of the National Bureau of Economic Research is to ascertain and to present to the public important economic facts and their interpretation in a scientific and impartial manner. The Board of Directors is charged with the responsibility of ensuring that the work of the National Bureau is carried on in strict conformity with this object.

2. To this end the Board of Directors shall appoint one or more Directors of Research.

3. The Director or Directors of Research shall submit to the members of the Board, or to its Executive Committee, for their formal adoption, all specific proposals concerning researches to be instituted.

4. No report shall be published until the Director or Directors of Research shall have submitted to the Board a summary drawing attention to the character of the data and their utilization in the report, the nature and treatment of the problems involved, the main conclusions, and such other information as in their opinion would serve to determine the suitability of the report for publication in accordance with the principles of the National Bureau.

5. A copy of any manuscript proposed for publication shall also be submitted to each member of the Board. For each manuscript to be so submitted a special committee shall be appointed by the President, or at his designation by the Executive Director, consisting of three Directors selected as nearly as may be one from each general division of the Board. The names of the special manuscript committee shall be stated to each Director when the summary and report described in paragraph (4) are sent to him. It shall be the duty of each member of the committee to read the manuscript. If each member of the special committee signifies his approval within thirty days, the manuscript may be published. If each member of the special committee has not signified his approval within thirty days of the transmittal of the report and manuscript, the Director of Research shall then notify each member of the Board, requesting approval or disapproval of publication, and thirty additional days shall be granted for this purpose. The manuscript shall then not be published unless at least a majority of the entire Board and a two-thirds majority of those members of the Board who shall have voted on the proposal within the time fixed for the receipt of votes on the publication proposed shall have approved.

6. No manuscript may be published, though approved by each member of the special committee, until forty-five days have elapsed from the transmittal of the summary and report. The interval is allowed for the receipt of any memorandum of dissent or reservation, together with a brief statement of his reasons, that any member may wish to express; and such memorandum of dissent or reservation shall be published with the manuscript if he so desires. Publication does not, however, imply that each member of the Board has read the manuscript, or that either members of the Board in general, or of the special committee, have passed upon its validity in every detail.

7. A copy of this resolution shall, unless otherwise determined by the Board, be printed in each copy of every National Bureau book.

(Resolution adopted October 25, 1926,
as revised February 6, 1933, and February 24, 1941)

LETTER OF TRANSMITTAL

NATIONAL BUREAU OF ECONOMIC RESEARCH, INC.,
New York, N.Y., October 17, 1961.

Hon. WRIGHT PATMAN,
Chairman, Joint Economic Committee,
House Office Building,
Washington, D.C.

DEAR REPRESENTATIVE PATMAN: On behalf of the National Bureau of Economic Research I am happy to transmit to you, in response to your request of September 5, 1961, the report "Postwar Cycles in Manufacturers' Inventories," by Dr. Thomas M. Stanback, Jr.

Dr. Stanback's report is the culmination of several years of careful and systematic research, which he began as a research associate at the National Bureau in 1955–56 and continued since despite the pressure of teaching duties. He is presently associate professor of economics at New York University. Fortunately the completion of his work on the study earlier this year coincided with the plans of the Joint Economic Committee for a comprehensive study of the subject of inventories. We are therefore glad to make the report available to the committee. The report will also be published separately by the National Bureau as one of its studies in business cycles.

As the report itself indicates, it has had the benefit of a thorough review by members of the National Bureau's staff and board. The cooperation of the Office of Business Economics of the Department of Commerce was invaluable. Of great assistance, too, in the planning and conduct of the study, was the earlier work by Prof. Moses Abramovitz, issued by the National Bureau in 1950, under the title "Inventories and Business Cycles." Many of Abramovitz' findings, based on prewar information, are verified in Stanback's study, some are modified, and a number of new results are reported.

We hope that the report will be of assistance to the committee in its investigation of this important subject.

Very truly yours,

SOLOMON FABRICANT,
Director of Research.

ACKNOWLEDGMENTS

This study was begun in the academic year 1955–56, while the author was a research associate at the National Bureau of Economic Research, and was continued thereafter under Bureau sponsorship. At almost every stage the work benefited from the assistance, criticism, and encouragement of members of the Bureau staff. My obligations are many—more than I can fully acknowledge here.

My greatest debt is to Geoffrey H. Moore, who followed the study from the beginning, giving unstintingly of his time in reading and criticizing the various versions of the manuscript. Ruth Mack, Moses Abramovitz, and Victor Zarnowitz comprised the staff reading committee; R. A. Gordon, Maurice Lee, and George B. Roberts, the Board of Directors' review committee. I am grateful to all of these persons for their careful reading of the manuscript and for the many helpful suggestions which were offered. Thanks go also to Dorothy Suchman, who was my research assistant; to Johanna Stern, who was helpful in many ways in assembling the data; and to Irving Forman, who drew the charts. Joan Tron's high standard of editorial craftsmanship contributed immeasurably to the final product. Finally, I wish to express my gratitude to my wife for her patience and confidence over the extended period of preparation of this study.

THOMAS M. STANBACK, Jr.

CONTENTS

CONTENTS

CONTENTS

CONTENTS

CHARTS

1

Introduction and Summary

Changes in inventory investment are widely regarded as a major indicator of cyclical instability in the American economy, and have been closely followed in recent years by economists, businessmen, and the press. This study deals principally with the behavior of manufacturers' stocks—the principal component of nonfarm inventories—since the end of World War II. Available aggregates for all manufacturers, durable-goods manufacturers, and nondurable-goods manufacturers, as well as certain commodity series, are used. Attention is concentrated on the period 1947–56, although certain parts of the analysis have been extended to the end of 1958 in order to include the 1957–58 business cycle contraction. Comparisons are also made with prewar behavior when information is available.

A major objective has been to test the relevance for the postwar years of the principal findings and hypotheses of Moses Abramovitz as set forth for the interwar years in his "Inventories and Business Cycles, With Special Reference to Manufacturers' Inventories." [1] Since his earlier investigation has influenced the approach and organization of this study, it is well to comment here on Abramovitz' work. His most important contributions were the determination of typical patterns of timing and the relative importance of movements in manufacturers' inventories during the interwar business cycles, the development of an explanation for the patterns he found, and the conclusion that the overall movement in manufacturers' stocks should, for purposes of analysis, be regarded as a complex of somewhat dissimilar movements of a number of different types of stocks.

In spite of severe limitations necessitated by principal reliance on annual data, Abramovitz was able to estimate the timing of stocks and inventory investment at business cycle turns, and to establish the general magnitude of movements in expansions and contractions.

In studying the behavior of the various components, he analyzed stocks successively at each stage of fabrication (i.e., purchased materials, goods in process, finished goods), breaking down these classes still further in an attempt to establish the nature and significance of the patterns of movement. Essentially he tried to determine the size of each type of stock and the factors which influenced its fluctuations, examining such commodity series as were available in order to check his hypotheses and shed additional light on cyclical characteristics.

The organization of the present study is similar to Abramovitz'. Chapter 2 examines the importance of nonfarm and manufacturers' inventory investment in the postwar and prewar periods. Chapter 3 analyzes the behavior of total stocks held by all manufacturers, durable-goods and nondurable-goods manufacturers, and by individual industries. In chapters 4, 5, and 6 the behavior of stocks by stage of fabrication is treated in the sequence of purchased materials, finished

[1] New York, National Bureau of Economic Research, 1950.

goods, and goods in process.   Chapter 7 summarizes the timing characteristics and describes the behavior of manufacturers' inventories as a composite of these three major types of stocks.   Chapter 8 examines the manner in which inventory investment movements contribute to cyclical instability.   Finally, an appendix is provided containing notes on sources and methods of processing the data, as well as the principal time series used.

For the convenience of the reader the conclusions in chapters 2 through 8 are summarized below:

Changes in nonfarm inventory investment, as indicated in chapter 2, have contributed significantly to business cycle contractions.   Measured on the basis of annual data, they have accounted for at least 42 percent of the decline in national product in every business cycle contraction of the interwar and postwar periods except that of 1929–32.   With this exception, there is no evidence that the role of movements in nonfarm inventory investment during business cycle contractions has changed significantly since the prewar period.

Movements in nonfarm inventory investment have contributed to changes in national product to a lesser degree during expansions than during contractions—a tendency which has increased since World War II.   This is due to the greater length of postwar expansion phases, as well as to the earlier occurrence of the peaks in inventory investment.

Movements in manufacturers' inventory investment have played a somewhat larger role since the war, accounting for 83 percent of those in nonfarm inventory investment, compared with 56 percent in the prewar period.   Although turns in manufacturers' inventory investment have led business cycle turns since the war, investment movements have conformed closely to general business contractions, the sharpest declines occurring between cyclical peaks and troughs.

Chapter 3 shows that total manufacturers' stocks have lagged behind business cycle turns from 1 to 8 months, in contrast to Abramovitz' estimate of a 6-to-12-month prewar lag.   Manufacturers' inventory investment has moved in well-defined cyclical patterns and has demonstrated a high degree of conformity to business cycles.   Timing of the total inventory investment series relative to business cycles varied from roughly coincident to a lead of 14 months.

The durable-goods inventory and investment series have been cyclically more sensitive than those of nondurable goods, conforming more closely to business cycle movements and moving with greater amplitude.   The explanation appears to be that the production and sale of these goods are subject to greater amplitude of movement and that fluctuations in these industries tend to occur at about the same time.   In addition, of stocks held at each stage of fabrication, durables appear to be more responsive to cyclical influences.

Manufacturers' inventories are significantly smaller relative to sales than before World War II.   Moreover, composition has changed— from approximately 40 percent purchased materials, 20 percent goods in process, and 40 percent finished goods before the war—to an estimated 38, 29, and 33 percent in 1952–53.   The principal reason for this change is the increased importance of the durable-goods industries which carry larger goods-in-process stocks.

The purchased-materials stocks discussed in chapter 4 conform well to cyclical movements, turning earlier at sales and business cycle

peaks than at troughs. Turns tend to coincide with business cycle
peaks and to lag at troughs. On the other hand, investment leads
all turns. In these movements the durables series show a higher
conformity and greater amplitude.

Abramovitz' theory, although it goes far to explain the general
behavior of purchased-materials inventories and investment, does not
provide for the occurrence of certain observed timing in the inventory
and investment series. Moreover, it fails to consider the possible
role of unfilled order backlogs, availability of materials, and price
behavior of purchased goods in influencing inventory behavior. In
an effort to provide a fuller explanation, these influences are examined.
It is noted that the amplitude of purchased-materials investment
movement appears to be related to the size and direction of movement
of unfilled order backlogs and that the timing of investment tends to
agree with certain measures of availability of materials. Price changes
though significant do not appear to play a vital causal role.

Finally, inventory objectives and purchasing policy of firms vary
cyclically, moving in general agreement with changes in availability
of materials and realized investment.

Postwar finished-goods behavior (ch. 5) was studied by analyzing
two sets of inventory data. The first was composed of data for 25
commodities, representing the largest component of finished goods:
staple made-to-stock commodities. The second was composed of
Department of Commerce industry data. Among the commodity
series, finished stocks are found to move in a strongly inverted fashion
relative to sales or output, but with a well-developed tendency to
turn and come into phase as the duration of the activity phase increases. The Department of Commerce industry data reveal a consistent tendency for stocks to lag behind sales and reference turns, but
movements are rarely of the completely inverted sort observed in the
commodity series. It is concluded that the staple made-to-stock
inventories contribute a strong tendency toward inverted behavior,
but that other categories offset inverted tendencies to a significant
degree.

Study of inventory investment data for the 25 commodities reveals
that investment moves in an inverted fashion relative to rates of
change in sales, but that peaks (troughs) in inventory investment lead
or turn coincidentally with troughs (peaks) in rates of change in
activity. Since peaks and troughs in the latter tend to occur well
before the end of each business cycle phase, inverted movements in
finished-goods inventory investment may be expected to terminate
relatively early in the business cycle phase. Analysis of finished-goods
inventory investment in the Department of Commerce series shows
this to be the case. Total manufacturers' finished-goods investment
turns roughly coincidently with business cycle turns or moves in an
inverted fashion (i.e., lags) for only a few months in the early part of
a business cycle phase.

Problems of deflation render conclusions regarding goods-in-process
behavior less dependable than those for purchased materials and
finished goods, but certain characteristics may be noted (ch. 6). The
deflated inventory series conform to business cycles with virtually
coincident timing at four of the six reference cycle turns, and inventory investment leads all business cycle turns. Analysis of timing
sequence among the industry series indicates that, for both inventory

and investment, goods in process lead or turn coincidently with purchased materials and lead the finished-goods series.

Although these findings are generally consistent with Abramovitz' theory, irregularities in timing appear, particularly among the individual industry investment series, which cannot be explained by his analysis. Moreover, durable-goods investment appears to be influenced by levels of unfilled orders in a manner similar to purchased materials. Three factors seem to contribute to this behavior. (1) The composition of postwar goods in process is different from that observed by Abramovitz. Owing to the increased role of durables, there is a much larger proportion of these stocks held by industries engaging in discontinuous processes—roughly 50 percent compared with his estimate of 36 percent. (2) Goods-in-process stocks in discontinuous-process industries are likely to be held in substantial quantities between stages. These stocks may be expected to rise and fall in a manner similar to that of purchased materials. (3) Goods held within stages need not fluctuate in as close conformity to changes in output as Abramovitz maintained.

In chapter 7, analysis of amplitude of investment movements reveals that inventory change has contributed significantly to cyclical instability at each stage of fabrication, the three components combining to form a total manufacturing inventory complex which is highly sensitive to cyclical forces. A summary of timing measures indicates that purchased-materials and goods-in-process inventories and investment tend to have similar timing characteristics, leading turns in the comparable finished-goods series. But the last lags behind the other investment series by no more than 6 months at four of the six business cycle turns, and shows almost no countercyclical tendencies.

A brief comparison of Abramovitz' estimates of prewar timing with postwar findings is presented. Where timing differences are noted, possible reasons for the differences are discussed.

Chapter 8 attempts to answer two fundamental questions: How do changes in inventory investment contribute to the cumulative forces of business cycle expansion and contraction? Is it possible that movements in inventory investment may spark the upswing or bring about the downturn, thereby constituting an underlying cause as well as an aggravating force?

In an examination of Lloyd Metzler's theory of the inventory cycle, it is noted that, in addition to the forces he discusses, inventory movements may be influenced by cyclical changes in the availability of goods and in the purchasing policies of firms. Inventory objectives may vary to a considerable degree as the expansion progresses and may be sharply revised when goods become readily available. Moreover, in making purchasing decisions, firms consider not only inventories on hand but also unfilled purchase orders. In the theory presented here it is held that changes in inventory objectives may contribute to cyclical instability and, under certain conditions, cause inventory investment to reverse, thereby contributing to a turn in the cyclical tide.

2

The Role of Inventory Investment in Business Cycles: A Preliminary View

In the present chapter it will be shown that during both the prewar and postwar periods, changes in nonfarm inventory investment have made a major contribution to changes in national product during contractions, and a significant but less important contribution during expansions. Typically, the impact during expansions is greatest in its early stages. Increases in inventory investment since World War II have comprised a significantly smaller part of rises in national product than they did before the war. Of great importance for the present study is the observation that movements in manufacturers' inventory investment during both expansion and contraction phases of the business cycle account for a major part of the changes in total nonfarm inventory investment.

INVENTORY INVESTMENT DURING CONTRACTIONS

Table 1 and charts 1 and 2 present evidence of the importance of nonfarm inventory investment movements in both prewar and postwar business cycles. Measured on the basis of annual data, the changes are found to have accounted for at least 42 percent of the decline in national product in every business cycle contraction except that of 1929–32.[1] Quarterly data, available for the postwar period only, indicate that changes in investment comprised 195, 62, and 35 percent of the declines in national product from the peak to the trough quarters of the recessions of 1948–49, 1953–54, and 1957–58.

---

[1] Inventory investment (i.e., the changes in stocks), like manufacturers' investment in durable equipment, is a component of gross national product. Accordingly, it is the change in inventory investment that must be compared with changes in GNP.

Postwar Cycles in Manufacturers' Inventories

TABLE 1.—*Changes in gross national product and nonfarm inventory investment,*
1919–60

EXPANSIONS

Business cycle phase	Change in GNP		Change in nonfarm inventory investment		Col. 3÷ col. 1 (percent)	Col. 4÷ col. 2 (percent)
	Annual data (1)	Quarterly data (2)	Annual data (3)	Quarterly data (4)	(5)	(6)
Prewar (billions of 1929 dollars):						
1919–20_____	+$1.4	(1)	+$0.4	(1)	29	(1)
1921–23_____	+14.6	(1)	+2.4	(1)	16	(1)
1924–26_____	+8.2	(1)	+1.5	(1)	18	(1)
1927–29_____	+7.6	(1)	+2.3	(1)	30	(1)
1932–37_____	+28.7	(1)	+5.7	(1)	20	(1)
Total, 1919–37_____	60.5	(1)	12.3	(1)	20	(1)
Postwar (billions of 1954 dollars):						
1946–48_____	+10.4	(1)	−6.1	(1)	−58	(1)
1949–53_____	+76.3	+$80.2	+3.7	+$9.5	5	12
1954–57_____	+45.5	+48.9	+2.8	+4.0	6	8
1958–60_____	+39.5	+48.2	+6.2	+9.0	16	19
Total, 1949–60 [2]_____	161.3	177.3	12.7	22.5	8	13
Average (prewar and postwar) [2]_____	----------	----------	----------	----------	14	(1)

CONTRACTIONS

Prewar (billions of 1929 dollars):						
1920–21_____	−$3.6	(1)	−$2.9	(1)	81	(1)
1923–24_____	+1.5	(1)	−3.2	(1)	−213	(1)
1926–27_____	+1.0	(1)	−1.3	(1)	−130	(1)
1929–32_____	−32.0	(1)	−5.3	(1)	17	(1)
1937–38_____	−3.1	(1)	−3.6	(1)	116	(1)
Total, 1920–38_____	−36.2	(1)	16.3	(1)	45	(1)
Postwar (billions of 1954 dollars):						
1948–49_____	−.4	−$4.3	−5.6	−$8.4	1,400	195
1953–54_____	−5.9	−11.1	−3.2	−6.8	54	62
1957–58_____	−7.3	−15.8	−3.1	−5.6	42	35
Total, 1948–58_____	13.6	−31.2	−11.9	−20.8	88	67
Average (prewar and postwar)_____	----------	----------	----------	----------	66	(1)

FULL CYCLES

Prewar (billions of 1929 dollars):						
1919–21_____	$5.0	(1)	$3.3	(1)	66	(1)
1921–24_____	13.1	(1)	5.6	(1)	43	(1)
1924–27_____	7.2	(1)	2.8	(1)	39	(1)
1927–32_____	39.6	(1)	7.6	(1)	19	(1)
1932–38_____	31.8	(1)	9.3	(1)	29	(1)
Total, 1919–38_____	96.7	(1)	28.6	(1)	30	(1)
Postwar (billions of 1954 dollars):						
1949–54_____	82.2	$91.3	6.9	$16.3	8	·9
1954–58_____	52.8	64.7	5.9	9.6	11	15
Total, 1949–58_____	135.0	156.0	12.8	25.9	9	17
Average (prewar and postwar)_____	----------	----------	----------	----------	20	(1)

[1] Not available.
[2] Expansion of 1946–48 is omitted.

NOTE.—Quarterly comparisons are based on business cycle reference dates.

Source: Prewar GNP data, compiled from Simon Kuznets, "National Product Since 1869" (NBER, 1946), table I–15; inventory data from Moses Abramovitz, "Inventories and Business Cycles" (NBER 1950), p. 568.
Postwar GNP and nonfarm inventory investment changes based on data in Survey of Current Business 1954 National Income Supplement and July 1961 issue.

CHART 1

GROSS NATIONAL PRODUCT, FINAL PURCHASES, AND INVENTORY INVESTMENT,
ANNUAL TOTALS, 1919–60

[Billions of dollars]

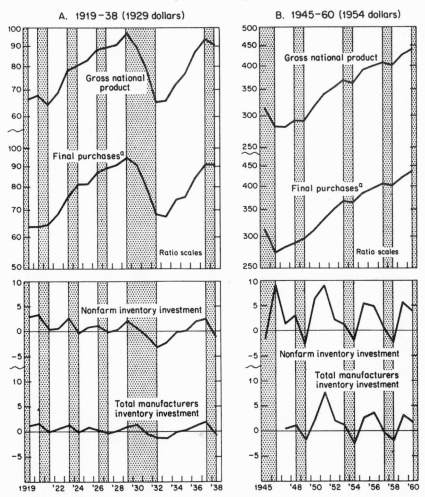

A. 1919–38 (1929 dollars)   B. 1945–60 (1954 dollars)

ᵃ Final purchases equal GNP less total inventory investment.
Shaded areas represent business contractions; unshaded areas, expansions.

Source: Prewar data for gross national product and final purchases, from tables I-15 and I-11, Simon
Kuznets, "National Product Since 1869," NBER 1946; for inventory investment, from Moses
Abramovitz, "Inventories and Business Cycles," NBER 1950. Postwar data from Department of
Commerce.

CHART 2

GROSS NATIONAL PRODUCT, FINAL PURCHASES, AND INVENTORY INVESTMENT,
QUARTERLY AT ANNUAL RATES, 1947–61

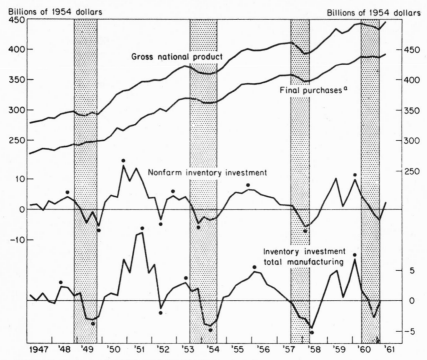

a Final purchases equal GNP less total inventory investment.
Shaded areas represent business contractions; unshaded areas, expansions.

Source: Department of Commerce.

It is difficult with certainty to rank the various contractions according to the relative importance of inventory investment movements, but comparison is facilitated by making use of final purchases (gross national product less nonfarm and farm inventory investment) rather than national product data. In table 2 changes in nonfarm inventory investment are compared with changes in final purchases; phases are ranked according to what appears to be the relative contribution of the former. It will be noted that in terms of annual data, final purchases rose during the contraction of 1948–49 and during all the prewar contractions except those of 1929–32 and 1937–38. Declines in inventory investment may, therefore, be regarded as the principal cause of contraction. The contractions of 1923–24 and 1948–49 belong at the top of the list in this respect, but it is debatable which should be accorded first place.

TABLE 2.—*Ranking of eight contractions according to magnitude of change in non-farm inventory investment relative to change in final purchases, 1920–58* [1]

Rank	Contraction	Change in nonfarm inventory investment		Change in final purchases		Col. 1÷ col. 3 (percent)	Col. 2÷ col. 4 (percent)
		Annual data	Quarterly data [2]	Annual data	Quarterly data [2]		
		(1)	(2)	(3)	(4)	(5)	(6)
1	1923–24	−3.2	(3)	+5.2	(3)	−61	(3)
2	1948–49	−5.6	−8.4	+7.6	+5.8	−74	−145
3	1920–21	−2.9	(3)	+.6	(3)	−483	(3)
4	1926–27	−1.3	(3)	+1.8	(3)	−72	(3)
5	1937–38	−3.6	(3)	−.2	(3)	180	(3)
6	1953–54	−3.2	−6.8	−3.8	−5.9	84	115
7	1957–58	−3.1	−5.6	−4.2	−10.1	74	55
8	1929–32	−5.3	(3)	−26.4	(3)	20	(3)

[1] Prewar data in 1929 prices. Postwar data in 1954 prices.
[2] Quarterly comparisons are based on quarterly reference cycle dates.
[3] Not available.

Source: For nonfarm inventory investment data see table 1. Prewar data for final purchases from Simon Kuznets, "National Product Since 1869," NBER 1946, tables I–15 and I–11. Postwar final purchases computed from GNP and nonfarm inventory investment data, see table 1.

In general, inventory investment has contributed in large measure to recessions both before and since the war, with no well-defined difference apparent in its importance in the two periods. Only in the contraction of 1929–32 was its role a relatively minor one.

INVENTORY INVESTMENT DURING EXPANSIONS

Table 1 reveals that changes in nonfarm inventory investment, though important, are significantly less so for expansions than for contractions. In all expansions, prewar and postwar, changes in nonfarm inventory investment average 14 percent of changes in national product, whereas the comparable figure for contractions is 66 percent.

Moses Abramovitz noted this difference in the relative importance of inventory investment in the prewar data, and gave as a possible explanation the fact that expansions are longer than contractions.[2] He observed that, ceteris paribus, the total change in the level of output may be expected to be greater the longer the phase, even though the rate of change may remain the same or decline. On the other hand, inventory investment is simply the rate of change in inventories in a given time period, and it is influenced by the rate of growth (or decline) of output in that period. Consequently it is not to be expected that the change in the levels of inventory investment in the terminal periods will be greater the longer the phase. It follows, therefore, that the share of change in inventory investment relative to the change in national product during a phase may not be expected to be as large for expansions as for the shorter contractions.

This is a cogent argument, and no doubt partially explains the phenomenon.[3] It is not the entire explanation however, for the generalization also holds for year-to-year changes within business cycle phases. In the interwar and postwar periods in only 2 years of

[2] Moses Abramovitz, "Inventories and Business Cycles, with Special Reference to Manufacturers Inventories," New York, National Bureau of Economic Research, 1950, p. 484.
[3] It may also help to explain why the share of inventory investment in the long and severe contraction of 1929–32 was so small.

10 Postwar Cycles in Manufacturers' Inventories

significant expansion (1927–28 and 1928–29) the change in nonfarm inventory investment constitutes as large a proportion of that in gross national product as in the year of sharpest disinvestment during the subsequent recession (table 3). Possible reasons for this important characteristic will be examined in chapter 8.

Another finding (table 3) is that increases in inventory investment relative to the increase in GNP tend to be larger in the early than in the later stages of expansions. This was true in three of the four prewar expansions which were of sufficient duration (i.e., 2 years or more) to permit observation and in three of the four postwar expansions.[4]

TABLE 3.—*Annual changes in gross national product and nonfarm inventory investment compared, 1919–38, 1945–60*

Years of—		Change in GNP during—		Change in nonfarm inventory investment during—		Col. 3÷ col. 1 (percent)	Col. 4÷ col. 2 (percent)
Expansion	Contraction	Expansion (1)	Contraction (2)	Expansion (3)	Contraction (4)	(5)	(6)
Prewar (billions of 1929 dollars)							
1919–20		+1.4		+0.4		29	
	1920–21		−3.6		−2.9		81
1921–22		+4.7		+.2		4	
1922–23		+9.9		+2.2		22	
	1923–24		+1.5		−3.2		−213
1924–25		+2.6		+1.1		42	
1925–26		+5.6		+.4		7	
	1926–27		+1.0		−1.3		−130
1927–28		+1.1		+.6		54	
1928–29		+6.5		+1.7		26	
	1929–30		−7.1		−1.4		20
	1930–31		−11.3		−1.8		16
	1931–32		−13.6		−2.0		15
1932–33		+.5		+.8		160	
1933–34		+6.7		+2.2		33	
1934–35		+4.6		+.3		6	
1935–36		+10.4		+1.9		18	
1936–37		+6.5		+.5		8	
	1937–38		−3.1		−3.6		116
Postwar (billions of 1954 dollars)							
1946–47		−0.2		−7.7		385	
1947–48		+10.8		+1.6		15	
	1948–49		−0.4		−5.6		1,400
1949–50		+25.4		+9.1		36	
1950–51		+23.7		+2.5		11	
1951–52		+11.7		−6.8		−58	
1952–53		+15.5		−1.1		−7	
	1953–54		−5.9		−3.2		54
1954–55		+29.6		+7.5		25	
1955–56		+8.2		−.5		−6	
1956–57		+7.7		−4.2		−55	
	1957–58		−7.3		−3.1		42
1958–59		+27.1		+8.0		29	
1959–60		+12.4		−1.8		−14	

Source: See table 1 for sources.

Finally, it will be noted (table 1) that changes in nonfarm inventory investment played a much larger part in prewar expansions (20 percent of total changes in gross national product) than in the postwar expansions (8 percent). Two possible explanations may be advanced. First, as already noted, postwar expansions have been longer than

---

[4] It will be noted in table 6 that for manufacturers' inventory investment the generalization held in each of the four prewar expansions for which comparison was possible and in three of the four postwar expansions.

prewar expansions. This added phase length would tend to reduce the role of changes in inventory investment. Second, peaks in inventory investment have displayed longer leads in postwar than in prewar expansions. Under such conditions, measurement of change in inventory investment from business cycle trough to peak understates the role of inventory investment during the postwar expansions.

In order to take account of differences in length of phase and of the earlier occurrence of peaks in inventory investment during the postwar period, changes in final purchases and inventory investment have been computed for both complete expansions and the first 2 years of expansions (table 4). Computing annual changes separately for the first 2 years of expansion compensates for differences in the length of phase. It also measures the change from the trough to the approximate investment peak in the two postwar expansions which were more than 2 years in duration.

TABLE 4.—*Changes in final purchases and nonfarm inventory investment, eight expansions, 1919–60*

Business cycle expansion	Length of expansion (years)	Change in—		Col. 3÷col. 2 (percent)
		Final purchases	Nonfarm inventory investment	
	(1)	(2)	(3)	(4)
		Billions of 1929 dollars		
1919–20	1	0	+0.4	
1921–23	2	+11.8	+2.4	20
1924–26	2	+6.1	+1.5	25
1927–29	2	+5.6	+2.3	41
1932–37	5 (2)	+22.9 (+6.3)	+5.7 (+3.0)	24 (48)
		Billions of 1954 dollars		
1946–48	2	+15.2	−6.1	−40
1949–53	4 (2)	+72.2 (+35.8)	+3.7 (+11.6)	5 (32)
1954–57	3 (2)	+42.3 (+31.7)	+2.8 (+7.0)	7 (22)
1958–60	2	+34.0	+6.2	18

Parenthetic entries are for 1st 2 years of expansion.

Source: See table 1 for sources.

During the initial 2-year interval the ratio of inventory investment change to change in final purchases was substantially larger than during the full expansions; it appears that the smaller role of changes in inventory investment during the postwar period is associated with the greater phase length and early occurrence of the investment peak. Among the three expansions which were longer than 2 years, the greatest change in inventory investment in the earlier years occurred in the prewar expansion of 1932–35. The next greatest occurred in the 1949–51 period which included the abnormal inventory accumulations of the early months of the Korean war. During the first 2 years of the 1954–57 expansion the relative magnitude of changes in inventory investment appears to have been roughly comparable to that of the 1921–23 and 1924–26 expansions. During the most recent expansion it was somewhat less.

MANUFACTURERS' INVENTORY INVESTMENT

Changes in manufacturers' inventory investment have been particularly significant during business cycles, especially in contractions. During the recessions of 1948–49, 1953–54, and 1957–58, they accounted for 79, 56, and 25 percent of the change in gross national product from the peak to the trough business cycle quarters (table 5). When the postwar and prewar annual data are compared, it is found that changes in this investment have contributed significantly to business cycles in both periods.

Manufacturers' inventory investment exhibits the same characteristics as were observed for nonfarm investment:

1. The contribution to instability has been greatest during contractions (table 5).

2. During expansions change in investment tends to reach a maximum during the first half of the expansion (table 6).

3. Investment has played a larger role in prewar than in postwar expansions (table 5).

This is not surprising, for movements in the two series have been similar, though not always identical, in both the prewar and postwar periods (charts 1 and 2). During the first two postwar expansions, both nonfarm and manufacturers' inventory investment established two peaks, a major one early in the phase and a lesser one toward the end. In both instances the earlier movement was essentially influenced by war. The sharp rise in investment from 1945 to mid-1946 represented necessary restocking of inventories which had been seriously depleted by the war, and the sharp upward movement from mid-1950 to mid-1951 was strongly influenced by the speculative psychology which prevailed during the early stages of the Korean war. In the 1954–57 expansion there was only a single upward movement in the two series, with peaks occurring during the first half of 1956.

TABLE 5.—*Changes in gross national product and manufacturers' inventory investment, 1919–60*

EXPANSIONS

Business cycle phase	Change in GNP		Change in manufacturers inventory investment		Col. 3 divided by col. 1 (percent)	Col. 4 divided by col. 2 (percent)
	Annual data	Quarterly data	Annual data	Quarterly data		
	(1)	(2)	(3)	(4)	(5)	(6)
Prewar (billions of 1929 dollars):						
1919–20	+$1.4	(1)	+$0.4	(1)	29	(1)
1921–23	+14.6	(1)	+1.4	(1)	10	(1)
1924–26	+8.2	(1)	+.6	(1)	7	(1)
1927–29	+7.6	(1)	+1.4	(1)	18	(1)
1932–37	+28.7	(1)	+3.3	(1)	11	(1)
Total, 1919–37	60.5	(1)	7.1	(1)	12	(1)
Postwar (billions of 1954 dollars):						
1946–48	+10.6	(1)	(1)	(1)	(1)	(1)
1949–53	+76.3	+$80.2	+3.0	+$5.6	4	7
1954–57	+45.5	+48.9	+2.2	+2.7	5	6
1958–60	+39.5	+48.2	+3.7	+6.2	9	13
Total, 1949–60 [2]	161.3	177.3	8.9	14.5	6	8
Average (prewar and postwar) [2]	----------	----------	----------	----------	9	(1)

CONTRACTIONS

Business cycle phase	Annual data (1)	Quarterly data (2)	Annual data (3)	Quarterly data (4)	(5)	(6)
Prewar (billions of 1929 dollars):						
1920–21	−$3.6	(1)	−$1.6	(1)	44	(1)
1923–24	+1.5	(1)	−1.6	(1)	−107	(1)
1926–27	+1.0	(1)	−.7	(1)	−70	(1)
1929–32	−32.0	(1)	−2.4	(1)	8	(1)
1937–38	−3.1	(1)	−2.7	(1)	87	(1)
Total, 1920–38	−36.2	(1)	−9.0	(1)	25	(1)
Postwar (billions of 1954 dollars):						
1948–49	−.4	−4.3	−3.0	−3.4	750	79
1953–54	−5.9	−11.1	−3.8	−6.2	64	56
1957–58	−7.3	−15.8	−1.6	−4.0	22	25
Total, 1948–58	13.6	−31.2	−8.4	−13.6	62	44
Average (prewar and postwar)	----------	----------	----------	----------	44	(1)

FULL CYCLES

Business cycle phase	Annual data (1)	Quarterly data (2)	Annual data (3)	Quarterly data (4)	(5)	(6)
Prewar (billions of 1929 dollars):						
1919–21	$5.0	(1)	$2.0	(1)	40	(1)
1921–24	13.1	(1)	3.0	(1)	30	(1)
1924–27	7.2	(1)	1.3	(1)	18	(1)
1927–32	39.6	(1)	3.8	(1)	10	(1)
1932–38	31.8	(1)	6.0	(1)	19	(1)
Total	96.7	----------	16.1	(1)	17	(1)
Postwar (billions of 1954 dollars):						
1949–54	82.2	$91.3	6.8	$11.8	8	13
1954–58	52.8	64.7	3.8	6.7	7	10
Total	135.0	156.0	10.6	18.5	8	12
Average (prewar and postwar)	----------	----------	----------	----------	12	(1)

[1] Not available.
[2] Expansion of 1946–48 omitted.

Source: See table 1 for sources of prewar data and postwar GNP data. Deflated manufacturers' inventory investment changes based on material from Department of Commerce.

TABLE 6.—*Annual changes in gross national product and manufacturers' inventory investment compared, 1919–38, 1945–60*

Years of		Change in GNP during		Change in manufacturers inventory investment during		Col. 3 divided by col. 1 (percent)	Col. 4 divided by col. 2 (percent)
Expansion	Contraction	Expansion (1)	Contraction (2)	Expansion (3)	Contraction (4)	(5)	(6)
		Prewar (billions of 1929 dollars)					
1919–20		+1.4		+0.4		29	
	1920–21		−3.6		−1.6		44
1921–22		+4.7		+.9		19	
1922–23		+9.9		+.5		5	
	1923–24		+1.5		−1.6		−107
1924–25		+2.6		+.9		35	
1925–26		+5.6		−.4		−7	
	1926–27		+1.0		−.7		−70
1927–28		+1.1		+.6		54	
1928–29		+6.5		+.9		14	
	1929–30		−7.1		+.2		−3
	1930–31		−11.3		−1.9		17
	1931–32		−13.6		−.7		5
1932–33		+.5		−.02		−4	
1933–34		+6.7		+1.2		18	
1934–35		+4.6		+.4		9	
1935–36		+10.4		+1.0		10	
1936–37		+6.5		+.7		11	
	1937–38		−3.1		−2.7		87
		Postwar (billions of 1954 dollars)					
	1945–46		−31.5				
1946–47		−0.2					
1947–48		+10.8		+0.7		6	
	1948–49		−.4		−3.0		750
1949–50		+25.4		+4.5		18	
1950–51		+23.7		+5.5		23	
1951–52		+11.7		−5.8		−50	
1952–53		+15.5		−.8		−5	
	1953–54		−5.9		−3.8		64
1954–55		+29.6		+5.2		18	
1955–56		+8.2		+1.0		12	
1956–57		+7.7		−4.0		−52	
	1957–58		−7.3		−1.6		22
1958–59		+27.1		+5.2		19	
1959–60		ₐ +12.4		−1.5		−12	

Source: See table 5 for sources.

The similarity in patterns of movement in the two inventory investment series is largely due to the fact that manufacturers' inventory investment is the major component of nonfarm inventory investment. Table 7 shows that manufacturers' stocks have comprised between 46 and 56 percent of nonfarm inventories in the prewar and postwar periods. Moreover, in six of the eight cycles, movements in manufacturers' inventory investment have been larger than would be expected on the basis of the proportion of total stocks held (in one case, they were equal). During the single cycle in which they were smaller, the 1924–27 episode, atypical countermovements in durable-goods inventory investment occurred, serving to dilute the intensity of movements in total manufacturers' inventory investment (see table 10, ch. 3).

TABLE 7.—*Analysis of relative size of cyclical changes in manufacturers' inventory investment, 1919–60*

Cycle	Manufacturers' inventories as percent of nonfarm inventories [1]		Change in manufacturers' inventory investment				Change in gross national product as percent of average gross national product contraction
			As percent of change in nonfarm inventory investment [2]			As percent of manufacturing inventories [1] contraction	
	Abramovitz-Kuznets	Department of Commerce	Expansion	Contraction	Total cycle		
Prewar:							
1919–21	46	----------	100	55	61	16	5.4
1921–24	48	----------	58	50	54	14	2.0
1924–27	49	----------	40	54	46	6	1.2
1927–32	50	----------	61	45	50	17	37.0
1932–38	53	54	58	75	65	19	3.9
Weighted average	50	----------	58	55	56	12	12.0
Postwar:							
1946–49	----------	55	[3] 91 (4)	54 (40)	[3] 73 (4)	8	.01
1949–54	----------	56	81 (59)	119 (91)	99 (72)	8	1.7
1954–58	----------	56	79 (68)	52 (71)	64 (70)	3	1.8
1958–60	----------	----------	60 (69)	----------	----------	----------	----------
Weighted average [5]	----------	55	70 (64)	71 (65)	83 (71)	6	1.4

[1] Cycle averages of inventories were used in these comparisons.
[2] Figures in parentheses are based on quarterly data.
[3] Measured from 1945 to 1948 in order to compare trough and peak inventory investment.
[4] Not available.
[5] Averages exclude 1946–48 expansion; include 3 expansions, 3 contractions, 2 full cycles.

Source: Prewar figures computed from data in Abramovitz, Inventories and Business Cycles, pp. 476, 568. Postwar figures from material provided by Department of Commerce. All data are deflated.

The continuing importance of postwar movements in nonfarm and manufacturers' inventory investment is especially interesting in view of the fact that stocks are smaller relative to the volume of sales and output than they were before the war. For the years 1919 to 1939 Abramovitz constructed indexes of year-end ratios of deflated manufacturing stocks to output.[5] Similar ratios have been computed here for the years 1947 through 1954. The 1947–54 average compares as follows with decade averages for the twenties and the thirties:

1920–29 _____ 103
1930–39 _____ 119
1947–54 _____ 77

Comparable data are not available for distributive and other firms but the fact that such stocks have also been reduced sharply relative to sales is attested to by their decreased share of total nonfarm inventories (table 7). It is concluded therefore, that although manufacturing and other nonfarm stocks are relatively smaller today than before the war, their movements have played an equivalent role in postwar business cycle contractions.

It should be kept in mind, however, that postwar recessions have been comparatively mild. Changes in inventory investment have been large relative to changes in gross national product (tables 1 and 5); but movements in national product during contractions have not been large relative to average levels of national product, and postwar changes in manufacturers' inventory investment have not been large in relation to the average size of stocks (table 7).

[5] Abramovitz, "Inventories and Business Cycles," p. 570.

3

Manufacturers' Inventories and Inventory Investment

Analysis of the Department of Commerce total stock series in the present chapter yields several important findings. Both total manufacturers' stocks and inventory investment are shown to have turned somewhat earlier in relation to business cycle turns since 1946 than Abramovitz indicated was characteristic of the prewar period. Nevertheless, movements in quarter-to-quarter change in inventories (i.e., inventory investment) have well-defined cyclical patterns in most of the series and show a high degree of conformity to both industry sales cycles and business cycles. Durable-goods series were cyclically more sensitive than those of nondurable goods, showing a higher conformity to business cycles and moving with greater amplitude. Stocks in durable-goods industries have been relatively larger since the war, and their increased importance has altered the composition of total stocks.

Timing Comparisons

During the 1946–58 period, total stocks lagged behind reference turns by 1 to 8 months (table 8 and chart 3), in contrast to Abramovitz' estimate of a 6-to-12-month prewar lag.[1] Total investment timing varied from roughly coincident to a lead of 14 months (table 9 and chart 4), compared to Abramovitz' coincident timing estimate.

[1] It will be noted that timing of the two most recent turns in table 8 is based upon book value data.

TABLE 8.—*Timing and conformity of manufacturers' total inventory at reference and activity turns; comprehensive series*

A. TIMING MEASURES [1]

Industry	Lead (−) or lag (+) in months—Business cycles					
	Peak November 1948	Trough October 1949	Peak July 1953	Trough August 1954	Peak July 1957	Trough April 1958
	Timing at reference turns					
Total, manufacturing	+4	+6	+2	+1	+2	+8
Durable goods industries, total	−14	+4	+2	+9	+3	+8
Nondurable goods industries, total	(2)	(2)	+2	+1	+1	+5
	Timing at activity (sales) turns					
Total, manufacturing	+6	+4	+2	−1	+8	+9
Durable goods industries, total	−15	+4	+2	+7	+9	+8
Nondurable goods industries, total	(2)	(2)	(3)	(3)	+7	+6

B. SUMMARY OF TIMING (16 INDUSTRY SERIES) [4]

	At business cycle peaks		At business cycle troughs	
	Number	Percent	Number	Percent
Leads, more than 3 months	6	22	2	7
Rough coincidences	12	45	10	37
Leads, 3 months or less	(8)	(30)	(3)	(11)
Coincidences	(0)	(0)	(0)	(0)
Lags, 3 months or less	(4)	(15)	(7)	(26)
Lags, more than 3 months	9	32	15	56

C. SUMMARY OF CONFORMITY [4]

	16 industry series		7 durable goods industries		9 nondurable goods industries	
	All turns	All turns except Korean	All turns	All turns except Korean	All turns	All turns except Korean
Comparisons with reference turns:						
Number of comparisons	96	64	42	28	54	36
Matching inventory turns	65	54	30	28	35	26
Percentage of matching turns	68	84	71	100	65	72
Comparisons with output turns:						
Number of comparisons	75	53	38	28	37	25
Matching inventory turns	54	48	30	28	24	20
Percentage of matching turns	72	91	79	100	65	80

[1] Inventory series have been deflated to 1956; 1957–58 turns based on undeflated data. Korean cycle reference turns are not shown, since there were no corresponding inventory turns.
[2] No corresponding inventory turn.
[3] Inventory turn occurs, but no sales turn.
[4] Analysis includes only deflated 1948–56 data.

Source: Based on material from Department of Commerce.

CHART 3

INVENTORIES AND SALES: TOTAL MANUFACTURING, DURABLE- AND NONDURABLE-
GOODS INDUSTRIES, 1945–61

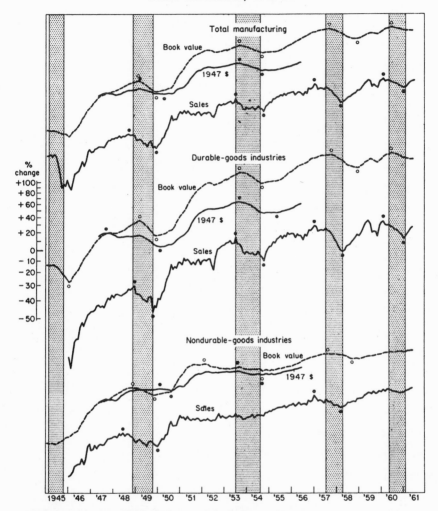

Shaded areas represent business contractions; unshaded areas, expansions.
Dots identify peaks and troughs of deflated inventory cycles; circles, of undeflated cycles. All sales data
are undeflated.

Source: Department of Commerce. Data deflated by the author.

It should be noted, however, that the prewar estimates were based
on year-end data and hence are necessarily less precise. Abramovitz
estimated from the annual data the range within which inventory
and inventory investment turns would lead or lag behind reference
turns on a monthly basis. Using his method, I have estimated the
range of timing for total manufacturers' deflated inventories from

postwar annual data. These estimates may be compared with actual timing as follows:

Reference turn	Timing	
	Estimated range	Actual
Peak November 1948	+3 to +12	+4
Trough October 1949	0 to +9	+6
Peak July 1953	+3 to +12	+2
Trough August 1954	+3 to +12	+1

The consensus of Abramovitz' findings for the prewar period was for longer lags than these. Two of his turns showed a minimum lag of 12 months. I agree with Abramovitz that lags were typically somewhat longer before the war, but it seems likely that the range was greater than he indicated. Evidence of this is to be found in Department of Commerce estimates of the book value of manufacturers total stocks (quarterly, 1926–38, monthly thereafter) and in National Industrial Conference Board estimates (monthly, 1929–44). Prewar timing measures for these series are as follows:

Date of reference turn	Timing at peak		Timing at trough	
	Department of Commerce	NICB	Department of Commerce	NICB
October 1926	−3½			
November 1927			−7½	
August 1929	+7½	+5½		
March 1933			+3½	+2½
May 1937	+4½	+6½		
June 1938			+12½	+12½

During the postwar period a tendency for the inventory series to turn earlier at peaks than troughs, as compared with both reference and activity series may be observed (table 8). This finding is less well established in the comprehensive series than in the individual industry series and is offered only as a tentative observation.[2]

Table 8 shows the timing of movements in the comprehensive series. In two sets of comparisons (the turns which were related to the recessions of 1948–49 and 1957–58) stocks show shorter lags at peaks than at troughs; in the remaining comparison they do not (see also chart 3). The departure from the observed tendency is not so damaging as might at first appear, for the trough in stocks has been marked at the technically lowest point of an almost flat-bottomed recession phase which extends 10 months after the date of the trough selected. In the industry data, the evidence is more impressive.

---

[2] In this chapter and the chapters which follow, inventory and inventory investment turns are compared both with turns in the comparable sales or output series and with business cycle reference turns. This is a necessary, if somewhat repetitious, procedure; inventory behavior in a given industry or group of industries must be presumed to be functionally related to economic activity as represented by sales or output (typically, the two move together closely). It is essential, therefore to relate movements in stocks or investment to activity. At the same time, in order to generalize regarding behavior of inventories during business cycles and to compare the timing of one inventory series with another, it is essential to make direct timing comparison with reference turns. In addition to the NBER business cycle reference turns, use has been made of the two subcycle reference turns established for the Korean war period by Ruth Mack. For a discussion of subcycles and the criteria involved in establishing subcycle chronology, see Ruth P. Mack, "Notes on Subcycles in Theory and Practice," *American Economic Review*, May 1957, pp. 161–174.

The summary of timing comparisons for the 16 series (table 8) shows that 47 percent of the peaks in the inventory series lagged behind reference peaks, whereas 82 percent of the inventory troughs lagged behind reference troughs.

The tendency for shorter lags at peaks holds for both of the two cycles for which industry data were studied (1948–49 and 1953–54). During the first postwar business cycle, 54 percent of inventory peaks lagged behind the reference peak, and 73 percent of inventory troughs lagged behind the reference trough. For the second cycle the figures were 42 and 92 percent, respectively.

We shall see, however, that the generalization does not extend to inventory investment which turns relatively early at activity and reference peaks and troughs. Some instances of earlier timing at peaks than at troughs may be noted, but there is no consistent pattern.

The tendency of quarterly inventory investment series (quarter-to-quarter change in inventories) to move in well-conforming cyclical patterns was found in most of the individual industry series for total stocks and, as we shall see in the following chapters, by stage of fabrication as well.

The relatively high degree of conformity of the total inventory investment series to business and output cycles is clearly evident from the summary of conformity measures given in table 9. Industry investment turns could be consistently related with corresponding reference turns in 86 percent of possible comparisons, and with output turns in 87 percent.[3] This conformity is of roughly the same magnitude as that noted for total stocks series in table 8 (68 and 72 percent, respectively).

---

[3] A principal method of measurement used in this study was to record the number of turns in inventory or investment series that could be "matched" with reference or activity turns, using NBER rules for matching. Peaks in a series are said to match reference (activity) peaks when there is no intervening trough in either the reference (activity) cycle or in the series in question.

TABLE 9.—*Timing and conformity of manufacturers' total inventory investment at reference and activity turns; comprehensive series*

A. TIMING MEASURES [1]

Industry	Lead (−) or lag (+) in months							
	Business cycle		Korean cycle		Business cycles			
	Peak (reference, November 1948)	Trough (reference, October 1949)	Peak (February 1951)	Trough (June 1952)	Peak (July 1953)	Trough (August 1954)	Peak (July 1957)	Trough (April 1958)
Timing at reference turns								
Total manufacturing	−6	−2	+3	−1	−2	0	−14	+1
Durable-goods industries, total	−6	−2	+6	−1	−2	−3	−20	+1
Nondurable-goods industries, total	−6	+7	+3	(2)	(2)	−9	−14	+4
Timing at activity (sales) turns								
Total manufacturing	−4	−4	(3)	(3)	−2	−2	−8	+2
Durable-goods industries, total	−7	−2	(3)	(3)	−2	−5	−14	+1
Nondurable-goods industries, total	−1	+4	+4	(2)	(4)	(5)	−8	+5

B. SUMMARY OF TIMING (16 INDUSTRY SERIES) [6]

	At business cycle peaks		At business cycle troughs	
	Number	Percent	Number	Percent
Leads, more than 3 months	12	----------	8	30
Rough coincidences	11	----------	15	56
Leads, 3 months or less	(8)	----------	(11)	(41)
Coincidences	(2)	----------	(0)	(0)
Lags, 3 months or less	(1)	----------	(4)	(15)
Lags, more than 3 months	5	----------	4	15

C. SUMMARY OF CONFORMITY [6]

	16 industry series		7 durable-goods industries		9 nondurable-goods industries	
	All turns	All turns except Korean	All turns	All turns except Korean	All turns	All turns except Korean
Comparisons with reference turns:						
Number of comparisons	96	64	42	28	54	36
Matching investment turns	83	55	40	28	43	27
Percentage of matching turns	86	86	95	100	80	75
Comparisons with output turns:						
Number of comparisons	75	53	38	28	37	25
Matching investment turns	65	49	38	28	27	21
Percentage of matching turns	87	92	100	100	73	84

[1] Inventory series have been deflated to 1956; 1957–58 turns based on undeflated data.
[2] Sales turn occurs but no well defined corresponding inventory investment turn.
[3] No sales turn occurs.
[4] No sales or inventory turn occurs.
[5] Inventory turn occurs, but no sales turn.
[6] Analysis includes only deflated 1948–56 data.

Source: Based on material from Department of Commerce.

CHART 4

INVENTORY INVESTMENT: TOTAL MANUFACTURING, DURABLE- AND NONDURABLE-GOODS INDUSTRIES, 1945–61

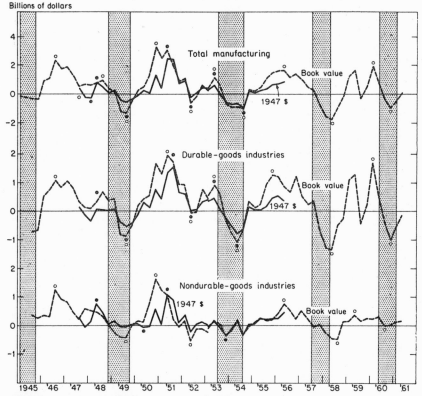

Shaded areas represent business contractions; unshaded areas, expansions.
Dots identify peaks and troughs of deflated cycles; circles, of undeflated cycles.

Source: Department of Commerce.   Data deflated by the author.

CYCLICAL SENSITIVITY OF DURABLE GOODS

Conformity measures point clearly to the greater cyclical sensitivity of durables.   Turns in the durable-goods inventory series (table 8) could be matched with reference turns (except Korean) in 100 percent of comparisons; among the nondurables, only 72 percent.   Similar figures for inventory investment (table 9) were 100 percent for durables and 75 percent for nondurables.

Amplitudes of fluctuations in inventory investment may be compared for durables and nondurables by means of a simple tabulation of the change from peak to trough and from trough to peak in investment-cycles.   Since total stocks of durable-goods industries on the average are not greatly in excess of nondurable (about 1.2 times as large) the results may be compared directly.   The following tabulation (in billions of 1954 dollars at annual rates) shows that the change in level of inventory investment was far greater for durables than for nondurables in all but one of the postwar phases for which deflated data were available.

Durables		Nondurables	
P–T I 49 to III 49	−2. 8	II 48 to II 49	−2. 9
T–P III 49 to III 51	+10. 3	II 49 to II 51	+4. 3
P–T III 51 to II 52	−9. 5	II 51 to III 54	−4. 4
T–P II 52 to II 53	+3. 9	III 54 to III 56	+2. 6
P–T II 53 to II 54	−6. 7	III 56 to II 58	−2. 9
T–P II 54 to I 56	+7. 9	II 58 to IV 59	+2. 6
P–T I 56 to II 58	−7. 3		
T–P II 58 to I 60	−10. 4		

This was not the result of one or two dominating series, but a highly representative performance. During the 1949 recession six of the seven durables inventory series showed declines of 10 percent or more from their peaks, whereas only five of the nine nondurables declined by this amount. During the 1953–54 recession five of the seven durables series declined 10 percent or more, but only one of the nondurables did so.[4]

Another characteristic of durables inventory movements is that the series move together; this makes for little muting of the impact through dissimilar and counteracting changes. This characteristic is clearly in evidence when diffusion indexes of percentage of series increasing were constructed for the durables and nondurables series. Among the durables the tendency for stocks to move together was indicated by very high scores (indicating that most series were rising) or very low scores (indicating that few series were rising), whereas among the nondurables the tendency for stocks to move in different directions was indicated by scores close to 50 percent. During the period extending from second quarter 1948 to second quarter 1955, scores were above 80 percent or below 20 percent more than half of the time for the durables and less than a sixth of the time for the nondurables.

There appear to be two types of causation for these well-established cyclical tendencies among the durables. In the first, the cyclical behavior appears to derive from greater fluctuations and more closely coordinated changes in activity among the several durables industries. In the second, the explanation lies in the composition of stocks; i.e., the inventories held at different stages of fabrication are of the types which are more responsive to cyclical forces.

The first point is readily established by applying the same test to output series that was used to show amplitude of movements in inventories. During the 1949 contraction, all seven durables output series declined by more than 10 percent of their cycle bases, whereas only three of the nine nondurables series declined by such amounts. During the 1953–54 recession, six of the seven durable output series declined by more than 10 percent, but only four of the nine nondurables declined by as much as this amount. In addition, diffusion indexes for output of durables showed a greater swing than nondurables during these two periods, indicating a closer intercorrelation in the movements of durables.[5]

The second type of causation will become apparent as the behavior of stocks at each stage of fabrication is analyzed, but the general argument may be stated here. Durables inventories are composed in a

---

[4] The declines were measured as percentages of the average level of stocks during each cycle.
[5] G. H. Moore, *Business Cycle Indicators*, Princeton for NBER, 1961, vol. I, pp. 283–284.

larger degree than nondurables of the types of stocks which move sensitively when manufacturing activity increases or decreases. Procurement of durable purchased stocks is largely demand oriented; it is not limited by supply conditions, as may be the case with certain nondurable agricultural raw materials. Durable goods-in-process stocks are held between stages (rather than within stages) to a much greater extent. It is these between-stage stocks which may be varied to the greatest extent with changes in demand conditions (chapter 6). Finally, durable goods are typically manufactured to order rather than to stock; this tends to cause finished stocks to respond more sensitively to cyclical forces.

By making use of Abramovitz' data, it is possible to determine the relative size of durable-goods manufacturers' stocks before the war and to learn whether they displayed as high a degree of responsiveness in that period. Table 10 shows the average proportion of total stocks made up by durables for each cycle from 1919 to 1958. In addition, it shows the proportion of the change in manufacturers' inventory investment in each phase which was caused by changes in durables investment. It can be concluded that durables stocks have constituted a larger share of total stocks in recent years, and have contributed in a greater measure to economic instability. The characteristic of high cyclical responsiveness, however, was well established in the earlier period.

COMPOSITION OF MANUFACTURERS' STOCKS

We have seen that total manufacturers' stocks are smaller relative to output than they were before the war. Census data and Department of Commerce statistics indicate, in addition, that their composition has been significantly altered. Abramovitz estimated the prewar composition of stocks as 40 percent purchased materials, 20 percent goods in process, and 40 percent finished goods. The Annual Survey of Manufactures shows the 1952–53 proportion to be approximately 38 percent purchased materials, 29 percent goods in process, and 33 percent finished goods.

The proportions differ considerably for the durables and the nondurables groups. In the period 1952–54 the composition of durable and nondurable manufacturers' stocks was approximately: [6]

	Purchased materials	Goods in process	Finished goods
Durables	30	40	30
Nondurables	44	14	42
Total	36	28	36

The major difference in composition of durables and nondurables is, of course, the large stock of goods in process held by the durables group. These in-process inventories account for the large stocks-to-sales ratios of the durables group (approximately 2.1 to 1 compared to 1.6 to 1 for nondurables). The stocks-to-sales ratios for purchased

---

[6] The composition of total stocks given here was obtained from Department of Commerce data and is slightly different from that in the Annual Survey of Manufactures. The difference is due principally to the fact that the former are reported on a firm basis and include some finished stocks held by company distributing organizations, whereas census data are reported by individual manufacturing plants.

materials and for finished goods do not differ significantly between the durables and nondurables groups.[7]

The change in composition of manufacturers' stocks from prewar to postwar appears to be explained largely by the shift toward durables. Using the prewar ratios of nondurables to durables inventories (table 10) which is about 2 to 1, the prewar composition (if composition within durables and nondurables had been the same as postwar) would be 39 percent purchased materials, 23 percent goods in process, and 37 percent finished goods. These percentages are quite close to the actual prewar figures (40–20–20) as estimated by Abramovitz.

The significance of the behavior of stocks at each stage of fabrication is determined by the size of each category and by the amplitude and cyclical pattern of its movement. Judged on the basis of size it is clear that each category may be considered to be of substantial importance. Analysis of cyclical conformity, timing, and amplitude will be presented in the chapters which follow.

TABLE 10.—*Analysis of percentage of change in total manufacturers' inventory investment accounted for by inventory investment of durables manufacturers, 1919–61*

Cycle	Durables inventory as percentage of total inventory (cycle average)	Percentage of change in manufacturers' inventory investment accounted for by durables inventory investment [1]	
		Expansion	Contraction
Prewar:			
1919–20–21	38	76	46
1921–23–24	37	83	40
1924–26–27	43	(²)	(²)
1927–29–32	36	28	52
1932–37–38	35	39	40
Postwar:			
1946–48–49	52	(²)	50 (68)
1949–53–54	54	97 (84)	92 (82)
1954–57–58	54	95 (93)	112 (88)
1958–60–61	(³)	78 (74)	(³)

[1] Figures in parentheses are based on quarterly data.
[2] Durables inventory investment out of phase with total manufacturers' inventory investment and reference cycle.
[3] Not available.

Source: Prewar figures computed from deflated data in Abramovitz, "Inventories and Business Cycles," pp. 564–565. Postwar figures are in 1954 dollars; data from Department of Commerce.

———

[7] The changed composition of goods in process is treated in detail in chapter 6.

4

Purchased-Materials Inventories and Inventory Investment

Abramovitz began his investigation of purchased-materials behavior by adopting a preliminary hypothesis that "stocks of raw materials generally grow and decline with manufacturing activity." [1] Although he recognized that movements in prices may play a role, this hypothesis provided the principal basis for his inquiry. Purchased materials were seen to move in response to changing levels of output, but with delays occasioned principally by lack of immediate availability of the materials in question. The analysis based upon this hypothesis consisted principally of estimating the length of the average period of delay in securing materials. This estimate was based on a special study made during the preparation of the 1929 Census of Manufacturers, which classified materials used by manufacturers according to their origins. [2] On the basis of this study Abramovitz concluded that "most raw materials stocks held by manufacturers are likely to vary positively with a short lag" and that total manufacturers' stocks of purchased materials might be expected to conform closely to business cycles, "lagging 3 months or somewhat more at turning points." [3] Moreover, movements in purchased-materials inventory investment were expected to be a lagged reflection of movements in the rate of change in output. Evidence at hand did not permit him to estimate how long the lag might be. He simply noted that "a lag of investment in raw materials behind the rate of change in output of even 6 months would still leave this class of investment leading business cycle turns by several months. This, of course, is presumably subject to considerable irregularity, especially near business peaks, corresponding to the irregularity in the timing of turns in the rate of change in output." [4] In an analysis of the behavior of 10 raw-materials inventory series, however, he found support for the tentative conclusions reached in his estimate of typical timing based on availability of materials. [5]

No study such as that used by Abramovitz is available for the postwar period, and there is no basis for an accurate comparison of

[1] Abramovitz, "Inventories and Business Cycles With Special Reference to Manufacturers Inventories," New York, NBER 1950, p. 178. His definition of raw materials as "goods purchased by manufacturers but not yet manipulated by their owners," is used in this study as a description of "purchased materials." It should be noted that purchased materials defined in this way include not only raw or semiprocessed materials, but also fully fabricated component parts, such as carburetors purchased by automobile manufacturers or small motors purchased by the producers of electric fans.
[2] Abramovitz divided these stocks into three groups according to source. The first group included commodities purchased from manufacturers or mines in this country. The stocks which were presumed to be available from suppliers on relatively short notice accounted for approximately two-thirds of all purchased materials used by manufacturers in 1929. A second group, comprising about 10 percent of the raw materials purchased by manufacturers, was composed of imports. These stocks are not easily adjusted to changes in requirements. The third group, accounting for approximately a quarter of manufacturers' raw materials, included products (principally agricultural) whose availability is subject to short-term movements that are independent of current demand. Abramovitz noted that materials in either of these last two classes might actually be quickly available if they were storable and typically held in large quantities by middlemen (e.g., cotton stored by cotton merchants). Ibid., pp. 184–187, 314.
[3] Ibid., p. 317.
[4] Ibid., p. 467.
[5] Ibid., pp. 192–239.

postwar and interwar composition of stocks. Fortunately, however, there is recent direct evidence relating to the availability of purchased materials. The National Association of Purchasing Agents has published monthly, since April 1955, statistics on purchasing leadtimes as reported by their members. Each respondent reports monthly the basis of its purchasing policy for principal purchased materials within one of the following categories: Hand-to-mouth buying, 30-day requirements, 60-day requirements, 90-day requirements, 120-day requirements, or more.

These NAPA statistics indicate that, in the main, purchased materials are readily available, but to a greater or lesser degree depending on the stage of the business cycle. This is apparent in the following data which show the percentage of purchasing agents reporting leadtimes of 60 days or less for production (purchased) materials in business cycle peak and trough months (see also chart 16):

Percent

Peak, July 1957 [1]_____ 75
Trough, April 1958_____ 91
Peak, May 1960_____ 79

[1] June data were used because no July data were published.

Clearly, Abramovitz' assumption that most purchased materials are available within a relatively short span of time is valid for the postwar period. But has this condition led to the type of inventory and investment behavior which he concluded would be the logical outcome of such ready availability? In the sections that follow we shall examine the behavior of purchased-materials inventory and inventory investment, note certain characteristics not envisioned by Abramovitz and inquire into the reasons for the observed behavior.

BEHAVIOR OF INVENTORIES

TIMING AND CONFORMITY OF INVENTORIES: COMPARISONS WITH SALES TURNS

The timing of purchased materials to sales turns, as shown in table 11, varies widely from turn to turn in the individual industry series and among the series at each peak and trough. Nevertheless, the conformity to sales turns is generally high and approximately the same for durables and nondurables industries (about 80 percent of sales turns can be matched by inventory turns in each category).

TABLE 11.—*Timing and conformity of manufacturers' purchased-materials inventories at sales turns*

A. TIMING MEASURES [1]

| Industry | Lead (−) or lag (+) in months, in zones associated with reference turns | | | | | |
	1948 peak	1949 trough	1953 peak	1954 trough	1957 peak	1958 trough
Total manufacturing	−1	+4	+1	+6	+10	+6
Durable-goods industries, total	−17	+4	+1	+8	+2	+4
Nondurable-goods industries, total	+4	+5	(2)	(3)	+7	+11
Primary metals	−6	+7	−1	+10		
Machinery (including electrical)	−17	+3	+1	+5		
Transportation equipment (including motor vehicles)	−24	+1	+1	+12		
Stone, clay, and glass	−2	+2	(2)	+13		
Food and beverages	−14	+6	(2)	+7		
Paper	+2	+13	(4)	(4)		
Chemical	+6	+9	(2)	+15		
Petroleum and coal	−13	+13	(2)	+12		
Rubber	+7	+7	0	+12		

B. SUMMARY OF TIMING (9 INDUSTRY SERIES) [1]

	At sales peaks	At sales troughs
Leads, more than 3 months	5	0
Rough coincidences	6	3
Leads, 3 months or less	(2)	(0)
Coincidences	(1)	(0)
Lags, 3 months or less	(3)	(3)
Lags, more than 3 months	2	13

C. SUMMARY OF CONFORMITY

| | 9 industry series | | 4 durable-goods industries | | 5 nondurable-goods industries | |
	All turns	All turns except Korean	All turns	All turns except Korean	All turns	All turns except Korean
Number of comparisons	44	34	20	16	22	18
Matching inventory turns	33	20	16	15	17	15
Percentage of matching turns	75	88	80	94	77	83

[1] Inventory series have been deflated to 1956. 1957–58 turns based on undeflated data. Timing of inventory turns for "Korean" cycle is not shown since there were only 3 inventory turns that could be matched with sales turns related to this episode. See table 12 for timing comparisons of inventory turns with "Korean" reference turns.
[2] No sales or inventory turns occurred. Most recent inventory turn to occur was peak in May 1952 associated with Korean war cycle.
[3] Inventory turn occurs, but no sales turn.
[4] Sales turn occurs but no inventory turn; preceding inventory peak was related to Korean war cycle. Inventory peaks occurred in series as follows: Nondurable-goods industries, November 1951; stone, clay, glass, March 1952; food and beverages, May 1951; chemical, June 1952; petroleum and coal, June 1952.

Source: Based on material from Department of Commerce.

In spite of diversity, there is a well-established characteristic in the timing of both the comprehensive and industry purchased-materials series during the 1948–54 period: turns in these series occur earlier relative to sales at peaks than they do at succeeding troughs. This is true for 24 of the 26 turns in the industry series that could be matched with a specific sales cycle, and for all turns in the deflated comprehensive series.

In addition, turns frequently lead at peaks, on some occasions by very substantial intervals. Lags at troughs are sometimes quite long, well over a year for certain of the industry series. Abramovitz made no provision for the occurrence of substantial leads in stocks relative to sales or output or for substantial lags at troughs. Purchased-materials stocks were presumed to be so clearly associated with output that only lags due to delays in procurement could occur.

Nevertheless, these timing characteristics find support in certain of his prewar data. The timing for three purchased materials which he believed behaved typically is as follows: [6]

	At peaks in activity				At troughs in activity			
	Number of—			Average lead (−) or lag (+) in months	Number of—			Average lead (−) or lag (+) in months
	Leads	Coincidences	Lags		Leads	Coincidences	Lags	
Raw cotton at mills	3	0	5	+1.5	0	1	6	+5.1
Raw silk at mills	1	0	3	+0.5	1	0	2	+1.0
Raw cattle hides at tanners	2	1	2	+1.2	1	0	3	+6.2
3 commodities	6	1	10	-----	2	1	11	-----

When timing comparisons are made at the 1957 peak and the 1958 trough the results are more ambiguous. The durables and nondurables series show shorter lags at peaks than at troughs, but the total manufacturing series shows a 10-month lag at the peak in the sales series and a 6-month lag at its subsequent trough. This paradoxical difference in the timing patterns of the aggregate and its two components is due, not to differences in the timing of durables and nondurables sales turns (which are virtually coincident), but to the fact that the two component inventory series do not decline significantly for a number of months following their peaks; in November 1957 they actually show simultaneous increases sufficient to cause the aggregate to register a peak in that month.

It is difficult to draw conclusions regarding this recent episode. The fact that the data have not been deflated and that prices did rise slightly at this time makes it not unlikely that appropriate deflation would have caused the series to show earlier turns at peaks. A second source of difficulty is the unusual behavior of manufacturing activity during this cycle. Output and sales reached peaks approximately half a year prior to the peak in general business activity, but showed no sharp decline until the business cycle turn. Under such conditions there was not, perhaps, the usual incentive to reduce stocks.

Nevertheless, on the basis of all the evidence, it seems justifiable to regard as significant the tendency for purchased materials to turn earlier at sales peaks than at troughs. Moreover, it is apparent that purchased materials may turn coincidentally with sales turns or even earlier and that lags at troughs may be of considerable duration.

---

[6] As indicated above, Abramovitz worked with a limited sample of 10 commodity series in investigating the behavior of purchased-materials stocks. Of these 10 series, only 8 were available in monthly or quarterly form; only the 3 shown appeared "to be supplied to manufacturers under conditions that afford the degree of responsiveness of supply to changes in demand that characterizes most raw materials purchased by manufacturers * * *," ibid., pp. 190, 393.

The 1957–58 experience does not invalidate these findings; it merely indicates that purchased materials inventory turns may lag at sales peaks as well as at troughs.

Timing and conformity of purchased-materials turns to business cycle turns (table 12 and chart 5) reveal tendencies similar to those pointed out above. Purchased-materials series typically turn earlier at business cycle peaks than at troughs. Among the industry series this earlier timing is manifested in leads or roughly coincident timing at peaks, and in lags at troughs. Thirteen peaks could be matched with business cycle reference peaks. Five of these turns led by more than 3 months, seven were roughly coincident, and only one lagged more than 3 months. (Rubber products lagged behind the reference peak of 1948 by 8 months.) Some of the leads were quite long, as much as 18 months. Eighteen troughs could be matched with business cycle troughs, of which 16 lagged more than 3 months and 2 were roughly coincident. Lags ranged from 3 to 16 months.

Using business cycle turns as a basis for comparison, the conformity rating of the durables is higher than that of nondurables. Purchased-materials stocks of durables show a somewhat higher conformity to sales turns associated with business cycle turns than the nondurable. In addition, the durable sales turns, themselves, conform better to business cycles; i.e., there are fewer "skipped" phases. The net result is that the durables purchased materials show a slightly higher conformity to business cycles, the four durables series matching business cycle turns in 15 of 16 possible comparisons, whereas nondurables matched in only 16 of 20.

TABLE 12.—*Timing and conformity of manufacturers' purchased-materials inventories at reference turns*

A. TIMING MEASURES [1]

	Lead (−) or lag (+) in months							
	Business cycle		Korean cycle		Business cycles			
Industry	Peak November 1948	Trough October 1949	Peak February 1951	Trough June 1952	Peak July 1953	Trough August 1954	Peak July 1957	Trough April 1958
Total manufacturing	−3	+6	+9	+4	+1	+8	+4	+5
Durable-goods industries, total	−16	+4	+13	+2	+1	+10	−4	+4
Nondurable-goods industries, total	−1	+8	+9	(2)	(2)	+7	+1	+10
Primary metals	−5	+7	(2)	(2)	−1	+10	--------	--------
Machinery (including electrical)	−16	+5	+14	+3	0	+7	--------	--------
Transportation equipment (including motor vehicles)	−18	+3	+9	+1	+1	+14	--------	--------
Stone, clay, and glass	−3	+4	+11	(2)	(2)	+6	--------	--------
Food and beverages	−16	+9	+3	(2)	(2)	+9	--------	--------
Paper	0	+10	+15	(2)	(2)	0	--------	--------
Chemical	+1	+6	+16	(2)	(2)	+8	--------	--------
Petroleum and coal	−17	+16	+16	(2)	(2)	+14	--------	--------
Rubber	+8	+10	(2)	(2)	0	+13	--------	--------

B. SUMMARY OF TIMING (9 INDUSTRY SERIES)

	At business cycle peaks	At business cycle troughs
Leads, more than 3 months	5	0
Rough coincidences	7	2
Leads, 3 months or less	(2)	(0)
Coincidences	(3)	(0)
Lags, 3 months or less	(2)	(2)
Lags, more than 3 months	1	16

C. SUMMARY OF CONFORMITY

	9 industry series		4 durable-goods industries		5 nondurable-goods industries	
	All turns	All turns except Korean	All turns	All turns except Korean	All turns	All turns except Korean
Number of comparisons	54	36	24	16	30	20
Matching inventory investment turns	40	31	20	15	20	16
Percentage of matching turns	74	86	83	94	67	80

[1] Inventory series have been deflated to 1956. 1957–58 turns based on undeflated data.
[2] No matching inventory turn.

Source: Based on material from Department of Commerce.

CHART 5

PURCHASED-MATERIALS INVENTORIES AND SALES: TOTAL MANUFACTURING,
DURABLE- AND NONDURABLE-GOODS INDUSTRIES, 1946–58

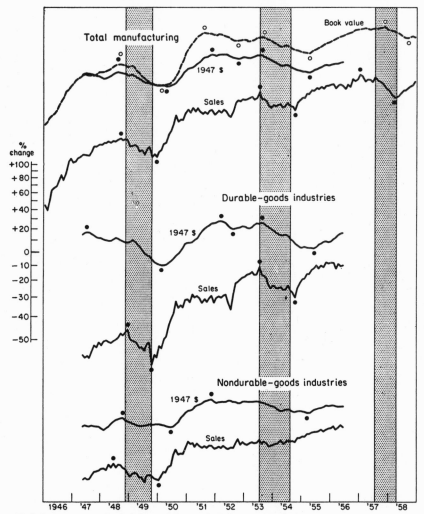

Shaded areas represent business contractions; unshaded areas, expansions.
Dots identify peaks and troughs of deflated inventory cycles; circles, of undeflated cycles. All sales data are undeflated.

Source: Department of Commerce.   Data deflated by the author.

When measured against Korean reference dates, turns in the comprehensive as well as the industry series show very long lags at peaks, quite in contrast to the leading tendency demonstrated at business cycle peaks.   It should be noted that the Korean cycle was unique in that manufacturers reported exceptionally high levels of order backlogs at the beginning of 1951 and that there was a marked difference in the behavior of durables and nondurables.   These matters will be discussed in a subsequent section.

BEHAVIOR OF INVENTORY INVESTMENT

The total manufacturers' purchased-materials investment series shows four cyclical movements from 1945 to 1954, two occurring in the course of each business cycle. (See Chart 6.) In each pair of investment cycles the first is the major movement. The second involves a relatively small increase prior to the sharp declines in both inventory investment and inventories proper which conform closely to the two business cycle recessions.

Differences between the behavior of durables and nondurables occurred during these two secondary movements. For the durables series, there was no significant resurgence of inventory investment immediately following the major movement which reached its peak in the third quarter of 1946, but there was a well-developed upswing (reaching its peak in the second quarter of 1953) following the major investment movement of 1949–50. On the other hand, the nondurables showed a much stronger investment cycle following the initial major postwar cycle, but no cyclical movement following the period of intensive inventory accumulation which reached its maximum level in the final quarter of 1950.

TIMING AND CONFORMITY OF INVESTMENT: COMPARISONS WITH SALES TURNS

The timing and conformity analysis presented in table 13 for the comprehensive and industry series not only substantiates the preceding observations but also provides detail on the essential timing characteristics and relative cyclical sensitivity of the durables and nondurables series.

Among the durables, two of the four industry series (machinery and transportation equipment) showed inventory investment expansion movements in 1948, which were merely declines in the rates of disinvestment, but all showed investment expansions conforming to the final stage of sales expansions that culminated in 1953. Among the nondurables the tendency was clearly different: all industry series showed inventory investment cycles in 1948, but none (except the rubber-goods series) conformed to sales movements in the latter half of the succeeding expansion.

TABLE 13.—*Timing and conformity of manufacturers' purchased-materials inventory investment to sales turns*

A. TIMING MEASURES [1]

Industry	Lead (−) or lag (+) in months, in zones associated with reference turns—Korean war							
	1948 peak	1949 trough	1951 peak	1952 trough	1953 peak	1954 trough	1957 peak	1958 trough
Total manufacturing	−4	−7	(²)	(²)	−2	−11	−17	+2
Durable-goods industries, total	−7	−5	(²)	(²)	−2	−2	−17	+1
Nondurable-goods industries, total	−1	−14	(²)	(³)	(³)	(²)	+4	+5
Primary metals	−6	−5	+8	+2	−2	0		
Machinery (including electrical)	[4]−7	−7	(²)	(²)	−7	−11		
Transportation equipment (including motor vehicles)	[4]−9	−7	(²)	(²)	−2	−11		
Stone, clay, and glass	−5	−4	0	+11	+4	+7		
Food and beverages	−4	+4	(²)	(²)	(⁵)	(⁵)		
Paper	0	+4	+3	+5	(³)	(³)		
Chemical	+2	+7	+5	(⁵)	(⁵)	−2		
Petroleum and coal	−1	−2	(³)	(³)	(⁵)	+11		
Rubber	+1	+10	(⁴)	(³)	(³)	−2	−5	

See footnotes at end of table, p. 35.

TABLE 13.—*Timing and conformity of manufacturers' purchased-materials inventory investment to sales turns*—Continued

B. SUMMARY OF TIMING AND CONFORMITY

Timing and conformity comparisons	9 industry series		4 durable-goods industries		5 nondurable-goods industries	
	All turns	All turns except Korean	All turns	All turns except Korean	All turns	All turns except Korean
Number of comparisons	42	34	20	16	22	18
Matching inventory investment turns	37	30	20	16	17	14
Percentage of matching turns	88	88	100	100	78	78
Leads, more than 3 months		13		11		2
Rough coincidences		10		3		7
Leads, 3 months or less		(6)		(2)		(4)
Coincidences		(2)		(1)		(1)
Lags, 3 months or less		(2)		(0)		(2)
Lags, more than 3 months		7		2		5

1 Inventory investment series have been deflated to 1956; 1957–58 turns based on undeflated data.
2 Inventory investment turn occurs, but there is no sales turn.
3 No turn occurs in either sales or inventory investment.
4 Peak was submerged—a decline in disinvestment.
5 Sales turn occurs but no matching inventory investment turn.

Source: Based on material from Department of Commerce.

CHART 6

PURCHASED-MATERIALS INVENTORY INVESTMENT, NEW ORDERS AND CHANGE IN INDEX OF INDUSTRIAL PRODUCTION, 1946–58

A. Total Manufacturing

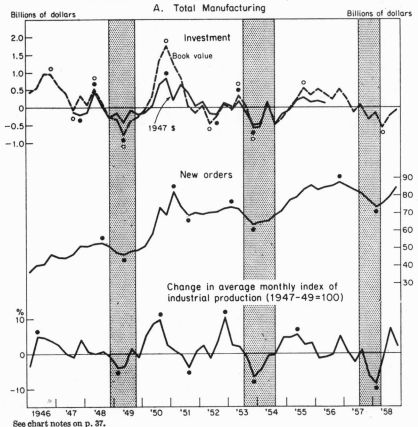

See chart notes on p. 37.

CHART 6—Continued

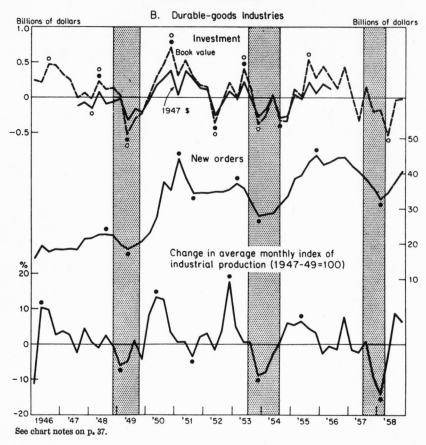

B. Durable-goods Industries

See chart notes on p. 37.

CHART 6—Continued

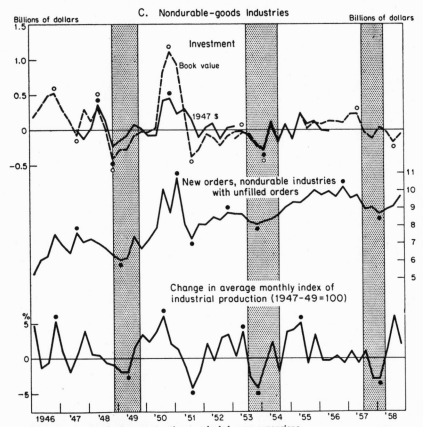

C. Nondurable-goods Industries

Shaded areas represent business contractions; unshaded areas, expansions.
Dots identify peaks and troughs of deflated investment cycles; circles, of undeflated cycles. All new orders data are undeflated.

Source: Investment and new orders data from Department of Commerce. Data deflated by the author. Industrial production series from Federal Reserve Board.

In general, conformity was higher among the durables: All 20 sales turns were matched by stock turns, whereas among the nondurables only 17 of the 22 sales turns could be matched. Moreover, the tendency to lead was much better established for durables than for nondurables. Only 2 of the 16 turns in the durables series which occurred at major sales turns (turns associated with business cycle turns) show a lag, whereas among the nondurables a lag appears in 7 of the 14 turns.

TIMING AND CONFORMITY OF INVESTMENT: COMPARISONS WITH REFERENCE TURNS

Comparison of inventory investment movements to business cycle turns provides additional evidence that this investment is sensitive to business cycle influences and, further, that the durables group is significantly more sensitive to these forces than the nondurables.

Turns in purchased-materials inventory proper could be matched with reference turns (including the Korean subcycle reference turns) in 40 of 54 possible comparisons (table 12). Table 14 shows that inventory investment turns could be matched in 44 of the 54 comparisons.

The durables show a perfect conformity score (inventory investment turns could be matched in each of the 24 comparisons). The nondurables could be matched in only 20 of 30 possible comparisons. Further, as was true in the comparisons with sales turns, the durables inventory investment showed a stronger tendency to lead: 15 of the 16 durables investment turns matched with business cycle reference turns led or turned roughly, coincidently, 10 of the 14 nondurables investment turns matched in the same way showed similar timing.

TABLE 14.—*Timing and conformity of manufacturers' purchased-materials inventory investment at reference turns*

A. TIMING MEASURES [1]

Industry	Lead (−) or lag (+) in months							
	Business cycle		Korean cycle		Business cycles			
	Peak November 1948	Trough October 1949	Peak February 1951	Trough June 1952	Peak July 1953	Trough August 1954	Peak July 1957	Trough April 1958
Total manufacturing	−6	−5	−3	+2	−2	−9	−23	+1
Durable-goods industries, total	−6	−5	−3	−1	−2	0	−23	+1
Nondurable-goods industries, total	−6	−11	−3	(2)	(2)	−6	−2	+4
Primary metals	(3)	−5	−6	+2	−2	0		
Machinery (including electrical)	[4] −6	−5	−3	−1	−8	−9		
Transportation equipment (including motor vehicles)	[4] 0	−5	+3	−1	−2	−9		
Stone, clay, and glass	−6	−2	+3	+5	+4	0		
Food and beverages	−8	+7	−3	−10	(2)	(2)		
Paper	−2	+1	+6	+5	(2)	(2)		
Chemical	−3	+4	+6	(2)	(2)	−9		
Petroleum and coal	0	+1	+15	(2)	(2)	+12		
Rubber	−3	+13	(3)	(2)	−2	−3		

B. SUMMARY OF TIMING AND CONFORMITY

Timing and conformity comparisons	9 industry series		4 durable-goods industries		5 nondurable-goods industries	
	All turns	All turns except Korean	All turns	All turns except Korean	All turns	All turns except Korean
Number of comparisons	54	36	24	16	30	20
Matching inventory turns	44	30	24	16	20	14
Percentage of matching turns	88	83	100	100	67	70
Leads more than 3 months		11		9		2
Rough coincidences:		14		6		8
Leads, 3 months or less		(8)		(3)		(5)
Coincidences		(4)		(3)		(1)
Lags, 3 months or less		(2)		(0)		(2)
Lags, more than 3 months		5		1		4

[1] Inventory series have been deflated to 1956. 1957–58 turns based on undeflated data.
[2] No matching inventory investment turn.
[3] This turn cannot be marked because data begin in early 1948. The data show, however, that there was a well-defined peak at least 6 months prior to reference peak.
[4] Peak was "submerged"—a decline in disinvestment.

Source: Based on material from Department of Commerce.

CYCLICAL AMPLITUDE OF INVENTORY INVESTMENT

In addition to their higher conformity to business cycles, the durables series also move with greater amplitude than the nondurables. This characteristic is clearly shown for inventory investment in table 15. When measured in relative terms, amplitude of total change (peak to trough or trough to peak) is found to be larger for durables in every phase. Relative changes computed on a per-month basis alter the results in only one phase: the abrupt contraction in nondurables from the second to the fourth quarters of 1948 is larger than for durables.

Purchased-materials stocks in durables industries are somewhat smaller than in nondurables, averaging around 40 percent of total purchased materials for the period as a whole, and this serves to reduce somewhat the cyclical impact of the sensitive durables inventory investment movements. When the magnitude of change in durables and nondurables inventory investment is measured in dollars rather than relative to inventory levels (table 15), the latter half of 1948 is once again the only phase in which the contraction in nondurables inventory investment is found to be larger than in durables.

TABLE 15.—*Amplitude of change in purchased-materials inventory investment cycles, by phase, 1948–58*

Industry	Peak–trough (1948–49)	Trough–peak (1949–50)	Peak–trough (1950–52)	Trough–peak (1952–53)	Peak–trough (1953–54)	Trough–peak (1953–55)	Peak–trough (1955–58)
	Total change (relative) [1]						
Total manufacturing	−7.15	+10.28	−7.82	+2.43	−4.57	+7.44	−7.20
Durable goods	−8.60	+14.94	−12.12	+7.23	−9.69	+12.72	−14.78
Nondurable goods	−8.27	+9.28			[2] −3.93	+6.38	−5.00
	Change per month (relative) [1]						
Total manufacturing	−0.60	+0.57	−0.37	+0.81	−0.38	+0.35	−0.34
Durable goods	−.72	+.83	−.67	+.60	−.65	+.61	−.70
Nondurable goods	−1.38	+.39			[2] −.44	+.42	−.13
	Total change (millions of dollars) [3]						
Total manufacturing	−843	+1,220	−1,017	+336	−627	+1,143	−1,136
Durable goods	−415	+700	−626	+406	−513	+921	−1,089
Nondurable goods	−588	+680			[2] −320	+507	−415
	Change per month (millions of dollars) [3]						
Total manufacturing	−70	+68	−48	+112	−52	+54	−54
Durable goods	−35	+39	−35	+34	−34	+44	−52
Nondurable goods	−98	+28			[2] −36	+34	−11

[1] Expressed as percentage of the mean level of inventories during the phase. Mean level is an average of the beginning and ending inventory levels of the terminal quarters of the phase.
[2] To permit comparision with change in durable goods, purchased-materials investment change in nondurable goods has been measured from the second quarter of 1953 to the first quarter of 1954.
[3] All 1948–54 data have been deflated (1947 dollars). Measures for the two most recent phases are based on undeflated (book value) data.

Source: Based on Department of Commerce data.

TIMING AND CONFORMITY OF INVESTMENT: COMPARISONS WITH RATES
OF CHANGE IN OUTPUT

Abramovitz' analysis led him to expect that rates of change in purchased materials would lag behind rates of change in output. Timing analysis of the postwar data tends to bear out this expectation. In table 16 all turns in rates of change in output for total manufactures and for durables manufacturers could be matched by turns in purchased-materials investment, typically with a lag of investment behind output. Timing was irregular, however, especially for the nondurables category. It ranged from coincident to a 12-month lag for total manufacturers, from a 3-to 9-month lag for durables, and from a 6-month lead to a 24-month lag for nondurables. The industry series shows the relationship to be closest where expected, among the durables (particularly the total machinery series), and to be poor or nonexistent among the five available nondurable series. The latter, by the nature of conditions under which materials are procured, would not be expected to show a close timing relation between rates of change in output and inventory investment. On the other hand, some of the lags are much too long to be explained in terms of delays in procurement and, for some of the series, irregularities in timing would seem to be too great to find a place in the theory. Also there are leads in the investment turns which are contradictory to Abramovitz' hypothesis.

FACTORS INFLUENCING THE BEHAVIOR OF PURCHASED MATERIALS

Thus far we have seen that Abramovitz' theory, although it goes far to explain the general behavior of purchased-materials inventories and investment, does not provide for the occurrence of certain observed timing relative to turns in sales, the business cycle as a whole, and rates of change in output.

TABLE 16.—*Timing of purchased-materials inventory investment to rates of change in output*

Industry	Lead (−) or lag (+), in months								Percent of months in phase, mid-1948 through 1958 [1]
	1949 troughs	1950 peaks	1951 troughs	1952 peaks	1953 troughs	1955 peaks	1958 troughs	Average timing	
Total manufacturing	+3	+3	+12	+6	0	+3	+3	+4.3	86
Durable-goods industries	+3	+6	+9	+6	+9	+3	+3	+5.6	82
Nondurable-goods industries	−6	+3	(2)	(2)	+3	+24	+6	(3)	(3)
Primary metals	−6	+6	+3	+6	+6	(2)	(2)	+3.0	---
Machinery (including electrical)	0	+3	+9	0	0	(2)	(2)	+2.4	---
Transportation equipment (including motor vehicles)	−6	+9	+9	+6	+3	(2)	(2)	+4.2	---
Stone, clay, and glass	+6	+12	(2)	(2)	+9	(2)	(2)	(3)	---
Paper	+9	+12	+15	(2)	(3)	(2)	(2)	(3)	---
Chemicals	+9	+12	(2)	(2)	0	(2)	(2)	(3)	---
Rubber	(2)	(2)	(2)	+6	+9	(2)	(2)	(3)	---

[1] Undeflated investment data used for 1956–58. Months in phase computed after adjustment for average timing.
[2] No timing comparisons were possible.
[3] Data lacked sufficient comparability for computation.

Source: Inventory investment computations based on material from Department of Commerce deflated by the author; output computations based on Federal Reserve Board Index of Industrial Production (Manufacturing). Food and beverages and petroleum and coal industries omitted because no timing comparisons were possible.

We may now ask if there are not other significant factors omitted by Abramovitz. Victor Zarnowitz has established that the durable-goods industries produce principally to order and that backlogs of unfilled orders vary in size in the course of the business cycle.[7] In addition, the National Association of Purchasing Agents data show that "lead times" for procurement of materials vary cyclically. Abramovitz' contention that inventory objectives are related to output levels makes no provision for the possible effect that changes in the size of unfilled order backlogs have upon the willingness of selling firms to hold purchased materials. Neither does his theory provide for the impact of altered conditions of availability upon the desired inventory levels of purchasing firms.

It is reasonable to suppose that both these phenomena are important. The necessity of carrying stocks arises principally from the need to avoid the penalties suffered when interruptions occur in production or in the delivery of merchandise by a firm to its customers. Production stoppages, slowdowns, or the inability to supply merchandise in the required type or amount within a time period considered convenient and reasonable by the purchaser entail additional production costs and result in lost sales. They may also damage customer relations thereby reducing the market share of the firm. Consequently, management acts to avoid such risks by carrying stocks in a quantity adequate to provide sufficient protection against delays in delivery by suppliers as well as protection against increases in its own sales requirements. Just what constitutes "sufficient" protection is a matter for individual managers to decide. There are costs and risks incident to carrying additional stocks (e.g., costs of storage and insurance, risk of obsolescence, and adverse price movements) which must be set against the protection they provide. On the basis of all these factors, it would be logical to assume that increased backlogs of unfilled orders (or other assurances of steady or rising future output) or deteriorating availability of materials add to the desirability of carrying additional purchased materials stocks and that decreased backlogs or increased availability reduce the need for stocks.

In the sections which follow these two factors, the level of unfilled orders and availability of materials, along with a third—price movements—are considered in detail.

UNFILLED ORDER BACKLOGS

Zarnowitz has noted that unfilled orders typically lead at peaks in activity, but turn roughly coincidently with activity troughs.[8]

After a major trading movement the large backlog of orders which will have accumulated can provide the basis for expanding shipments for some months, even while the backlog is declining. On the other hand, such a lead is not likely to occur during the latter part of a recession, since any increase would immediately tend to increase the level of production and, where inventories of finished stocks are held or the period of production is short, the level of shipments.

It follows that during late expansion, declining backlogs of orders constitute an invitation to trim any purchased-materials stocks that

---

[7] Victor Zarnowitz, "The Timing of Manufacturers' Orders During Business Cycles," in *Business Cycle Indicators*, Geoffrey H. Moore, editor, Princeton for NBER, 1961, vol. I, pp. 426, 451.
[8] Ibid., p. 451.

may have accumulated excessively during the preceding speculative period. Of course, declining order backlogs seldom signal the oncoming recession as clearly as they may appear in retrospect to have done, but they serve at least to put the manufacturer on his guard. Once made, the decision to curtail stocks is implemented with relative ease. Existing purchase orders may be canceled or, more probably, delivery postponed. Seen in this light changing levels of unfilled orders appear as a reasonable explanation of the observed early turns in purchased-materials stocks at business cycle peaks.

In late recession, however, there will be no comparable influence to exert pressure for larger stocks. Although new orders may turn up before the end of the recession phase, there will be little incentive to press for a higher level of purchased-material stocks until unfilled orders have begun to accumulate. When the decision to add to stocks is finally made, there still remains the delay occasioned by processing the orders and making delivery.

Although these observations may account for the observed lagging tendency of purchased-materials stock turns at troughs, they do not explain the duration of some of these lags. This may occur for any, or all, of the following reasons. (1) Since postwar recessions have been a year or less in duration the reduction of stocks which were at excessive levels during expansion may not have been completed. (2) The manufacturer may be expected to be less aggressive in raising purchased-materials stock levels in early expansion than he is in lowering these stocks in early contraction, since he is not under the same pressure to do so. The beginning of recession is accompanied by demands to conserve working capital, by a rapid increase in availability of goods (this point is discussed at length below), and by expectations of more favorable terms of purchase. In the early months after the trough, however, the manufacturer has no assurance that the incipient recovery will not collapse; prices are not as yet firming appreciably, and materials can still be procured with relatively little delay. (3) The manufacturer may fail to foresee the extent of the pickup as he places his purchase order and an undesired liquidation of inventories occurs; for this reason he underestimates. There is no evidence to indicate which of these is most important, but it is not unreasonable to suppose that all have played a part.

It will be observed in chart 7 that upward movements in purchased-materials inventory investment are substantial only when the increases in new orders are sufficiently in excess of the increases in shipments to bring about rapid accumulations of order backlogs, or when large order backlogs are not significantly reduced by current shipments at the time that a new surge in orders occurs. This generalization sheds light on the great bulge in total purchased-materials investment which occurred in 1946 and the small amplitude (relative to the very large increases in new business) of the second investment cycle which immediately preceded the 1948–49 recession. Similarly, it is helpful in explaining the huge movement in purchased-materials investment in 1950 and the relatively small movement which occurred just prior to the business cycle peak of August 1953. In each of these cases the major movements occurred under conditions of large and rising backlogs. The succeeding smaller movements, however, occurred under conditions of declining backlogs even though the upward movements of new orders were quite sizable.

CHART 7

MANUFACTURERS' UNFILLED ORDERS, RATIOS OF UNFILLED ORDERS TO SALES,
NEW ORDERS, AND PURCHASED-MATERIALS INVESTMENT, 1946–58

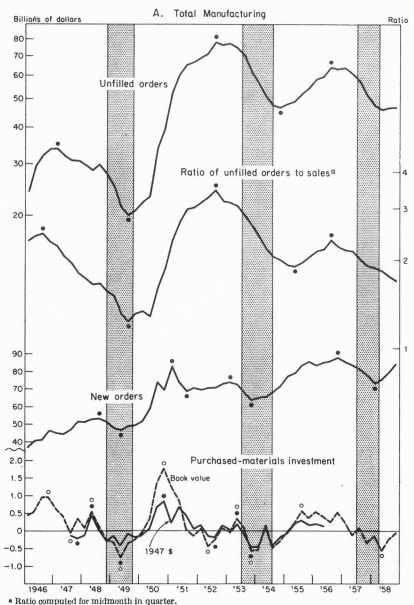

A. Total Manufacturing

a Ratio computed for midmonth in quarter.

See chart notes on p. 45.

CHART 7—Continued

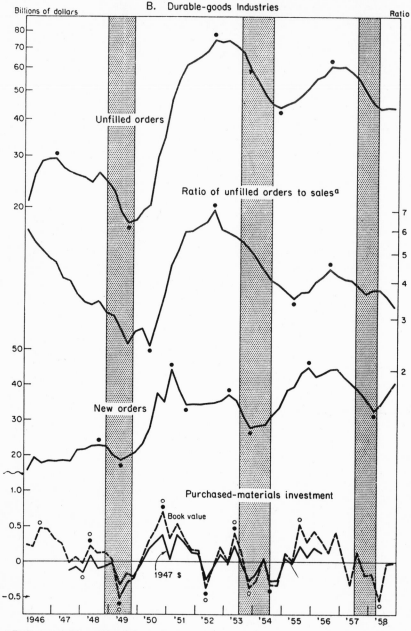

B. Durable-goods Industries

Billions of dollars

Ratio

Unfilled orders

Ratio of unfilled orders to sales[a]

New orders

Purchased-materials investment

Book value

1947 $

1946 '47 '48 '49 '50 '51 '52 '53 '54 '55 '56 '57 '58

[a] Ratio computed for midmonth in quarter.

See chart notes on p. 45.

CHART 7—Continued

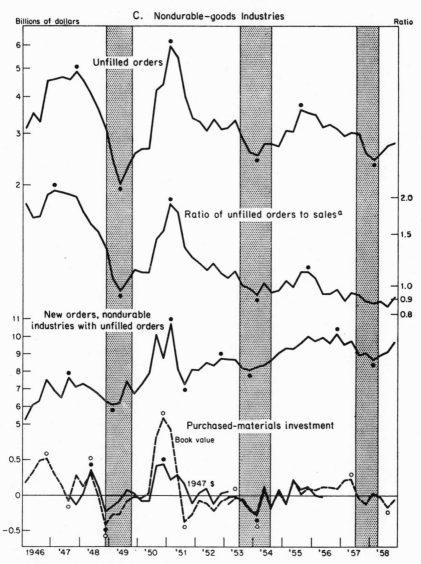

C. Nondurable-goods Industries

* Ratio computed for midmonth in quarter.

Shaded areas represent business contractions; unshaded areas, expansions.
Dots identify peaks and troughs of deflated investment cycles; circles, of undeflated cycles. All other data are undeflated.

Source: Department of Commerce. Data deflated by the author.

In addition, an explanation is provided for the previously observed differences in the behavior of durables and nondurables purchased-materials investment preceding the business cycle peaks of 1948 and 1953. It will be recalled that in the former of these two episodes, durables purchased-materials stocks were declining for months prior to the peak in shipments, with an inventory cycle evident after mid-1947 only in the rate at which disinvestment occurred; but nondurables showed a well-developed second postwar cycle in purchased-materials investment from third quarter 1947 to fourth quarter 1948. In 1952–53, the opposite was the case; nondurables declined after fourth quarter 1950, with only small irregular movements in inventory investment noted, whereas durables displayed a well-established cycle from second quarter 1952 to fourth quarter 1953.

The explanation is to be found in the differences in order backlogs during these two periods (chart 7). In the months immediately following the war, durables and nondurables experienced sharp increases in orders which were sufficient to carry unfilled orders to record peacetime heights. Under these conditions manufacturers increased their stocks of purchased materials sharply. Following this initial wave of demand there was a second wave (i.e., expansion of new orders) which occurred in both durables and nondurables (chart 6), but with quite dissimilar developments. In the nondurables the resurgence in demand in the last half of 1947 resulted in a sustained level of unfilled orders at close to record heights through the first quarter of 1948 (chart 7) and was the occasion for a second investment cycle in purchased materials.[9] In the durables, the second wave of demand which began in late 1947 and continued through most of 1948, though relatively much more substantial than that in nondurables, was easily accommodated as manufacturers reconverted from wartime operation. The result is striking: durables unfilled orders fell almost continuously from the beginning of 1947 until the end of the recession, and there was only a submerged second cycle in the deflated purchased-materials investment series.

Beginning in 1949, both categories experienced upward movements continuing through the two great surges in buying in the third quarter of 1950 and first quarter of 1951, prompted by the Korean war; but after early 1951, movements in the two categories were dissimilar. When it was discovered that there were not to be important consumer shortages, the demand for a variety of nondurables declined and a well-defined recession in the related nondurables industries occurred. New orders fell sharply until 1951, when sales reached a trough. The recovery from this recession, which reached a peak in 1953, was comparable in amplitude of movement to that of 1947–48. The volume of goods demanded was not sufficient, however, to increase the level of unfilled orders, and sales which had been sustained previously by order backlogs gradually declined in spite of the increase in the volume of new business. Under these conditions deflated purchased-materials investment declined throughout the latter part of the business cycle expansion.

In the durables category, defense orders sustained shipments and output to the degree that no well-marked recession developed, although there was a sharp downward movement in new orders from first to

---

[9] It will be noted that a peak in unfilled orders was reached in November 1947, but order backlogs fell very little until after March 1948.

third quarter 1951. The backlog of unfilled orders rose continuously until September 1952 and remained at approximately this level until April 1953. Under these conditions the upsurge in new orders which lasted until May 1953 brought a concomitant increase in purchased-materials investment.

The relation between the level of unfilled orders and the vigor of inventory investment suggests that the capacity level may play a significant role in inventory investment and in the strength of recovery movements in the manufacturing sector. During a period characterized by extensive industrial overcapacity it is not to be expected that there will be a substantial accumulation of unfilled orders.[10] Under such conditions firms would tend to refrain from any substantial purchased-materials investment. This attitude, if generalized, would work significantly against the development of a full-fledged recovery.

AVAILABILITY OF MATERIALS

Fortunately, there are data on cyclical variations in availability of materials used by industrial firms. These data are found in vendor performance statistics collected by the Purchasing Agents Association of Chicago, and in quarter-to-quarter changes in total manufacturers' unfilled orders (Department of Commerce).

The vendor performance series is derived from monthly reports, submitted by member agents, in which each respondent states whether vendors' deliveries are slower, about the same, or faster than in the preceding month.[11] These reports have been consolidated into a diffusion index by combining for each month the percentage of agents reporting increased delays in delivery with one-half of the percentage reporting no change.

The index presumably records the approximate rate of change in availability of materials. When the value of the index is greater than 50, a rising series indicates that availability of materials is declining at an accelerating rate and a declining series indicates continued deterioration, but at a decreasing rate. Conversely, when the index value is less than 50, a declining series indicates accelerated improvement in supply conditions, and a rising series, that the rate of improvement is slackening.

The series for manufacturers' unfilled orders provides essentially the same type of information. Unfilled orders are the accumulated difference between new orders received (less cancellations) and shipments. In a given period, the change in the level of unfilled orders will be the difference between the volume of received orders and the volume of shipments. If orders exceed shipments, unfilled orders will rise, and the larger backlog of unfilled orders will often make it necessary for the firm to quote longer delays to its customers. If, on the other hand, the firm is able to reduce the backlog, it may be able to reduce delays in delivery.

Accordingly, the rates of change in unfilled orders should provide a measure of the acceleration of deterioration, or of improvement in

---

[10] An upward movement in orders would result in some accumulation of unfilled order backlogs because there is a necessary period which must elapse in the production process. This period prevents the outflow (shipments) from equaling the inflow (orders) as long as the inflow is rising. The unfilled orders which thus accumulate, however, are likely to be quite small in comparison to the backlogs which would arise with similar demand conditions and significant constraints upon increases in output.

[11] This series should not be regarded as merely an index of regional supply conditions, for firms in the highly diversified Chicago industrial area purchase from suppliers located throughout the United States.

supply conditions, in the same manner as does the vendor performance series.   Such differences between the behavior of the two series as may appear, should stem from the difference in coverage,[12] or from the fact that one is a value series, and thus affected by price changes, whereas the other is a diffusion index unaffected by price.

It is interesting that these are the same unfilled orders data which were examined in relation to the inventory objectives of selling firms. But the logic is apparent: high or rising unfilled order backlogs bring assurance of a high level of operation to the seller, but to the buyer they bring delays in delivery and problems of procurement.   As a result, both seller and buyer find justification for high levels of purchased-materials stocks.   The converse holds for low or rapidly falling backlogs.

When the vendor performance and unfilled orders series are compared they are found to move in a similar manner.   The troughs associated with the three business cycle recessions are coincident on two occasions and differ by only 3 months on the other.   The major peaks in each of the 1950–51 and 1955 series are 6 months apart on one occasion, and 3 months on the other (chart 8 and table 17).

In addition to these major movements, the vendor performance series records very clearly two brief upswings, one beginning in 1947, the other beginning in 1952.   These movements are less well defined in the unfilled orders series.

Another basis for comparing the series is the date at which they fall below the zero line, indicating the beginning of overall improvement in supply conditions, or rise above it, indicating the start of overall deterioration.   The two series show close timing agreement in the dates at which supply conditions begin to become worse (chart 8).   At two of these comparisons (third quarter 1949 and third quarter 1958), the turns are coincident; at the remaining one (late 1954), timing varies by 3 months.   In comparisons of points at which supply conditions improve, the series agree less well.   On one occasion (late 1946–early 1947), timing varies by 6 months; in the other comparisons, the unfilled orders series lags by 18 months (1951–52) and by 12 months (1955–56).   A possible explanation for these substantial lags is that the total unfilled orders series, in contrast to the diffusion index in which each firm has equal weight, reflects in a larger measure the sluggish movements of order backlogs related to Government defense contracts (the extended lag following May 1951) and producers' durable equipment (the lag in 1956).

---

[12] The vendor performance series is based upon a sample whose coverage cannot be measured precisely, although it is restricted to the performance of manufacturers who supply industrial concerns.   The unfilled orders series is well defined as to coverage but provides information on all manufacturers, regardless of their role as suppliers.

TABLE 17.—*Timing of vendor performance series to quarterly change in unfilled orders and unfilled-orders-to-shipments ratios, all manufacturers, 1947–58*

	Trough	Peak	Trough	Peak	Trough	Peak	Trough	Peak	Trough
Turns in vendor performance [1]	May 1947	August 1948	May 1949	August 1950	February 1952	August 1952	November 1953	August 1955	February 1958
Turns in quarter-to-quarter change:									
Total manufacturers unfilled orders.	0	0	0	+6	−3	−3	0	+3	−3
Unfilled-orders-to-shipments ratios.	0	0	0	+6	−3	0	+3	+12	−6

[1] Percent of purchasing agents (Chicago area) reporting increased delays in delivery plus one-half of those reporting no change.

Source: Vendor performance series compiled from statistics collected by Purchasing Agents Association of Chicago; other series based on material from Department of Commerce.

CHART 8

VENDOR PERFORMANCE AND CHANGE IN UNFILLED ORDERS AND RATIOS OF
UNFILLED ORDERS TO SALES, ALL MANUFACTURERS, 1946–58

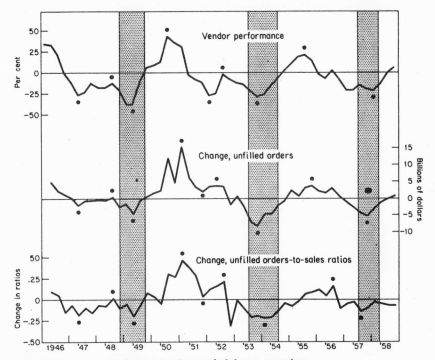

Shaded areas represent business contractions; unshaded areas, expansions.
Dots identify peaks and troughs of specific cycles.
Data are quarterly. For description of vendor performance series, see table 17. Change in unfilled
orders data are end-of-quarter to end-of-quarter. Changes in unfilled orders-to-sales ratios are from mid-
puarter month to midquarter month.

Source: Vendor performance data from Purchasing Agents Association of Chicago; other data from Department of Commerce.

Another method by which the unfilled orders data may be made to
reflect supply conditions is to express them as a ratio to current
shipments. Such a ratio should measure the average delay (in
months), assuming that the current rate of shipments is a reliable
measure of current ability to supply goods.

There are two possible objections to this measure, however. First,
production requires a significant interval. The current rate of
shipments is therefore influenced by previously existing demand
conditions and does not necessarily represent accurately the current
ability of manufacturers to fill orders. Second, these data measure
shipments by manufacturers who produce to stock out of finished
goods as well as by manufacturers who produce to order. Accordingly, the total shipments series may be a faulty standard of current
ability to make shipment on order.

Quarter-to-quarter changes in ratios of unfilled orders to shipments
are presented in chart 8, and appropriate timing measures in table 17.
Timing of this series is substantially the same as that for the rates of
change in unfilled orders except in one comparison, the peak in 1956.

The turns in the data proper show less close agreement, but there is no substantial difference except at the most recent turn.

The behavior of these series demonstrates certain cyclical characteristics which are apparent in each of the three postwar business cycles:

1. Availability of materials reaches its maximum at approximately the trough of the business cycle and begins to deteriorate with the beginning of recovery, or very shortly thereafter. In no instance does either the vendor performance series or the unfilled orders rates-of-change series rise above the zero line prior to the reference trough. Supply conditions deteriorate at an accelerating rate during early expansion and then at a diminishing rate.

2. By mid-expansion, supply conditions begin to improve, although the high levels of unfilled orders in the three observed expansions attest to substantial delays. The improvement may proceed at varying rates, but it is continuous throughout the latter half of the expansion.

3. In the final months of expansion and during early recession, availability improves at an accelerating rate. The maximum rate of improvement is attained before the end of the recession.

PRICE MOVEMENTS

Although it is not within the scope of this study to analyze the behavior of prices, it seems reasonable to suppose that there exists a more than incidental relationship between cyclical movements in prices of purchased materials and changes in the rates of their accumulation. During periods of rising demand, tightening supply, and rapid inventory accumulation, price increases are likely to occur. Under certain conditions such price rises may, in turn, set off inventory buying which will give rise to still further pressure upon prices; under other conditions the interaction with inventory movements might be expected to be small.

Recent work by Victor Zarnowitz sheds new light on the conditions which may cause cyclical price movements. Zarnowitz has advanced and tested the hypothesis that "in industries in which a high or substantial share of output is produced to order, price change is a positive function of the change in the [unfilled order] backlog volume." [13] He finds, as set forth in a recent progress report, that for major industries which have a relatively high degree of competition, high coefficients of correlation between price change and backlog change may be noted. But "in industries with heavily predominant elements of imperfect competition or oligopoly the association between price changes and backlog changes, while still positive, is rather weak." [14] Zarnowitz concludes that "while the response of prices is thus found to be in the direction consistent with the hypothesis, its extent is often small, e.g., the elasticities of price change with respect to backlog change are mostly low (less than unity for all the major manufacturing industries examined with the exception of textile-mill products)." [15]

These findings suggest two points which are relevant to the present study: (1) For many industries, especially in the durable goods sector where inventory investment movements are most volatile, the influence of price changes on inventory behavior may be of rela-

[13] 40th Annual Report of the National Bureau of Economic Research, New York, 1960, pp. 40-41.
[14] Ibid.
[15] Ibid.

tively little importance; and (2) the relationship between price movements and changes in unfilled order backlogs is consistent with and lends support to the hypothesis that the amplitude of movement in purchased-materials inventory investment is conditioned by the level and rate of change of unfilled orders.

The conditions of "excess demand" which, Zarnowitz finds, accompany price fluctuations are the same as those which prompt a high level of inventory accumulation, because (*a*) the price changes which are observed and anticipated by purchasing firms stimulate inventory accumulation, (*b*) the delivery problems which accompany such market conditions make additional purchased-materials stocks desirable, and (*c*) inventory accumulation itself influences price movements (i.e., there is a reciprocal relationship).

INVENTORY OBJECTIVES AND THE PURCHASING PROCESS

In the foregoing section it was shown that the availability of materials fluctuates cyclically. The next task is to examine series which provide evidence of the manner in which inventory objectives and purchasing policy are affected.

MOVEMENTS IN NEW ORDERS AND PURCHASED-MATERIALS INVESTMENT

There is a strong tendency for purchased-materials investment to move in a manner similar to new orders. For the comprehensive data, this is evident at most turns during the entire period. Among three of the industry series [16] one (machinery) shows similar movements throughout the period, a second (transportation equipment), for part of the period, and a third (primary metals) displays a considerable degree of irregularity.

It will be noted (table 18 and chart 6) that the important departures from good conformity occurred during periods when unusual conditions existed. The inventory investment series for total manufactures, durables, and transportation equipment all show lags of 9 months behind new orders at the 1952 investment troughs. This appears to be due principally to the exceptionally large backlog of unfilled orders among the durables which did not diminish significantly until after mid-1952. Under these conditions purchased-materials investment declined very sluggishly, the contraction finally terminating in a sharp downward movement of both stocks and investment in the second quarter of 1952. The abruptness of this decline may be at least partially attributed to the extensive steel strike which occurred at that time and which reduced the flow of this raw material for almost 2 months.

---

[16] Of the nine industry classifications for which stage of fabrication inventory data are available, it was possible to procure new orders figures for only three: primary metals, total machinery, and total transportation equipment.

TABLE 18.—*Timing of purchased-materials inventory investment to new orders* [1]

Industry	Lead (−) or lag (+) in months in zones associated with reference turns							
	Korean war						Percent of months in phase	
	1948 peak	1949 trough	1951 peak	1952 trough	1953 peak	1954 trough	Mid-1948 through 1955	Mid-1948 through 1958
Total manufacturing	−3	0	−3	+9	+3	0	79	76
Durable-goods industries, total	−3	0	−3	+9	+3	0	80	86
Nondurable-goods industries, total	+9	−3	−3	0	+6	+3	83	79
Primary metals [2]	(3)	−3	−6	+3	0	+6	60	(3)
Machinery (including electrical)	0	0	−3	0	−6	+3	87	(3)
Transportation equipment (including motor vehicles)	+6	+3	0	+9	+12	+3	63	(3)

[1] Inventory investment series are quarterly data. Computations were based on undeflated inventory data to permit comparisons with new orders material for which no deflation was possible. As a matter of caution a comparison was made based on deflated inventory data. The results were approximately the same as those shown. New orders data are quarterly totals.
[2] This series showed 2 extra cycles not found in new orders.
Not available.

Source: Based on material from Department of Commerce.

In addition to this departure from close agreement, the transportation-equipment investment series also shows a 12-month lag behind new orders at its last (second quarter 1953) peak. Here again the explanation would appear to be found in the behavior of order backlogs, for unfilled orders continued to rise in the transportation equipment industry after they had turned down elsewhere. New orders for transportation equipment turned down after the second quarter of 1952, but remained above the level of shipments until the end of the first quarter 1953.

Although all turns in new orders for primary metals could be matched from 1949 on, there were two extra cycles in the investment series with the result that overall conformity was low. The poor conformity of the primary metals series cannot be explained on the same grounds as given for the transportation equipment series, but no close conformity should be expected. Producers of primary metals utilize basic ores and other raw materials which are procured only with considerable delay. It is not to be anticipated that investment in these stocks will move as sensitively as the inventory investment of machinery manufacturers, for example, whose purchased-materials stocks are drawn to a considerable degree from standardized, readily available metals and metal parts.

I have extended the analysis to the 1956–58 period for total manufacturers, total durables, and total nondurables. Chart 6 shows the related new orders and inventory investment series moving together in what appears to be the same close relationship noted for the earlier period. Table 18 substantiates this: the percentages of months in phase are not significantly altered by adding the data for these three more recent calendar years.

But why does this close association between orders and purchased-materials investment exist? If the new orders data are looked upon as a purchase orders series, their close relationship to purchased-materials inventory investment are revealed: [17] (a) When manufacturers are attempting to increase stocks at increasing rates they will tend to increase purchase orders above previous levels; (b) when manufacturers are attempting to decrease the rate of accumulation of purchased stocks, but either desire or permit them to continue to rise, they will tend to place smaller orders than previously; (c) during periods when manufacturers are attempting to reduce stocks outright, they will reduce their orders still more; and (d) when manufacturers are allowing their stocks to continue to fall but are attempting to decrease the rate of liquidation they will increase the size of their orders.

Thus it is clear that the pattern of new orders placed will be strongly influenced by action taken to adjust inventories. Moreover, the effect should occur in a roughly instantaneous fashion. In late expansion when manufacturers wish to reduce the rate of inventory accumulation or decrease stocks outright, they will reduce orders placed and request delays of goods currently scheduled for delivery. It may not be within the power of these ordering firms to halt immediately the increase in purchased materials, for they are likely to be committed to their suppliers for a sizable quantity of goods scheduled for future delivery. It would be surprising, however, if they could not sharply alter the rate of accumulation on very short notice. Similarly, in late recession manufacturers who wish to reduce the rate of decline in purchased-materials stocks or to increase them outright will immediately increase orders. Again, the manufacturer may not be able, nor may he desire to halt instantaneously the direction of movement in purchased stocks, but he should be able to alter sharply the rate of liquidation.

CYCLICAL CHANGES IN PURCHASING POLICY

The data relating to cyclical behavior of buying policy originates in reports to the National Association of Purchasing Agents regarding current purchasing policy. Firms are reported as purchasing predominantly on a hand-to-mouth basis, on the basis of 30-day requirements, 60-day requirements, 90-day requirements, 6-month requirements, 1-year requirements or more. The data have been consolidated into two categories: percentage of firms purchasing on the basis of current requirements (30 days or less) and percentage purchasing on the basis of more than current requirements (60 days or more). The latter series is presented in chart 9.

Although this time series is not long, it provides considerable information on the cyclical variations which occur in purchasing policy. The first data became available in January 1950, only 3 months after the reference trough in late 1949. We are able to observe, therefore, almost the entire expansion of 1949–53, the complete expansion of 1954–57 and the first year of the most recent expansion, as well as the recessions of 1953–54 and 1957–58. Of particular

[17] The Department of Commerce new orders series concern orders received but there are two reasons why such data may reflect new orders placed as well. (1) To the extent that the orders reported as received originate with other firms within the same industry they are, of course, authentic purchase orders data for that industry. The larger the industry group, the more likely is this to be the case. (2) To the extent that orders received by manufacturers give rise to purchase orders which have the same pattern of timing, new orders received may be regarded as a proxy for purchase orders placed by reporting firms. Evidence that firms tend to place purchase orders synchronously with the receipt of new orders has been presented by Ruth Mack and Victor Zarnowitz. See Ruth P. Mack, "Consumption and Business Fluctuations," New York, 1956 and Ruth P. Mack and Victor Zarnowitz, "Causes and Consequence of Changes in Retailers' Buying," American Economic Review, March 1958, 18–49.

CHART 9

PURCHASING POLICY, VENDOR PERFORMANCE, TOTAL MANUFACTURERS' PUR-
CHASED-MATERIALS INVESTMENT AND NEW ORDERS, 1946–58

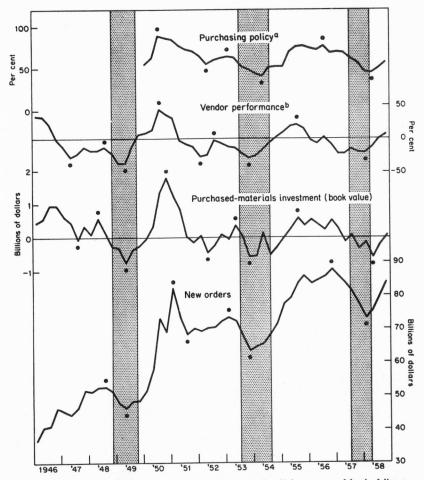

ᵃ Purchasing policy series is percent of purchasing agents reporting 60 days or more delay in delivery.
January 1950 to April 1955 data cover all purchases; subsequent data, production materials only.
  ᵇ For description of series see table 17.

Shaded areas represent business contractions; unshaded areas, expansions.
Dots identify peaks and troughs of specific cycles.

Source: Purchasing policy series compiled from National Association of Purchasing Agents data.   Vendor
performance series compiled from Purchasing Agents Association of Chicago data.   Other series compiled
from Department of Commerce data.

interest is the behavior of the purchasing-policy series in early expansion and during recession.   In each of the three expansions, observable
in whole or in part, the early months are characterized by very sharp
increases in the percentage of firms purchasing on the basis of more
than current requirements.   Between January and June of 1950 (the
remainder of the year is excluded because of the crisis buying which
accompanied the outbreak of Korean hostilities) the percentage of
firms purchasing on this long-range basis rose from 53 to 69 percent.

In the period June 1954 to December 1955, it rose from 41 to 80 percent,[18] and from April 1958 to April 1959, it rose from 43 to 68 percent.

It will also be noted that during the two complete expansions observed, the percentage of firms purchasing in the 60-day-or-longer range reached a maximum by midphase. The range of purchase began to shorten well before the reference peak, but the sharpest drop occurred during the period extending approximately from the reference peak month to the date of the reference trough. In the period from May 1953 to May 1954, the series fell from 64 to 40 percent; and in the period from May 1957 to February 1958, it fell from 71 to 41 percent.

Taken together the series representing purchasing policy, supply conditions, new orders, and purchased-materials investment provide valuable insight into the processes by which inventory objectives fluctuate in the course of the business cycle.[19]

As already observed, movements in the new-orders series appear, to a significant extent, to reflect buyers' efforts to adjust stocks; i.e., a rising volume of orders would seem to reflect attempts of buyers to decrease the rate of disinvestment in purchased goods or to increase the rate of investment; and a declining volume of orders, attempts to reduce the rate of investment in purchased goods or to increase the rate of disinvestment. Of course, the new-orders data are comprised principally of purchases for production or for resale rather than for inventory accumulation; in general, their rise and fall must be largely in response to changes in final demand. Nevertheless, inventory investment demand is superimposed upon this demand, and the data give evidence that the former influences significantly the timing of turns in the aggregate order series. This was inferred in the previous section from the similarity in the timing of turns in new orders and in purchased-materials investment. It is now supported further by the close agreement between timing of both of these series and the purchasing-policy series.

---

[18] The data are not perfectly comparable throughout, however. Prior to May 1955 agents submitted reports in which all types of purchases were combined. From May 1955 forward, reports were made on the basis of three categories: production materials, maintenance and materials repair, and capital expenditures. Only data covering production materials buying are shown for this latter period.

[19] This discussion is based on chart 9 and table 19, which concern vendor-performance, purchasing-policy, orders, and purchased-materials investment series.

TABLE 19.—*Timing comparisons: Vendor performance, purchased-materials investment, total manufacturers new orders, purchasing policy series, 1946–58*

A. TIMING TO PURCHASING POLICY SERIES

Series compared	Peak, August 1950	Trough, May 1952	Peak, February 1953	Trough, May 1954	Peak, August 1956	Trough, May 1958
Vendor performance	0	−3	+6	−6	−12	−3
Purchased materials investment	+3	0	+3	−6	−12	0
Total manufacturers' new orders	+6	−9	0	−6	+3	−3

B. TIMING TO PURCHASED MATERIALS INVESTMENT SERIES

Series compared	Trough, August 1947	Peak, May 1948	Trough, May 1949	Peak, November 1950	Trough, May 1952	Peak, May 1953	Trough, November 1953	Peak, August 1955	Trough, May 1958
Vendor performance	−3	+3	0	−3	−3	−9	0	0	−3
Purchasing policy	(1)	(1)	(1)	−3	0	−3	+6	+12	0
Total manufacturers' new orders	(2)	+3	0	+3	−9	−3	0	+15	−3

1 Not available.
2 No turn.

Sources: Vendor performance data compiled from statistics collected by Purchasing Agents Association of Chicago; purchasing policy series compiled from data published by the National Association of Purchasing Agents. Other series based on material from Department of Commerce.

In general, during periods in which total new orders are rising, the purchasing-policy series is also rising (i.e., the typical purchase range is lengthening), thereby indicating that the volume of orders placed during these periods of expanding trade is rising in relation to current operating requirements. It is at this time that realized disinvestment is declining sharply (in the very early months of expansion) or realized investment is rising (as the expansion progresses).

During periods in which total new orders are falling, the purchasing-policy series, declines, revealing that the volume of purchase orders is falling in relation to current operating requirements (i.e., the typical purchasing range is shortening). During such periods realized investment is found to be decreasing (or realized disinvestment increasing).

The inference that the rise and fall in orders reflects, to a significant degree, the efforts of firms to alter the rate of accumulation or de-accumulation of stocks, is supported by the fact that orders lead turns in business cycles. Since turns in manufacturers' shipments, as well as turns in retailers' sales, show no similar tendency to lead cycle turns, it may be presumed that the early turns in orders do not reflect a reversal in end-use demand, but rather an attempt by businessmen to adjust their stocks or their purchase commitments.

In addition, the role played by supply conditions in cyclical variations in purchasing policy is an important one. To be sure, it is not possible to distinguish conclusively between cause and effect here: supply conditions deteriorate because purchasing policy alters and orders increase; purchasing policy may change and orders may increase in turn, because supply conditions deteriorate. Yet, the similarity of movement in the vendor-performance and purchasing-policy series indicates some degree of causation in the role played by supply conditions, particularly in the light of the functions exercised by purchasing executives.[20] It is difficult to imagine that the changes in vendor performance observed in the data do not prompt executives to revise their inventory target levels. Indeed, if purchasing agents were not influenced by such considerations, one of their major associations would not collect and publish the data on vendor performance examined here.

The influence of supply conditions may operate in two ways during expansions: (1) Deterioration in supply conditions makes it more difficult to achieve inventory objectives, so realized inventory investment will be somewhat less than that desired; and (2) deterioration in supply conditions influences the inventory objective itself.

The second is by no means a simple concept. If it were, we might expect to find that the purchasing range would be rising as long as availability is deteriorating; that is, as long as the vendor-performance series lies above the zero line. In fact, however, the turn in the purchasing-policy series occurs at approximately the same time as that in the vendor-performance rate-of-change series.

One can only speculate regarding the explanation of this intriguing relationship. One suggestion is that purchasing agents may view the declining rate of deterioration in vendor performance as a signal that delivery conditions will begin to improve in the near future, and thus, via a change in anticipations, the range of purchase is shortened.

SUMMARY AND CONCLUSIONS

Although there are variations in the behavior of individual industry series, certain characteristics of purchased-materials behavior appear to be clearly established. Purchased-materials stocks conform well to cyclical movements, turning earlier at sales and business cycle peaks than at troughs. Turns in the comprehensive series tend to coincide with business cycle peaks and lag at business cycle troughs. This timing characteristic does not carry over to inventory investment behavior: the comprehensive investment series show leads at all business cycle turns. In these movements the durables series show a higher conformity and a greater amplitude of movement.

The well-established tendency of inventory investment turns to lead reference turns during the period under study is of major significance for business cycle analysis. In late expansion the decline in the level of inventory investment has constituted a source of declining demand for the factors of production, and during late recession the decline in the rate of disinvestment has provided a source of new strength in the economy. To the extent that these observations are typical, purchased-materials investment may be regarded as one of those highly strategic forces which serve to turn the cyclical tide.

Abramovitz' theory does not provide for the occurrence of certain observed timing in the inventory and investment series. Moreover, it fails to consider the possible role of unfilled-order backlogs, availability of materials, and price behavior of purchased goods in influencing inventory behavior. In an effort to provide a fuller explanation, these influences were examined.

---

[20] Note that the two series are reported by different purchasing agent groups, so that they are, at least statistically, independent.

The amplitude of movements in purchased-materials investment was found to be related to the size and direction of movement of manufacturers' unfilled-order backlogs. Series reflecting availability of materials were constructed from the vendor-performance data of the Purchasing Agents Association of Chicago and from unfilled-orders data. From the behavior of these series it was observed that—

(1) Availability of materials reaches its maximum at approximately the trough of the business cycle and begins to deteriorate with the beginning of recovery, or shortly thereafter. Supply conditions deteriorate at an accelerating rate during early expansion and then at a diminishing rate.

(2) By midexpansion, supply conditions begin to improve although there are still substantial delays in delivery.

(3) In the final months of expansion and during early recession availability improves at an accelerating rate. The maximum rate of improvement is attained before the end of the recession.

There is evidence that industrial prices move in response to the same conditions of demand and supply that influence purchased-materials inventory investment. It is reasonable to suppose that they not only respond to such forces but also play a causal role. However, for many industries, especially in the durable-goods sector, the influence may be relatively small.

In a final section, the behavior of inventory objectives and purchasing policy was observed in relation to the availability of materials and realized inventory investment. Data relating to leadtime of purchase show that the cyclical behavior of purchasing policy is well-developed; the series move in a manner similar to that of the series reflecting availability of materials. Moreover, the timing of the purchasing-policy series agrees rather closely with that of manufacturers' new orders and purchased-materials inventory investment. Taken together these series tell of a sensitive process by which rising inventory objectives and deteriorating supply conditions are matched by rising orders and an ever-increasing rate of inventory accumulation in the earlier stages of expansion. Reversal begins in late expansion, but the sharpest declines in inventory objectives, orders, and realized inventory investment, as well as the sharpest improvement in supply conditions, occur during recession.

5

Finished-Goods Inventories and
Inventory Investment

In analyzing the behavior of finished goods, Abramovitz distinguished two major types: finished goods made to order and finished goods made to stock. The second category was subclassified according to whether the production cycle of the commodity was governed by demand or by conditions of raw materials supply, and according to whether the finished products were perishable items or staples. This classification may be outlined as follows:

I. Goods made to order.
II. Goods made to stock:
    A. Goods whose production cycles are governed by demand:
        1. Perishables.
        2. Nonperishable staples.
    B. Goods whose production cycles are governed by the supply of raw materials:
        1. Perishables.
        2. Nonperishable staples.

Abramovitz drew no conclusions regarding the timing of finished-goods inventories as a whole, but instead dealt with the behavior of the component classifications. Goods made to order he saw as tied to the level of output.[1] Of those goods whose production cycle is governed by demand, nonperishable staples would tend to move inversely to the rate of manufacturing and to business cycles; perishable goods, even if produced to stock, would be expected to vary with the volume of business, moving with, perhaps, a moderate lag. Goods whose output is governed by supply would not be expected to be cyclically sensitive. Their behavior would be influenced by the conditions of supply and the degree of perishability of the product.

Knowledge of the relative importance of these several components may be gained by examining the composition of finished stocks, comparing Abramovitz' estimates for the prewar period with postwar estimates. Such an investigation is made in this chapter; it is followed by an analysis of inventory behavior which deals first with the largest component, staple (nonperishable) made-to-stock finished goods whose production is governed by demand, and then with total finished goods. In subsequent sections inventory investment behavior is treated in a similar manner.

COMPOSITION OF STOCKS

Abramovitz' estimates of the size of the various components was based largely on an analysis of finished goods within each industrial

---

[1] The statements contained in this paragraph are based on Abramovitz, "Inventories and Business Cycles, With Special Reference to Manufacturers Inventories," New York, November 1950, pp. 240-241.

breakdown of the 1939 Census of Manufactures. He used the following classification:

1. Finished goods whose raw materials were procured from the agricultural sector:
    (a) perishable.
    (b) nonperishable staple.
2. Finished goods whose raw materials were procured from the nonagricultural sector:
    (a) perishable.
    (b) nonperishable staple.

His investigation was made on the assumption that commodities whose raw materials were procured from the agricultural sector would have production cycles that were supply determined and from the nonagricultural sector, production cycles that were demand determined. The assumption results in an underestimate of the demand determined category, in that there are important industries using agricultural raw materials that are not supply dominated (e.g., cotton textiles). The approach does, however, indicate the importance of nonfarm goods which, by and large, can be reliably classified as demand dominated. Moreover, it makes possible the identification of those industries for which agricultural raw materials are most important, and permits, through an inquiry into the nature of their production processes, the determination of whether their fluctuations are supply or demand influenced.

A duplication of Abramovitz' techniques, making use of 1947 Census of Manufactures data, revealed the following:

1. The staple demand dominated category was by far the largest; it is estimated at roughly 66 percent. Staple finished goods whose raw materials are procured from the nonagricultural sector accounted for 55.3 percent of total finished stocks; some produced from agricultural raw materials, but clearly demand dominated, accounted for 10.3 percent more.[2]

2. Those industrial categories using agricultural raw materials which may be supply influenced, and whose finished stocks are staple, accounted for about 23 percent of total finished goods. They included principally the food, beverage, and tobacco industries which are probably the least sensitive to business cycles.

3. The perishables are a relatively small category. Perishable finished goods whose raw materials are agricultural were estimated to be 9.1 percent; those with nonagricultural raw materials, 2.4 percent.

This classification of census material provides no insight into the size of the made-to-order category, but there is reason to believe that it is relatively small. Abramovitz estimates that it is no more than 15 to 25 percent of total finished goods stocks in spite of the fact that a much larger volume of business is done on a production-to-order basis.[3]

---

[2] I estimate that in 1947 the staple finished stocks held in the textile industry accounted for 5.8 percent of total finished goods; in the apparel industry, 3.1 percent, and in the leather goods industry, 1.4 percent. All are demand-oriented industrial activities, although, according to Abramovitz' classification, they make important use of agricultural raw materials.

[3] I found finished stocks-to-sales ratios for goods made to order to be much lower than similar ratios for goods made to stock, indicating that the magnitude of the former is much smaller than might be implied by the importance of the practice of producing to order (see footnote 7 below). For an analysis of the importance of production to order as a postwar practice in American manufacturing see Victor Zarnowitz, "The Timing of Manufacturers' Orders During Business Cycles," in *Business Cycle Indicators*, vol. I, Princeton for NBER, p. 426.

If we accept Abramovitz' rough estimate that 15 to 25 percent of finished stocks are made to order and deduct this from the 66 percent of total finished stocks previously designated as the staple demand dominated category, then staple made-to-stock finished goods in industries whose production cycles are demand dominated comprise from 41 to 51 percent of total finished goods. This estimate, combined with the percentages of perishables and the supply-dominated staples given above, provide an estimated composition of finished goods in 1947 which is compared with Abramovitz' estimates for 1939 in table 20.

Two observations may be helpful in interpreting the subsequent analysis of finished goods behavior. The first is that demand-dominated, nonperishable, made-to-stock finished goods, though important, are less so than before the war. This change in composition should make for somewhat less inverted behavior in the entire category. The second is that the estimate of made-to-order finished goods may well be too low. I have accepted Abramovitz' very tentative figure in the absence of other evidence, but a larger made-to-order category is quite possible in view of the increased importance of durables (produced principally to order) in the postwar period. Of course, a larger made-to-order component would also tend to reduce inverted behavior in the entire finished-goods category.

TABLE 20.—*Estimated composition of finished goods stocks, 1939 and 1947*

Components of finished goods stocks	1939 (percent)	1947 (percent)
Goods made to order	15–25	15–25
Goods made to stock	75–85	75–85
Goods whose production cycles are governed by demand:		
Perishables	(¹)	2
Nonperishable staples	50–60	41–51
Goods whose production cycles are governed by supply:		
Perishables	(¹)	9
Nonperishable staples	16	23

¹ Total perishables were estimated to be 9 percent. There was no breakdown.

Source: For 1939 estimates see Abramovitz, "Inventories and Business Cycles," p. 246; 1947 estimates were prepared from 1947 Census of Manufactures data.

In evaluating the significance of composition we must keep in mind that there does not exist in practice the sharp distinction between firms producing to stock and firms producing to order that is implied by the preceding classification. One finds new cases in which the producer sells entirely on an immediate delivery basis out of stock already on hand, and relatively few in which there is no production except to order. There will usually be at least some orders taken for subsequent delivery; and the practice of producing to stock may vary from that of a firm which produces a line of standardized items, selling freely from stock, but studying closely such orders for future delivery as it receives as a guide in planning production—to the firm which produces almost entirely against orders, but allows a relatively small quantity of buffer stocks to fall and rise against the cyclical tide.

Nevertheless, manufacturers do tend to operate predominantly on either a produce-to-stock or produce-to-order basis. Evidence that variability of practice may exist within these well-established classifications is found in the results of tests performed by Victor Zarnowitz, which revealed that made-to-stock and made-to-order activities could be distinguished by the size of average ratios of stocks to unfilled orders over a period of years. Working with a variety of manufacturing activities and industry groups which had previously been reliably classified as producing principally to stock or to order, Zarnowitz found that the stock-to-unfilled-orders ratios fell into a well defined dichotomy: ratios for the made-to-order series had average values substantially below the level of 1; ratios for the made-to-stock series, values above 1.[4] Zarnowitz also notes that, "according to the ratios * * * industries which sell mainly from future output are decidedly dominant in the composite of all durable manufactures. In contrast, production to stock apparently prevails within the aggregate of nondurable goods industries." [5]

THE STAPLE, MADE-TO-STOCK INVENTORY SERIES

Abramovitz studied the behavior of demand-dominated staples made to stock with a sample of 18 nonfarm commodities.[6] In the present study, 25 series, representing a variety of activities, are analyzed. Among them are postwar extensions of some of Abramovitz' original 18 series. The only available commodities which have been omitted are those which would have given roughly duplicate coverage (e.g., additional lumber series, some other categories of gas heaters, men's hosiery).

Abramovitz' 18 series, as well as the 25 here, may be regarded as representing activities in which production is principally to stock rather than to order, although several of the postwar series would seem to be on the borderline.[7]

TIMING AND CONFORMITY OF STOCKS DURING ACTIVITY CYCLES

The 25 commodity series display well-developed timing and conformity characteristics. They tend to move with good conformity in a strongly inverted fashion relative to activity (see table 21).[8] Ninety-one inventory turns may be matched with the 109 activity turns on an inverted basis.[9] In a large majority of the comparisons (64 out of 91) the inverted turns in stocks were roughly coincident with activity turns. The remaining comparisons were about equally divided between leads and lags of 4 or more months. Average timing for all comparisons on an inverted basis was approximately coincident.

[4] Zarnowitz, in Business Cycle Indicators, vol. I, p. 426.
[5] Ibid.
[6] We shall have occasion to refer frequently to this category of finished goods. For the sake of convenience it shall be designated henceforth simply as "staples made to stock."
[7] In attempting to apply the Zarnowitz test to the 25 series it was found that only 8 have unfilled orders data available. Of these, seven (gas domestic heating stoves, bathtubs, lavatories, southern pine lumber, oak flooring, paper, and ladies full-fashioned hosiery) are clearly made-to-stock activities with stocks-to-unfilled-orders ratios ranging from 1.39 to 5.15. The other series—paper products—is a borderline case with a ratio of 0.62.
  In an effort to classify the remaining series, stock-to-sales ratios were tested as an alternative basis of classification. The series for which both types of ratios were available were ranked first according to Zarnowitz' average stocks-to-unfilled-orders ratios, and then according to average stocks-to-sales ratios during the period 1948–55. The ranks were identical.
  Using the stocks-to-sales in lieu of stocks-to-unfilled-orders ratios it was then possible to classify the entire sample. With 2 exceptions (newsprint, 0.29, and wood pulp, 0.10) all of the series had stock-to-sales ratios considerably larger than the border-line paper products (stocks-to-sales ratio, 0.42); 16 had ratios above 1, 20 above 0.70.
[8] I attempted to use shipments (sales) data where possible to represent activity, and was able to secure such data for 20 of the 25 commodities. For the remaining commodities, output data were used. As Abramovitz has shown, the two give very similar results. See Abramovitz, "Inventories and Business Cycles," p. 248.
[9] Immediately following the war there occurred a long period of finished-goods inventory buildup. No inverted behavior of stocks took place until the recession of 1948–49. For this reason the comparisons were not begun on an inverted basis until the beginning of the 1948–49 recession period.

TABLE 21.—*Timing and conformity of 25 commodities at activity turns, 1947–55*

A. TIMING AND CONFORMITY MEASURES

Stocks	Indicator of activity	Activity turns [1]	Turns matched [1]	Extra turns	Percent months out of phase [2]
1. Gas domestic stoves	Shipments	5	5		80
2. Gas ranges	do	5	5		74
3. Warm air furnaces	do	5	5		87
4. Domestic refrigerators	do	5	5		77
5. Electric ranges	do	5	3		84
6. Lavatories	do	5	5		96
7. Kitchen sinks	do	3	3		90
8. Bathtubs	do	5	5		87
9. Southern pine lumber	do	5	5		79
10. Oak flooring	do	3	3	2	56
11. Glass containers	do	5	5		72
12. Refined copper	do	3	3	2	55
13. Slab zinc	do	3	3		61
14. Lead	do	5	3		49
15. Portland cement	do	0	0	5	([3])
16. Women's hosiery	do	4	4	1	62
17. Auto tires	do	5	3		54
18. Newsprint at mills	do	2	1	3	([4])
19. Paper, all grades	do	3	2		58
20. Total rayon	do	5	5		90
21. Synthetic rubber	Production	5	5		62
22. Lubricants	do	3	3		72
23. Wood pulp at mills	do	3	2		51
24. Cotton cloth, unsold mill stock	Cotton consumption at mills.	5	5		89
25. Flat rayon fabrics	Production	5	3		35

B. SUMMARY OF TIMING AND CONFORMITY [1]

	Number
Number of activity turns	109
Matching turns	91
Leads, 4 or more months	14
Rough coincidences	64
Leads, 1–3 months	(22)
Coincidences	(11)
Lags, 1–3 months	(31)
Lags, 4 or more months	13
Average timing all turns	+.08

[1] Only turns beginning with the trough in activity corresponding to the trough of the 1948–49 recession have been used in this analysis. Conformity and timing measures are based on inverted timing.
[2] First major peak to final major trough.
[3] No activity turns.
[4] No 1948–49 cycle.

Source: Line 1: Facts for Industry, series M51E, Department of Commerce; lines 2, 3: Facts for Industry series M51N; lines 4, 5: data from National Electrical Manufacturers Association, with restrictions on publishing; lines 6, 7, 8: Facts for Industry series M51H; lines 9–15, 17–19, 21, 22: Survey of Current Business, various issues and supplements; line 16: National Association of Hosiery Manufacturers, annual reports; line 20: Textile Organon, various issues; line 23: Facts for Industry, series FF1, 14A, line 24: various issues of Textile Hi-Lights, American Cotton Manufacturers Association (data for cotton consumption at mills from Survey of Current Business); line 25: data from National Federation of Textile Manufacturers, with restrictions on publication.

Abramovitz' investigations established for the prewar period the hypothesis that staples made to stock would tend to conform to activity cycles in an inverted fashion, but that the tendency for stocks to move in the opposite direction from sales and output would weaken as the phase increased in duration. This length-of-phase hypothesis was demonstrated by an analysis of timing in inventory turns compared, on an inverted basis, to the timing of turns in corresponding indicators of manufacturing activity. When leads and lags in the inverted stock series were classified according to the length of their comparable activity phases, it was found that the percentage of leads in the stock turns increased as the duration of the phase increased; the average timing changed from a lag for phases of 12 months and under, to a lead which became progressively larger as the activity phase lengthened beyond 12 months.[10]

When the same test was performed for the postwar data, the hypothesis was sustained both for expansions and contractions, with some indications that the postwar turns occurred slightly earlier. Sufficient observations for analysis could be made for only two categories of phase duration, 12 months and under, and 13 to 24 months. For these two categories leads of 1 or more months occurred in 30 and 50 percent of total timing comparisons, in contrast to 19 and 43 percent for similar prewar timing computations. The average postwar timing (inverted) was a lag of 1.2 months for activity phases of 12 months and under, and a lead of 1.05 months for those of 13 to 24 months, compared with average prewar lags of 6.1 months and 0.7 month, respectively.[11]

TOTAL FINISHED GOODS INVENTORIES

For the period from 1945 to 1958, it is clear (see chart 10) that total finished stocks conform positively to sales cycles, lagging by a number of months at most turns. During the relatively short sales contraction phases lags in the inventory series make for essentially inverted timing, but during the longer expansion phases the two series move in the same direction in most months. It is for this reason that the timing comparisons in table 22 are made on a positive, rather than an inverted basis.

TIMING AND CONFORMITY OF STOCKS: COMPARISONS WITH SALES AND REFERENCE TURNS

Timing comparisons for finished goods inventory turns are shown in table 22 for the comprehensive and the nine-industry series, along with measures indicating the degree to which cyclical movements in finished goods conform to cycles in the sales series. The total manufacturing and durables series conformed positively to major turns in sales activity in 1948–49, 1953–54, and 1957–58, but displayed long lags at five of the six turns (table 22 and chart 10). It is interesting that the nondurables inventory series shows a longer lag than the durables series at only one of the four comparisons; the lag is actually shorter on two occasions. Zarnowitz' finding that the practice of producing to stock is much more prevalent among nondurables would lead us to expect significantly longer lags in this series at all turns. There is no direct evidence to explain the observed behavior. It is possible that it may reflect the fact that nondurables sales do not fluctuate as vigorously as those of durables. If inverted movements in staples made to stock are regarded as largely due to unanticipated changes in sales, it is to be expected that the duration of inverted behavior (i.e., the duration of the lag of inventories behind sales) would be influenced by the extent to which sales fluctuate.

[10] Ibid., pp. 249–256.
[11] Ibid., p. 253.

CHART 10

FINISHED-GOODS INVENTORIES AND SALES: TOTAL MANUFACTURING, DURABLE-
AND NONDURABLE-GOODS INDUSTRIES, 1946–58

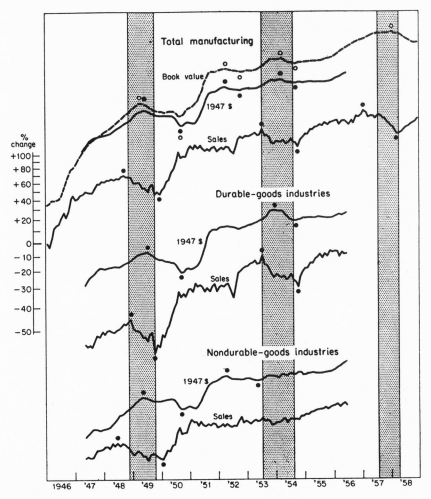

Shaded areas represent business contractions; unshaded areas, expansions.
Dots identify peaks and troughs of deflated inventory cycles; circles, of undeflated cycles. All sales data
are undeflated.

Source: Department of Commerce. Data deflated by the author.

Postwar Cycles in Manufacturers' Inventories

TABLE 22.—*Timing and conformity of manufacturers' finished goods inventories at sales turns*

A. TIMING MEASURES [1]

Industry	Lead (−) or lag (+) of inventories to sales, in months, in zones associated with business cycle reference turns					
	1948 peak	1949 trough	1953 peak	1954 trough	1957 peak	1958 trough
Total, manufacturing	+9	+9	+8	−1	+12	+9
Durable goods industries, total	+7	+11	+5	−1	+12	+9
Nondurable goods industries, total	+11	+8	(2)	(2)	+12	+6
Primary metals	+7	3 +20	+9	+13	------	------
Machinery (including electrical)	+8	+9	+5	+15	------	------
Transportation equipment (including motor vehicles)	−21	+9	+3	+5	------	------
Stone, clay, and glass	+10	+9	(2)	(2)	------	------
Food and beverages	3 +20	+9	−3	+2	------	------
Paper	3 +20	3 +21	(4)	(4)	------	------
Chemical	+14	3 +20	(2)	(2)	------	------
Petroleum and coal	+7	+8	+12	+6	------	------
Rubber	+13	+15	+2	+7	------	------

B. SUMMARY OF TIMING AND CONFORMITY

Timing and conformity comparisons	9-industry series	4 durable goods industries	5 nondurable goods industries
Number of comparisons at business cycle turns	34	16	18
Matching inventory turns	30	14	16
Percentage of matching inventory turns	88	88	89
Leads more than 3 months	1	1	0
Rough coincidences	4	1	3
Leads 3 months or less	(1)	(0)	(1)
Coincidences	(0)	(0)	(0)
Lags 3 months or less	(3)	(1)	(0)
Lags more than 3 months	25	12	13

[1] Inventory series have been deflated to 1956, 1957–58 turns based on undeflated data. Timing comparisons are based on a positive relationship between cyclical movements. Timing of inventory turns for "Korean" cycle is not shown since there were no inventory that could be matched with sales turns related to this episode. See table 23 for timing comparisons of inventory turns with Korean reference turns.
[2] Sales turn occurs, but no matching inventory turn.
[3] Timing relationship is completely inverted· turn is coincident with subsequent sales turn.
[4] No turn occurs in either sales or inventories.

Source: Based on material from Department of Commerce.

For the Korean period it is difficult to measure the timing of manufacturing and total durables inventory movements because the related sales series show only a period of retardation rather than actual decline.[12] If, however, sales turns were marked from diffusion index series showing accumulated net increases (total manufactures sales series: peak February 1951, trough February 1952; total durables sales series: peak February 1951, trough November 1951), we would note inverted inventory movements throughout the contraction periods.

When we turn to the industry measures, the major impression is the consistent tendency for finished-stocks series to lag behind sales turns; lags are noted at 28 of the 30 possible comparisons. The duration of these inverted movements varies considerably, however, particularly among the nondurables. The five nondurables series

[12] Sales failed to contract because expanding defense shipments in key durable-goods industries offset declines elsewhere in the economy. If diffusion indexes based on durable-goods industry group-sales volume (quarterly) are constructed, the behavior of the aggregate sales series appears in a different light. The number of industries with expanding sales falls sharply from 90 percent in the first quarter of 1951 to 46 percent in the second, and remains well below the 50-percent level through the first quarter of 1952. As would be expected, the contraction is more pronounced in the nondurables group, but the diffusion indexes of the durables sales series show a contraction to below 50 percent during the second and third quarters of 1951 and no marked expansion until the first quarter of 1952.

available for study give a picture of erratic behavior, with long lags at the first major turns, and short lags, roughly coincident turns, or nonconforming movements at the last major turns.

Timing comparisons with reference turns are not significantly different from those with sales turns (table 23). Relatively earlier timing at business cycle peaks than troughs is noted for 22 of the 30 comparisons of industry series with business cycle reference turns, but the tendency is not well established in the comprehensive series.

It may be concluded from this analysis that total finished-goods stocks tend to lag behind sales and reference turns with considerable variation in timing. The completely inverted timing noted in the staple made-to-stock series is not observed in the total finished-stock series. Lacking additional evidence, we must conclude that the staple made-to-stock inventories contribute a strong tendency toward inverted behavior, but that the other categories of finished goods move more readily with sales, thereby offsetting inverted tendencies to a very significant extent. The net result is the strongly lagged timing which has been observed.

TABLE 23.—*Timing and conformity of manufacturers' finished-goods inventories at reference turns*

A. TIMING MEASURES [1]

Industry	Lead (−) or lag (+) in months							
	Business cycle		Korean cycle		Business cycles			
	Peak, November 1948	Trough, October 1949	Peak, February 1951	Trough, June 1952	Peak, July 1953	Trough, August 1954	Peak, July 1957	Trough, April 1958
Total manufacturing	+7	+11	+14	+4	+8	+1	+6	+8
Durable-goods industries, total	+8	+11	(2)	(2)	+5	+1	+6	+9
Nondurable-goods industries, total	+6	+11	+14	+10	(2)	(2)	+6	+5
Primary metals	+8	+20	(2)	(2)	+9	+13	------	------
Machinery (including electrical)	+10	+11	(2)	(2)	+4	+17	------	------
Transportation equipment (including motor vehicles)	−12	+11	+12	+15	+3	+7	------	------
Stone, clay, and glass	+9	+11	(2)	(2)	(2)	(2)	------	------
Food and beverages	+14	+12	+13	+3	+6	+4	------	------
Paper	+18	+18	(2)	(2)	(2)	(2)	------	------
Chemical	+9	+16	(2)	(2)	(2)	(2)	------	------
Petroleum and coal	+7	+11	(2)	(2)	+12	+7	------	------
Rubber	+8	+18	(2)	(2)	+2	+9	------	------

B. SUMMARY OF TIMING AND CONFORMITY

Timing and conformity comparisons	9 industry series		4 durable-goods industries		5 nondurable-goods industries	
	All turns	All turns except Korean	All turns	All turns except Korean	All turns	All turns except Korean
Number of comparisons	54	36	24	16	30	20
Matching inventory turns	34	30	16	14	18	16
Percentage of matching inventory turns	63	83	67	88	60	80
Leads more than 3 months	------	1	------	1	------	0
Rough coincidences	------	2	------	1	------	1
Leads 3 months or less	------	(0)	------	(0)	------	(0)
Coincidences	------	(0)	------	(0)	------	(0)
Lags 3 months or less	------	(2)	------	(1)	------	(1)
Lags more than 3 months	------	27	------	12	------	15

[1] Inventory series have been deflated to 1956; 1957–58 turns based on undeflated data.
[2] Sales turn occurs but no matching inventory turn.

Source: Based on material from Department of Commerce.

THE STAPLE, MADE-TO-STOCK INVENTORY INVESTMENT SERIES

In studying finished-goods investment, once again we turn first to the important staple made-to-stock category before proceeding to the analysis of total finished-goods investment behavior as revealed in the Department of Commerce data.

In his study, Abramovitz used the NBER technique of dividing each activity cycle into nine separate stages. Levels of stocks were measured at each stage and inventory investment was computed by measuring the change per month between stages with eight intervals occurring in each cycle (four during expansion, four during contraction).

For the postwar period changes in these stocks have been computed on a strictly chronological basis (for each calendar quarter). The timing of each peak or trough (i.e., the lag from the beginning of the activity phase to the turn in the investment series) has been computed as a percentage of the duration of the activity phase during which it occurs. To provide a framework as similar to Abramovitz' as possible, the resulting timing measures have been arranged so that each expansion and contraction in activity is divided into four parts called quartile intervals. To time inventory investment, frequency distributions have been prepared, showing the proportion of inventory investment peaks occurring during each quartile interval of activity-contraction phases, the proportion of troughs occurring during each quartile interval of activity-expansion phases, and the percentage of all turns occurring in the first, second, third, and fourth quartile intervals of their respective activity phases (table 24).

TABLE 24.—*Distribution of timing of inventory investment turns (inverted) by quartile intervals of activity cycles, 25 finished goods, 1947–55*

Investment turns	Percent of turns during quartile intervals of activity phase				Mean length of phase (months)
	1st quartile interval	2d quartile interval	3d quartile interval	4th quartile interval	
Investment peaks, all activity contractions.	21	26	21	32	-----------
Cumulated percentage-----------------	(21)	(47)	(68)	(100)	-----------
Investment troughs, all activity expansions.	33	19	33	14	-----------
Cumulated percentage-----------------	(33)	(52)	(85)	(100)	-----------
Investment peaks or troughs, all activity phases----------------------------------	25	21	25	24	-----------
Cumulated percentage-----------------	(25)	(46)	(71)	(100)	-----------
Investment peaks:					
1948–49 contraction phases-------------	13	26	30	30	14
1951–52 contraction phases-------------	19	19	14	48	12
1953–54 contraction phases-------------	40	27	20	13	11
Investment troughs:					
1949–51 expansion phases-------------	52	0	29	19	20
1952–53 expansion phases-------------	7	47	40	7	15

NOTE.—The above analysis is based upon 93 observations of timing of finished-goods inventory investment turns. With only 5 exceptions all investment peaks occurred during activity contractions and all investment troughs during activity expansions. The exceptions may not be regarded as significant departures from this typical timing relationship: 4 inventory investment turns occurred from 1 to 3 months prior to the activity phase with which an inverted comparison could be made. These turns were classified as falling within the 1st quartile interval of the subsequent activity phase. The other exception was an investment peak which lagged the corresponding activity trough by 1 month. This turn was classified as falling within the 4th quartile interval of the preceding activity phase.

Source: See table 25.

The measures show that almost half (46 percent) of the investment series reached peaks or troughs by the middle of their respective activity phases (measured on an inverted basis), and well over two-thirds (71 percent) during the first three quartile intervals. The results are not greatly different for frequency distributions made separately for expansions and contractions: the expansions showed only a slightly higher percentage (52 percent) of turns occurring during the first two quartiles, and the contractions, a slightly lower percentage (46 percent) during the same period.

Such measures of the relative timing of peaks and troughs are, of course, not completely comparable with medians of average rates per month from stage to stage, but they would seem to bear out Abramovitz' general conclusion that inventory investment in this class of stocks which moves against the tide of activity expansion or contraction levels off or declines in the second half, and certainly by the fourth quarter, of the phase.

Despite tendencies generally consistent with Abramovitz' findings, these measures provide some evidence of earlier turns in activity cycle phases than existed in the prewar period. It will be noted that a fourth of the peaks or troughs in the inverted inventory investment movements occur during the first quartile interval of all activity phases. This is in sharp contrast to the typical patterns shown by Abramovitz, in which the inverted movement of inventory investment has either not yet begun or has scarcely begun during the early stages of the phase.[13]

INVENTORY INVESTMENT AND RATES OF CHANGE IN ACTIVITY

In the above discussion the timing of made-to-stock inventory investment was related to turns in activity proper. Turning now to the timing of investment and peaks or troughs in activity rates of change, it is reasonable to suppose on a priori grounds that the relationship will be an inverted one. Very abrupt changes in the flow of shipments would be expected to result in abrupt changes in made-to-stock goods and could easily lead to coincident inverted timing of turns in rates of activity and inventory investment change.

There are situations, however, in which the inverted turns in investment might lag or lead, as well as be coincident with turns in rates of change in shipments. Suppose, for example, that increases or decreases in the level of shipments take place very gradually and that manufacturers are strongly disposed to retain past rates of production. Under these conditions fluctuations in rates of change in shipments might play a role secondary to the increasing discrepancy between monthly shipments and output, with the result that the peak or trough in inventory investment would occur late in the phase (when the discrepancy reached a maximum), very probably lagging behind the peak or trough in rates of change in activity. On the other hand, it could be assumed that manufacturers are attempting to keep as tight a rein on finished-goods inventories as possible. They may allow only such inverted movements in stocks to occur as are absolutely necessary to meet the requirement that output be maintained at a high enough level during recession to avoid the loss of valuable workers through excessive layoffs, and at a low enough level during

---

[13] *Ibid.*, pp. 413–414.

expansion to minimize costly overtime work. Under such conditions large changes in inventories would occur principally as a result of inability to anticipate changes in shipments. Peaks or troughs in inventory investment might occur coincidently (on an inverted basis) with those in rates of change in shipments if the latter were large and abrupt. But if the efforts to control stock levels were partially successful, it is quite possible that the inverted inventory investment movement would be checked before the movement in shipment rates of change had reached its peak or trough, with the result that peaks or troughs (inverted) in inventory investment would lead those in activity rates of change.

In chart 11 a quarter-by-quarter record of the incidence of peaks and troughs in inventory investment and rates of change in activity is presented for the 25-commodity sample. It will be noted that peaks or troughs in investment tend to occur in clusters and that there is a well-developed inverted relationship between these turns and those in rates of change in activity (which also tend to cluster). Concentrations of peaks or troughs in inventory investment occur either coincidently or lead (on an inverted basis) those in rates of change in activity.

This tendency was also apparent when the commodity series were examined individually. The results of all timing comparisons for the 25 series are summarized below. Investment peaks and troughs led or turned coincidently with those in rates of change in activity for all but 16 percent of these comparisons, leads (41 percent) and coincident turns (43 percent) being about equally divided. The tendency was well established for both expansions and contractions.

	Leads	Coincidences	Lags	Total
Timing at peaks in rate of change in activity:				
Number of investment troughs compared	15	17	10	42
Percent of investment troughs compared	36	40	24	100
Timing at troughs in rate of change in activity:				
Number of investment peaks compared	28	28	7	63
Percent of investment peaks compared	44.5	44.5	11	100
Timing at all turns in rate of change in activity:				
Number of investment turns (inverted) compared	43	45	17	105
Percent of investment turns (inverted) compared	41	43	16	100

No directly comparable study has been made for the interwar period but Abramovitz' stage-by-stage analysis of rates of change in stocks and in activity during activity cycles provides a basis for examining this timing relationship during the earlier period. Abramovitz has presented summary statements for median rates of change for all expansions and contractions observed regardless of duration, and also for expansions or contractions of 12 months and under, 13 to 24 months, 25 to 36 months, and over 36 months.

Most relevant to this discussion are his profiles for activity phases of 12 months and under, and 13 to 24 months (our postwar data show almost no activity phases longer than 2 years in duration). Patterns of rates of change for these two periods of activity phase duration show quite clearly that turns in inventory investment (i.e.,

CHART 11

FINISHED-GOODS INVENTORY INVESTMENT AND CHANGE IN MANUFACTURING
ACTIVITY: 25 COMMODITIES

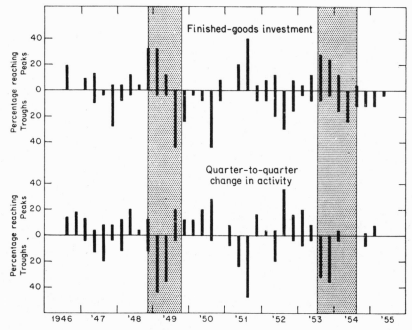

Shaded areas represent business contractions; unshaded areas, expansions.

Source: Compiled from seasonally adjusted industry data. For details on commodity series see table 21.

median rates of change in stocks) occurred coincidently with or
lagged behind (on an inverted basis) turns in rates of change in
activity. There were no leads: [14]

	Peak: Rate of change in activity	Trough: Inventory investment
Expansions:		
Phases 12 months or less	Stages IV–V	Stages IV–V.
Phases 13 to 24 months	Stages I–II	Stages III–IV.

	Trough: Rate of change in activity	Peak: Inventory investment
Contractions:		
Phases 12 months or less	Stages VII–VIII	Stages VIII–IX.
Phases 13 to 24 months	Stages VI–VII	Stages VI–VII.

Here, once again, is evidence that inventory investment has turned
earlier in the postwar period. Abramovitz' prewar data show that
timing of inverted investment turns was coincident or lagging. The
postwar data for this class of stock show a marked tendency for peaks

[14] This summary of timing is based on charts 78 and 79, ibid., pp. 413, 414. According to the NBER
techniques used by Abramovitz, stages I and IX are the terminal troughs of a cycle, stage V is the peak,
and stages II to IV and VI to VIII are intermediate stages of the expansion and contraction phases.

and troughs in investment to lead or turn coincidently with troughs and peaks in rates of change in activity.

RELATION BETWEEN STAPLES MADE TO STOCK AND TOTAL MANUFACTURERS' FINISHED GOODS

The discussion of inventory investment thus far has dealt in some detail with staples made to stock. It has already been shown that this is the largest finished-goods category (comprising perhaps as much as one-half of finished stocks). Moreover, it is probable that cyclical fluctuations in these stocks display the greatest relative amplitude. Staple made-to-stock inventories act as buffers, allowing the firm to operate without a complete synchronization of output and shipments. Stocks are permitted to rise or fall as changes in demand bring disturbances in this balance and as, subsequently, such imbalances are corrected. In contrast, made-to-order stocks are merely awaiting shipment. In most instances changes in their level can be little more than a reflection of ease or difficulty in making shipment or of changes in customers' preferences as to actual date of delivery. Finally, perishable goods, by definition, can be neither large nor cyclically sensitive, and supply-dominated stocks can hardly be expected to fluctuate cyclically. In view of the evident size and significance of staple made-to-stock inventories, the question now arises as to whether there might be a generalized investment pattern among the made-to-stock commodity series which would closely resemble the pattern in the aggregative Department of Commerce series. In order to test this hypothesis a diffusion index of the commodity series was constructed by computing quarterly the percent of series in which inventory investment increased (i.e., increases in stocks were larger, or decreases smaller, than in the preceding period) and accumulating the net percentage increases (percentage of series expanding minus 50) from quarter to quarter. Such a diffusion index approximates the aggregate behavior of the series included.

The resulting series, graphed in chart 12, shows a striking resemblance to the Department of Commerce series for total manufacturers' finished-goods investment series. The two display almost identical movements, coinciding in their turning points at five of the six turns and differing by only one quarter at the remaining turn.[15]

This presents a curious picture: there is ample evidence that the 25 commodity series for which the diffusion index was constructed represent activities in which goods are predominantly produced to stock; yet inventory investment for these series behaved like that for aggregate and durables manufacturing in which a large portion of output is produced to order.

---

[15] A strong upward trend may be noted in the diffusion index series, which is in sharp contrast to the trend-free behavior of the series for manufacturers' finished goods. The trend in the former series is not surprising in view of the type of data being observed. In preparing these series, quarterly computations were made of the net percentage of inventory investment series rising and the results accumulated. The average extent of participation in expansion and contraction periods is roughly the same (i.e., the typical quarterly amplitude of movement appears to be about the same for expansions and contractions), but the longer duration of the expansion periods gives the cumulative series an upward trend. Such a trend is impossible, of course, in the series showing quarter-to-quarter change in total manufacturers' finished goods, since disinvestment must be shown below the zero line.

CHART 12

FINISHED-GOODS INVESTMENT: TOTAL MANUFACTURING AND CUMULATED NET
PERCENTAGE OF INVESTMENT SERIES EXPANDING (25 COMMODITIES)

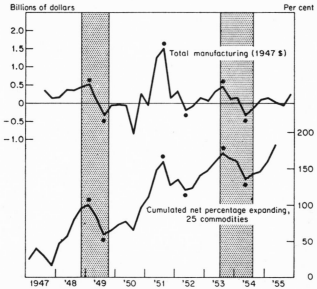

Shaded areas represent business contractions; unshaded areas, expansions.
Dots identify peaks and troughs of specific cycles.

Source: Total manufacturers' finished-goods investment series compiled from Department of Commerce data deflated by the author. For details on commodity series see table 21.

Two explanations of this agreement between the series are possible. The first is that total inventory investment was dominated by changes in the volume of finished goods made to stock; goods produced to order were quickly shipped and their variations played a negligible part in determining overall investment. The second is that inventory investment for made-to-order and made-to-stock finished goods share the same pattern.

The latter explanation is unacceptable; to adopt it is to say that inventories of goods produced to order show their sharpest rate of increase after shipments have begun to fall off and their sharpest rate of decrease after shipments have begun to rise. The statistical evidence is meager, but it does not point toward such behavior: Abramovitz found one made-to-order series, steel sheets, in which inventory investment moved with rates of change in sales, leading turns in sales proper. I have located one postwar series, steel barrels and drums, and here movements were irregular and of small amplitude.

The conclusion is that finished goods made to stock have much the greater amplitude of movement and that they dominate finished goods inventory investment. In short, the pattern and timing of inventory investment in our 25 made-to-stock series agree with that of total manufacturers' finished-goods investment because the movements that we see in the latter are predominantly reflections of movements in the former.

When the timing of inventories proper was compared by a similar means, however, the resemblance was less close. Turns in the cumulative diffusion index of the 25 commodity inventory series coincided with the Department of Commerce manufacturers' series in three of the five comparisons, but lagged by 3 and 6 months at the remaining comparisons.[16] It would seem that the influence of the other categories of finished goods is demonstrated here. As stated previously, it is to be expected that these other stocks will move more promptly with cyclical changes in activity than do the staple made-to-stock inventories, and that they will cause the aggregate finished-goods inventory movements to turn somewhat earlier. The stamp of the made-to-stock group remains, however, dominating the patterns in rates of change in the aggregate finished-goods series.

Total Finished-Goods Inventory Investment

INVESTMENT AND RATES OF CHANGE IN SALES

We may now ask whether total finished-goods inventory investment, which moves with similar timing to its staple made-to-stock component during business cycles, has a like tendency to move in an inverted fashion with turns in rates of change in sales.

Chart 13 and table 25 show that, for the period beginning in mid-1947, there is a strong tendency for total finished-goods investment, as well as its durable and nondurable components, to move in an inverted manner in relation to rates of change in sales, but to turn and come into phase at least several months before the turn in the latter series. There are two instances in which the lead is a year or more in duration. The first occurs in third quarter 1949, when the trough in investment leads by 12 months the peak in rate of change in sales.[17] The second occurs during the 1954–58 cycle, when the peak in inventory investment leads the trough in rate of change in sales by 18 months in the total manufacturers' and nondurables series and by 27 months in the durables. It should be noted, however, that the movements in the investment and sales series are inverted during roughly the first year and a half of the expansion. It is only during the latter part of the expansion that we note departure from the earlier pattern.

---

[16] If the timing of the Department of Commerce and the commodity series are compared with their respective activity series, the relatively greater inverted tendency of the commodity series becomes even more apparent, for the commodity activity series tended to turn relatively early in the business cycle phase (see footnote 20).

[17] There was a second trough in investment, of even greater magnitude, in third quarter 1950, accompanying the outbreak of the Korean war. This movement was of only one quarter duration, however, and the trough has been marked at the earlier date. On the other hand, it is apparent that the peak in rate of change in sales, marked as third quarter 1950, could not have occurred earlier than second quarter 1950 had there been no such outbreak.

CHART 13

FINISHED-GOODS INVENTORY INVESTMENT AND QUARTER-TO-QUARTER CHANGE IN
SALES, 1946–58

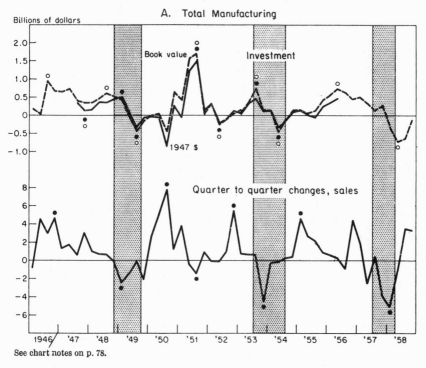

A. Total Manufacturing

See chart notes on p. 78.

CHART 13—Continued

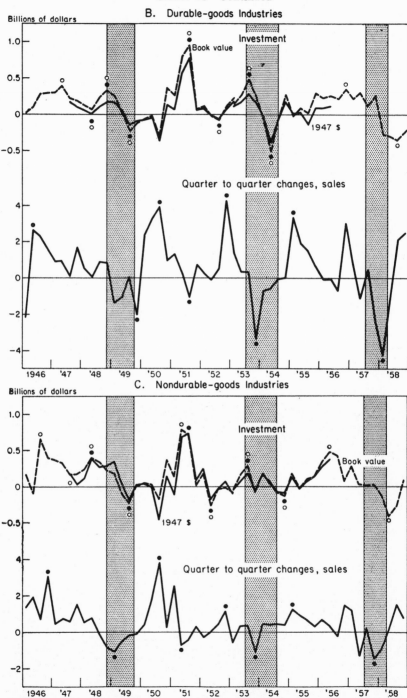

Shaded areas represent business contractions; unshaded areas, expansions.
Dots identify peaks and troughs of deflated inventory cycles; circles, of undeflated cycles. All sales data
are undeflated.

Source: Department of Commerce. Data deflated by the author.

TABLE 25.—*Timing of finished-goods investment to rate of change in sales*

Date of turns in rate of change in sales			Timing of finished-goods investment (inverted)		
Quarter	Year		Total manufacturing	Durable goods	Nondurable goods
I	49	(Trough)[1]	0	−12	−9
III	50	(Peak)	−12	−12	−12
III	51	(Trough)[2]	0	0	+3
IV	52	(Peak)	−6	−3	−6
IV	53	(Trough)	−3	−3	−3
I	55	(Peak)	−9	−9	−3
I	58	(Trough)[3]	−21	−15	−18

[1] For durable goods, date was 4th quarter 1949.
[2] For nondurable goods, date was 2d quarter 1951.
[3] For nondurable goods, date was 4th quarter 1957.

Source: Based on material from Department of Commerce.

TIMING OF INVESTMENT DURING BUSINESS CYCLES

The postwar tendency of turns in inventory investment (inverted) to lead or coincide with turns in rates of change in activity provides a basis for generalization regarding the typical timing of investment during business cycles.

There is considerable evidence available relating to the timing characteristics of rates of change in activity. Abramovitz studied the behavior of rates of change in activity during reference cycles for 57 prewar series and noted well-established tendencies: "The rate of growth in output reaches a high point considerably before the end of expansion, a trough considerably before the end of contraction." [18] During the postwar period this same tendency has been quite apparent in rates of change in total manufacturing sales, as may be seen from the following chronology of turns: [19]

	Reference turns (quarterly basis)	Quarter-to-quarter change, total manufacturing sales
Expansion	IV 1945 to IV 1948	Peak IV 1947.
Contraction	IV 1948 to IV 1949	Trough I 1949.
Expansion	IV 1949 to I 1951 [1]	Peak III 1950.
Contraction	I 1951 [1] to II 1952 [1]	Trough III 1951.
Expansion	II 1952 [1] to II 1953	Peak IV 1952.
Contraction	II 1953 to III 1954	Trough IV 1953.
Expansion	II 1954 to III 1957	Peak I 1955.
Contraction	III 1957 to II 1958	Trough I 1958.

[1] Based on subcycle reference turns. See note 2, ch. 3.

It may be concluded, therefore, that since peaks and troughs in inventory investment tend to lead (on an inverted basis) these early-occurring turning points in rates of change in sales, their timing will cause inventory investment to move with the tide of business during

---

[18] Abramovitz, "Inventories and Business Cycles," p. 378.
[19] This tendency is also applicable to rates of change in output. During the postwar period quarter-to-quarter changes in total manufacturers' sales and output have had approximately the same patterns of movement with coincident or near coincident timing. Such data are not available for the prewar period, but Abramovitz studied shipments and output for 10 nonfarm (made-to-stock) commodities and demonstrated the "very close connection between the rates of production and shipment of manufactured staples." Ibid., pp. 248, 250-251.

most, if not all, business cycle phases.[20]   Accordingly, timing comparisons are made with sales and reference turns on a positive basis in the sections which follow.

TIMING AND CONFORMITY OF INVESTMENT: COMPARISON WITH SALES TURNS

A somewhat higher conformity was noted for investment than for inventories proper with no significant difference in the conformity of the durables [and nondurables series.   Of the 42 [sales [turns in the industry sales series, including turns related to the Korean cycle, 41 (all 20 of the durables and all but 1 of the 22 nondurables) could be matched by investment turns.[21]   Timing varied, showing no consistent tendency to lead or lag.   Approximately half of the turns in the individual-industry series (21 of 41) occurred roughly coincidently with sales turns; among the others, lags of more than 3 months (14) were more prominent than leads of more than 3 months (6).   The comprehensive series bear out this timing tendency.   For total manufactures, timing ranges from a lead of 8 months to a lag of 6 months during the 1948–58 period (see also chart 11).

TABLE 26.—*Timing and conformity of manufacturers' finished-goods inventory investment at sales turns*

A. TIMING MEASURES [1]

Industry	Lead (−) or lag (+) in months, in zones associated with reference turns								
	1948 peak	1949 trough		Korean war		1953 peak	1954 trough	1957 peak	1958 trough
		Turns prior to mid-1950	Turns after mid-1950	1951 peak	1952 trough				
Total manufacturing	+5	−4	+8	(2)	(2)	+1	−5	−8	+2
Durable goods industries, total	−1	−2	+10	(2)	(2)	+1	−5	−2	+4
Nondurable-goods industries, total	−1	−5	+7	(2)	(2)	(2)	(2)	−8	+2
Primary metals	+5	(3)	+10	+2	+2	+1	−3		
Machinery (including electrical)	+2	−1	+8	(2)	(2)	−1	−5		
Transportation equipment (including motor vehicles)	−9	−7	(3)	(2)	(2)	+1	−2		
Stone, clay, and glass	+4	(3)	+8	+3	+8	−2	+4		
Food and beverages	−3	−5	+7	(3)	(3)	−8	+7		
Paper	+5	+1	+13	+3	+8	(3)	(3)		
Chemical	+8	+7	+13	+5	+2	+2	−2		
Petroleum and coal	+2	+4	(3)	(2)	(2)	+10	+2		
Rubber	+1	+1	+7	(2)	(4)	(2)	−11		

See footnotes at end of table, p. 81.

[20] It may be asked why, if there has been such a marked tendency for inverted turns in staple, made-to-stock investment series to occur early in business cycle contractions and expansions, there was not a greater concentration of turns in investment during the early stages of activity phases (see table 24).   The answer appears to be that the sample is composed of series for which activity has shown a pronounced tendency to turn prior to business cycle turns, but which displayed roughly the same timing of movements in activity rates of change as the total manufacturing series.   This was verified by analysis of diffusion indexes of activity and of rates of change in activity.   The former series led total manufacturers' sales but the latter turned roughly coincidently with rates of change in these sales.

[21] Timing comparisons presented a special problem for the period following the recession of 1948–49.   In five of the nine industry series, troughs in inventory investment occurred prior to the second quarter of 1950, but during the third quarter there were second and deeper troughs which were related to the sudden upsurge in sales at the outbreak of the Korean war.   These later troughs would probably not have occurred had there been no outbreak of hostilities, [but there is no certainty of this.   For this reason, and in order to present as accurate a picture of timing as possible, measures for both troughs have been included.   (See table 26.)

B. SUMMARY OF TIMING AND CONFORMITY

Timing and conformity comparisons	9 industry series		4 durable-goods industries		5 nondurable-goods industries	
	All turns	All turns except Korean	All turns	All turns except Korean	All turns	All turns except Korean
Number of comparisons	42	34	20	16	22	18
Matching inventory investment	41	33	20	16	21	17
Percentage of matching turns	98	97	100	100	95	94
Leads more than 3 months [5]	6	6	3	3	3	3
Rough coincidences	21	16	11	8	10	8
Leads 3 months or less	(7)	(7)	(5)	(5)	(2)	(2)
Coincidences	(0)	(0)	(0)	(0)	(0)	(0)
Lags 3 months or less	(14)	(9)	(6)	(3)	(8)	(6)
Lags more than 3 months [5]	14	11	6	5	8	6

[1] Inventory investment series have been deflated at 1956. 1957–58 turns based on undeflated data.
[2] Inventory investment turn occurs, but there is no sales turn.
[3] Sales turn occurs but no matching inventory investment turn.
[4] No turn occurs in either sales or inventory investment.
[5] In the 1949 revival zone, investment troughs prior to mid-1950 have been used in the timing measures when 2 troughs occurred.

Source: Based on material from Department of Commerce.

TIMING AND CONFORMITY OF INVESTMENT: COMPARISON WITH REFERENCE TURNS

It may be concluded from table 27 that finished-goods investment is very sensitive to cyclical forces. Conformity to reference cycles is very high: of 54 possible comparisons 52 turns could be matched with reference turns.

With overall conformity so high it is not surprising that there is little difference between that of durables and nondurables. It will be noted that investment turns could be matched with reference turns on occasions when no sales turns occurred, indicating that investment was responsive to cyclical forces even when these forces were not sufficiently strong to bring about full-fledged movements in the related sales series.[22]

There is one observation that deserves special mention: timing of investment turns shows less variation among the several industry series when compared to reference turns than when compared to sales turns. (See the timing measures in table 26 and table 27 for any given peak or trough.) This suggests further evidence of the relations between inventory investment and rates of change in sales. Analysis of the individual series indicates that turns in rates-of-change-in-sales movements tended to occur at about the same time in most of the series during the period studied. Some indirect evidence of this may be seen by observing the comprehensive series in chart 13: timing of turns in the durables and nondurables rates-of-change-in-sales series is coincident in five comparisons, and varies by only 3 months in the other two. Since turns in rates of change in sales occur at about the same time, comparisons of inventory investment with reference turns which were fixed points in time give roughly the same degree of agreement among the revised series as would timing

[22] These "extra" turns may be noted in table 26. In most instances they relate to the "Korean" cycle which has already been discussed, but there is one investment cycle, in the paper products industry, which is related to the 1953–54 business cycle peak and trough.

comparisons with rates of change in the respective sales series. Apparently, this relationship is closer than with movements in the series for sales proper.

TABLE 27.—*Timing and conformity of manufacturers' finished-goods inventory investment at reference turns*

A. TIMING MEASURES [1]

Industry	Business cycle peak, Nov. 1948	Business cycle trough, October 1949		Korean cycle		Business cycles			
		Turns prior to mid-1950	Turns after mid-1950	Peak, February 1951	Trough, June 1952	Peak, July 1953	Trough, August 1954	Peak, July 1957	Trough, April 1948
Total manufacturing	+3	−2	+10	+6	−1	+1	−3	−14	+1
Durable-goods industries, total	0	−2	+10	+6	+2	+1	−3	−8	+4
Nondurable-goods industries, total	−6	−2	+10	+6	−1	+1	+3	−14	+1
Primary metals	+6	(²)	+10	+6	+2	+1	−3	-------	-------
Machinery (including electrical)	+3	+1	+10	+6	+1	−2	−3	-------	-------
Transportation equipment (including motor vehicles)	0	−5	+10	+3	+2	−2	−3	-------	-------
Stone, clay, and glass	+3	(²)	+10	+6	+2	−2	−3	-------	-------
Food and beverages	−6	−2	+10	+6	+2	+1	+9	-------	-------
Paper	+3	−2	+10	+6	+8	+7	+6	-------	-------
Chemical	+3	+4	+10	+6	+2	+1	+3	-------	-------
Petroleum and coal	+3	+7	-------	+3	−1	+10	+3	-------	-------
Rubber	−3	(²)	+10	+12	(²)	(²)	−9	-------	-------

B. SUMMARY OF TIMING AND CONFORMITY

Timing and conformity comparisons	9 industry series		4 durable-goods industries, all turns	5 nondurable-goods industries, all turns
	All turns	All turns except Korean		
Number of comparisons	54	36	24	30
Matching inventory turns	52	35	24	28
Percentage of matching turns	96	97	100	93
Leads more than 3 months [3]	4	4	1	3
Rough coincidences [3]	30	21	17	13
Leads, 3 months or less	(11)	(10)	(7)	(4)
Coincidences	(1)	(1)	(1)	(0)
Lags, 3 months or less	(18)	(10)	(9)	(9)
Lags, more than 3 months [3]	18	10	6	12

[1] Inventory series have been deflated to 1956; 1957–58 turns based on undeflated data.
[2] No matching inventory investment turn.
[3] In making comparison with the reference trough of October 1949, investment troughs prior to mid-1950 have been used in the timing measures where 2 troughs occurred.

Source: Based on material from Department of Commerce.

AMPLITUDE OF DURABLES AND NONDURABLES INVESTMENT DURING CYCLES

Measures of amplitude of movements in finished-goods inventory investment reveal that the relative amplitude of the durables series is greater than that of nondurables. This is readily seen in table 28. Total change in relation to size of stocks, is greater for durables than for nondurables in five of the seven phases examined. Nondurable finished-goods stocks, however, are considerably larger than durables stocks, and total investment movements in the nondurables series are larger in five of the seven phases.

TABLE 28.—*Amplitude of change in finished-goods inventory investment cycles, by phase, 1948–58*

Industry	Peak-trough (1948–49)	Peak-trough (1949–50)	Peak-trough (1950–52)	Peak-trough (1952–53)	Peak-trough (1953–54)	Peak-trough (1954–56)	Peak-trough (1956–58)
	Total change (relative) [1]						
Total manufacturing	−7.72	+15.95	−13.51	+4.92	−5.83	+6.93	−7.60
Durable goods	−7.35	+19.44	−15.74	+6.43	−11.23	+10.16	−7.60
Nondurable goods	−9.37	+13.55	−12.40	+4.88	−3.56	+6.74	−9.00
	Change per month (relative) [1]						
Total manufacturing	−1.29	+.66	−1.13	+.41	−.65	+.29	−.32
Durable goods	−.82	+.81	−1.31	+.71	−1.25	+.34	−.36
Nondurable goods	−.62	+.56	−1.38	+.33	−.24	+.37	−.38
	Total change (millions of dollars) [2]						
Total manufacturing	−835	+1,321	−1,703	+666	−790	+1,190	−1,436
Durable goods	−315	+908	−815	+360	−668	+856	−700
Nondurable goods	−561	+923	−920	+379	−278	+602	−882
	Change per month (millions of dollars) [2]						
Total manufacturing	−139	+76	−142	+55	−88	+49	−60
Durable goods	−52	+38	−68	+40	−74	+29	−33
Nondurable goods	−37	+38	−102	+25	−18	+33	−37

[1] Expressed as percent of the mean level of inventories during the phase. Mean level is an average of beginning and ending level of inventories of the terminal quarters of the phase.
[2] All 1948–54 data have been deflated (1947 dollars). Measures for the two most recent phases are based on undeflated (book value) data.
Source: Based on material from Department of Commerce.

SUMMARY

Abramovitz emphasized the fact that finished stocks are of several different types, each possessing quite different cyclical characteristics. Analysis of postwar composition reveals that finished goods whose production cycles are governed by supply comprise less than one-third of the total. The major part, from 41 to 51 percent of the total, is made up of staple made-to-stock inventories. Goods made to order are estimated at 15 to 25 percent of the total. According to Abramovitz, staple made-to-stock goods may be expected to move in an inverted fashion relative to sales, made-to-order stocks will move in positive conformity, and the remainder will be cyclically insensitive or erratic.

Postwar finished-goods behavior was studied by analyzing two sets of inventory data. The first was composed of data for 25 staple, made-to-stock commodities, representing the largest component of finished goods. The second was composed of Department of Commerce industry data for nine industry groups and for comprehensive groupings. Among the commodity series, finished stocks were found to move in a strongly inverted fashion relative to sales or output, but with a well-developed tendency to turn and come into phase as the duration of the activity phase increased. The Department of Commerce industry data revealed a consistent tendency for stocks to lag behind sales and reference turns, but movements were rarely of the completely inverted sort observed in the commodity series. The conclusion drawn was that the staple made-to-stock inventories contribute a strong tendency toward inverted behavior, but that other categories offset inverted tendencies to a significant degree.

Study of inventory investment data for the 25 commodities revealed that investment moved in an inverted fashion relative to rates of change in sales, but that peaks (troughs) in inventory investment led or turned coincidently with troughs (peaks) in rates of change in activity. Since peaks and troughs in rates of change in activity tend to occur well before the end of each business cycle phase, the inverted movements in inventory investment may be expected to terminate relatively early in the business cycle phase. Analysis of finished-goods inventory investment in the Department of Commerce series shows this to be the case. Total manufacturers' investment turns roughly coincidently with business cycle turns or moves in an inverted fashion (i.e., lags) for only a few months in the early part of a business cycle phase.

6

Goods-in-Process Inventories and Inventory Investment

For his study of goods-in-process behavior, Abramovitz once again divided the category into its major components and sought to determine the typical behavior of each. In the present chapter, a discussion of Abramovitz' system of classification and the theory which he developed is followed by an observation of the behavior of goods-in-process stocks and investment as revealed in Department of Commerce data. A third section develops possible reasons for observed differences in actual and hypothesized behavior and presents a revised theory.

Amplitude of movements in purchased materials, goods-in-process, and finished-goods investment are compared in chapter 7. As noted in this chapter, however, significant movements in goods-in-process investment are found only in the durables series. Nondurables in-process investment moves erratically and with little amplitude.

Abramovitz' Theory of Goods-in-Process Behavior [1]

Abramovitz classified these stocks under two heads, those held within and those held between stages of manufacture. On the basis of an analysis of production processes, and from information in a special Federal Trade Commission survey for 1939, relating to size of goods-in-process stocks held by specific industries, he estimated that 37.7 percent of goods-in-process stocks were held by continuous process industries which characteristically hold them within stages; 36.1 percent by discontinuous process industries with large holdings of in-process stocks between stages; and2 6.2 percent by industries with a mixture of·continuous and discontinuous processes. He pointed out that if inventories in the mixed industries were about equally divided between stocks held within and stocks held between stages, roughly half of all goods in process would be held in each.

Goods-in-process behavior in the continuous process industries was determined by several hypothetical models which showed that the timing of turns in these stocks is dependent upon the timing pattern of inputs and the length of the production period. On the basis of this analysis Abramovitz concludes that: "In such industries stocks of goods in process cannot lag behind production. On the contrary, they are likely to lead. The lead, however, cannot exceed an interval equal to a production period; that is, it cannot exceed the time elapsing between the moment work is begun upon a prospective unit of output in a manufacturing establishment and the time it is ready for delivery." [2]

Regarding the goods in process held by discontinuous and mixed industries, he points out that "In other [than continuous] manu-

---

[1] The following account is based upon Abramovitz, "Inventories and Business Cycles, with Special Reference to Manufacturers Inventories," New York, NBER, 1950, pp. 160–177, 380–388.

[2] Ibid., p. 380. Abramovitz estimates the average length of the production period in American industry to be 25 days, pp. 171–174.

facturing industries, the relation need not be rigid; yet even here there is a bias in favor of a positive relation between production and goods in process. For only surplus stocks between stages can move inversely to output. The stocks within the various stages of discontinuous industries must still move together with activity in their respective stages. Since activity in these stages is closely bound together, so must output and goods in process within the various stages. Finally, it must be remembered that surplus stocks between stages need not move inversely to output; they only may do so.

"* * * there is, in fact, a very powerful set of forces impelling (all) goods in process as here defined, to move together with output in manufacturing as a whole." [3]

The analysis of goods-in-process investment follows along similar lines. Emphasis is given to the behavior of in-process stocks within stages. For these goods Abramovitz finds that investment will not lag behind the rate of increase in output and is likely to lead, but not by more than one production period.[4] He holds that goods "between stages" in discontinouous industries may or may not act in the same fashion, "when they do not, the effect is probably to cause goods in process in the aggregate to respond to changes in activity somewhat more tardily than they otherwise would. Hence investment in goods in process as a whole is likely to lead the rate of growth of production by less than investment in continuous industries does. It may even lag by a short interval. It seems best, therefore, to say merely that investment in goods in process and the rate of growth of output turn at nearly the same time." [5]

GOODS-IN-PROCESS INVENTORIES

Before examining the Department of Commerce data on goods-in-process inventories, it should be noted that the problems of deflation here are much greater than those encountered with purchased-materials and finished-goods data. Goods in process are not bought and sold and there is no market price for them. Their value for accounting purposes is determined by cost-accounting techniques which estimate the value of labor and overhead applied to the purchased materials. For the inventory data there are, therefore, no price indexes from which deflators can be constructed, nor any clues to the composition of goods in process (i.e., the proportions which are are in early, middle, and late stages of production) which would permit assumptions as to the value added.

These restrictions reduce the effectiveness of the analysis, but do not preclude learning from the data. Crude deflators can be devised which will permit us to observe whether or not cyclical characteristics found in the undeflated series are sufficiently well stamped upon the data to remain apparent after making an arbitrary allowance for possible price effect. Furthermore, the undeflated data may be examined and, where there are a large number of observations, generalizations may be made concerning well-established characteristics.

---

[3] Ibid., p. 165.
[4] Ibid., p. 387.
[5] Ibid., p. 387.

Comprehensive goods in process series were deflated by using an average of the purchased-materials and finished-goods deflators. It was not deemed worthwhile to prepare deflators for the individual industry series, but timing and conformity measures of the undeflated series were prepared, as well as a summary of the timing sequence of their turns when related to turns in undeflated purchased materials and finished goods.

MAJOR PATTERNS OF MOVEMENT IN STOCKS

The undeflated goods-in-process inventory series for total manufacturing shows three well-marked cyclical movements from 1945 to 1958 (chart 14). There is, however, no movement in the series which would indicate conformity to the cyclical forces accompanying the Korean period.

Deflation alters the total manufacturing series significantly in only one phase. The timing of the first cycle peak occurs 14 months earlier in the deflated than in the corresponding undeflated series (table 29). The undeflated-durables series which has the same pattern of movement as total manufacturing is affected in the same way.

In the undeflated nondurables series the cyclical patterns are less clearly defined. The pattern of the first cycle is approximately the same as that of the undeflated total manufacturing series, but movements are smaller. From June 1951 to the second peak in June 1953 a series of irregular movements occurs, and the contraction which follows is of very small amplitude. When the nondurables data are deflated, the resulting series moves so irregularly, prior to mid-1953, that no cycle turns can be marked. The contraction of 1953–54 remains, however, with timing approximately the same as in the undeflated series.

CHART 14

GOODS-IN-PROCESS INVENTORIES AND SALES: TOTAL MANUFACTURING, DURABLE-
AND NONDURABLE-GOODS INDUSTRIES, 1946–58

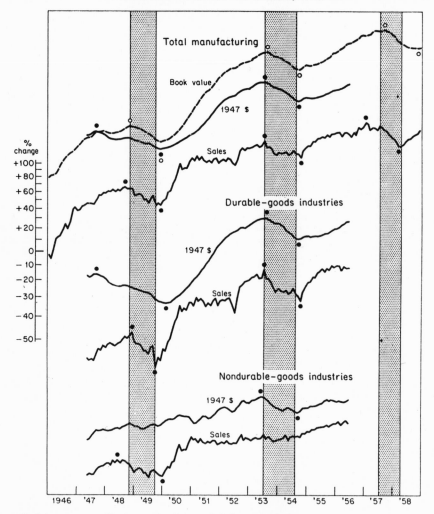

Shaded areas represent business contractions; unshaded areas, expansions.
Dots identify peaks and troughs of deflated inventory cycles; circles, of undeflated cycles. All sales
data are undeflated.

Source: Department of Commerce. Data deflated by the author.

TABLE 29.—*Timing and conformity of manufacturers' goods-in-process inventories at output and sales turns*

A. TIMING MEASURES

Industry	Lead (−) or lag (+), in months, in zones associated with reference turns							
	1948 peak	1949 trough	Korean war		1953 peak	1954 trough	1957 peak	1958 trough
			1951 peak	1952 trough				
Timing of inventories to output turns								
Deflated inventory data:								
Total manufacturing	−10	+1	[1]	[1]	0	+5	----	----
Durable-goods industries, total	−10	+4	[1]	[1]	+1	+5	----	----
Nondurable-goods industries, total	[2]	[2]	[2]	[2]	−1	+9	----	----
Undeflated inventory data:								
Total manufacturing	+4	+1	[1]	[1]	+1	+5	+1	+7
Durable-goods industries, total	+5	+4	[1]	[1]	+1	+5	0	+7
Nondurable-goods industries, total	+5	+6	[2]	[2]	−1	+9	+5	+7
Industry series (undeflated):								
Primary metals	+4	+7	[2]	[2]	+4	0	----	----
Machinery (including electrical)	−1	+7	[1]	[1]	−8	+10	----	----
Transportation equipment (including motor vehicles)	−6	+2	[1]	[1]	0	0	----	----
Stone, clay, and glass	+3	+9	[2]	[2]	+2	+16	----	----
Food and beverages	[1]	[1]	[1]	[1]	[1]	[1]	----	----
Paper	+6	+4	+8	+13	[3]	[3]	----	----
Chemical	−13	+9	−8	−10	+1	+7	----	----
Petroleum and coal	+5	+7	[3]	[2]	[2]	0	----	----
Rubber	[4]	+7	+20	[2]	[2]		----	----
Timing of inventories to sales turns								
Deflated inventory data:								
Total manufacturing	−12	0	[1]	[1]	0	−1	----	----
Durable-goods industries, total	−15	+4	[1]	[1]	+1	−1	----	----
Nondurable-goods industries, total	[2]	[2]	[1]	[1]	[3]	[3]	----	----
Undeflated inventory data:								
Total manufacturing	+2	0	[1]	[1]	+1	−1	+8	+8
Durable-goods industries, total	0	+3	[1]	[1]	+1	−1	+7	+7
Nondurable-goods industries, total	+5	−2	[1]	[1]	[3]	[3]	+12	+7
Industry series:								
Primary metals	+2	+7	[2]	[2]	+2	−1	----	----
Machinery (including electrical)	−12	+1	[1]	[1]	−6	+5	----	----
Transportation equipment (including motor vehicles)	−5	+2	[1]	[1]	0	−2	----	----
Stone, clay, and glass	+3	+3	[2]	[2]	+3	+16	----	----
Food and beverages	[2]	[2]	[1]	[1]	[2]	[2]	----	----
Paper	+6	+2	+8	+7	[3]	[3]	----	----
Chemical	+6	+9	−5	−11	+2	+7	----	----
Petroleum and coal	+5	+4	[3]	[3]	[2]	[2]	----	----
Rubber	[4]	+3	+8	[1]	[2]	−3	----	----

B. SUMMARY OF CONFORMITY TO OUTPUT

	9 industry series		4 durable-goods industries		5 nondurable-goods industries	
	All turns	All turns except Korean	All turns	All turns except Korean	All turns	All turns except Korean
Number of comparisons	39	29	20	16	19	13
Matching inventory turns	31	26	16	16	15	10
Percentage of matching turns	79	90	80	100	79	77

[1] No turn occurs in either activity or inventories.
[2] Activity turn occurs, but no matching inventory turn.
[3] Inventory turn occurs, but there is no activity turn.
[4] Not available.

Source: Based on material from Department of Commerce.

TIMING AND CONFORMITY OF STOCKS: COMPARISON WITH OUTPUT AND
SALES TURNS

In table 29 timing and conformity measures are presented for the
undeflated and deflated comprehensive series and for the undeflated
industry series. Timing comparisons were made with turns in output
as well as sales to facilitate subsequent discussion of the relations
between stocks and the rate of output.

The movements described above conform to all movements in
output and sales for the total manufacturing and durables comprehensive series. Timing is virtually coincident for all turns in the
undeflated series prior to the revival in 1958. Deflation alters the
timing no more than 1 month, except for the 1948 peak when the
turn in stocks occurs slightly over a year earlier.

In the nondurables undeflated comprehensive series the turns conform to the output and sales turns associated with the business cycle,
but not to those associated with the Korean cycle. For the two turns
which remain in the nondurables series after deflation, the timing is
approximately the same.

Among the undeflated industry series, 29 of the 39 turns in output
have matching stock turns, but timing is irregular. There appears
to be a tendency for stocks to lag behind output, but a number of
leads are noted. On the whole the durables conform better and show
more consistent timing.[6]

TIMING OF STOCKS DURING BUSINESS CYCLES

In table 30 timing of both the deflated and undeflated comprehensive series is compared with reference turns. With the exception
of the first peak the deflated total manufacturing and durable stocks
series turn roughly coincidently with business cycle (reference) turning points. The deflated nondurables series, of course, conforms only
to the 1953-54 business cycle turns.

Since the undeflated goods-in-process industry series may not be
relied upon to give an accurate picture of timing of cyclical movements,
the sequence of turns in these series has been related to comparable
turns in the purchased-materials and finished-goods series. The
cyclical behavior of these last two types of stocks has already been
described, and it is assumed that the patterns of sequence observed
in the undeflated series, if well established, will provide an acceptable
approximation of those which would be found to obtain if deflation of
all the series could be properly carried out.[7]

---

[6] There is a tendency for the durables series to show earlier turns relative to output and sales peaks than
they do at troughs. The characteristic does not appear, however, in the nondurables comprehensive series.

[7] This assumption is, of course, open to the criticism that price effects (upward during expansion, downward during contraction) may tend to find their way into inventory values in a time sequence in which
purchased materials show the effect first, followed by goods in process and finished goods. I have not
noticed such a tendency in deflating the purchased-materials and finished-goods series, however.

TABLE 30.—*Timing of manufacturers' goods-in-process inventories at reference turns* [1]

Industry	Lead (−) or lag (+) in months					
	Business cycle		Business cycles			
	Peak, November 1948	Trough, October 1949	Peak, July 1953	Trough, August 1954	Peak, July 1957	Trough, April 1958
Deflated inventory data:						
Total manufacturing	−14	+2	0	+1		
Durable-goods industries, total	−14	+4	+1	+1		
Nondurable-goods industries, total	(2)	(2)	−1	+1		
Undeflated inventory data:						
Total manufacturing	0	+2	+1	+1	+2	+7
Durable-goods industries, total	+1	+4	+1	+1	+1	+7
Nondurable-goods industries, total	0	+1	−1	+1	+6	+6

[1] There were no turns conforming to "Korean" cycle reference dates.
[2] No matching turn in inventories.

Source: Based on material from Department of Commerce.

Accordingly, turns in the individual industry goods-in-process series have been compared first with turns in purchased materials and then with those in finished goods.

Comparisons with purchased-materials turns

	Number	Percent
Total comparisons of goods in process	34	100
Leads, 4 or more months	11	32
Rough coincidences	18	53
Leads, less than 4 months	(11)	(33)
Coincidences	(2)	(6)
Lags, less than 4 months	(5)	(14)
Lags, 4 or more months	5	15

Comparisons with finished-goods turns

	Number	Percent
Total comparisons of goods in process	24	100
Leads, 4 or more months	15	62
Rough coincidences	5	21
Leads, less than 4 months	(2)	(9)
Coincidences	(2)	(8)
Lags, less than 4 months	(1)	(4)
Lags, 4 or more months	4	17

The typical relationships are apparent. Goods-in-process stocks turn at approximately the same time as purchased materials in over half the observations; but there is a tendency to lead. This is firmly established in relation to finished-goods turns, with leads noted in 71 percent of the comparisons—4 months or more in 62 percent.

These findings are consistent with the comparisons of timing in the deflated comprehensive series. To the extent that we may generalize from these postwar observations, goods in process may be expected to lead or coincide with business cycle peaks and to coincide or lag by a short interval at troughs.

GOODS-IN-PROCESS INVENTORY INVESTMENT

The overall behavior of total manufacturers' inventory investment in goods in process (chart 15) resembles in several respects that of purchased-materials investment (chart 16). During the period 1945–49 the patterns of movements in the two undeflated series are similar. Investment moves sharply upward until mid 1946, declines, and rises to a second and lesser peak in the first half of 1948. Thereafter each series declines to a trough in 1949. Following this last trough, goods-in-process behavior differs from that observed in the purchased-materials series. There is a major upward movement in goods-in-process investment lasting until the second quarter of 1951, following which there occurs an erratic, generally declining movement until the second quarter of 1953, and then a sharp drop to the trough in 1954.[8]

CHART 15

GOODS-IN-PROCESS INVENTORY INVESTMENT: TOTAL MANUFACTURING, DURABLE-
AND NONDURABLE-GOODS INDUSTRIES, 1946–58

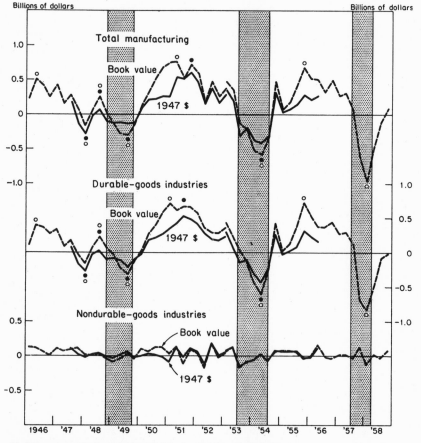

Shaded areas represent business contractions; unshaded areas, expansions.
Dots identify peaks and troughs of deflated cycles; circles, of undeflated cycles.

Source: Department of Commerce. Data deflated by the author.

[8] The pattern of movement in the deflated series is essentially the same except that the peak in 1948 becomes "submerged" and the peak in 1951 occurs 6 months later.

The purchased-materials series during this last period shows a very sensitive reaction to cyclical forces in the economy in 1951–52, declining sharply to a well marked trough in the second quarter of 1952.

The durables goods-in-process series (undeflated and deflated) show the same general pattern as total manufacturing, except that there are no irregular movements in 1952–53 (chart 16). The nondurables series, on the other hand, show a much less well-defined pattern, being especially choppy from the beginning of 1951 to the second quarter of 1953, so that peaks and troughs cannot be marked with confidence.

TIMING AND CONFORMITY OF INVESTMENT: COMPARISON WITH OUTPUT, SALES, AND REFERENCE TURNS

The movements described for total manufacturing and durable-goods investment are reflected in the timing measures shown in table 31. Among the industry series most of the output turns may be matched by those in inventory investment, but the timing is irregular.

TABLE 31.—*Timing and conformity of manufacturers' goods-in-process inventory investment at output and sales turns*

A. TIMING MEASURES

Industry	Lead (−) or lag (+) in months, in zones associated with reference turns							
	1948 peak	1949 trough	Korean War		1953 peak	1954 trough	1957 peak	1958 trough
			1951 peak	1952 trough				
Timing of investment to output turns								
Deflated data:								
Total manufacturing	+1	−3	(1)	(2)	(3)	+1	--------	--------
Durable-goods industries, total	+1	−2	(1)	(2)	(3)	+1	--------	--------
Nondurable-goods industries, total	(2)	(2)	(3)	(3)	(2)	(2)	--------	--------
Undeflated data:								
Total manufacturing	+1	−3	(1)	(2)	(3)	+1	−21	−2
Durable-goods industries, total	+1	−2	(1)	(2)	(3)	+1	−21	−2
Nondurable-goods industries, total	(2)	(3)	(3)	(2)	(2)	(2)	(2)	(2)
Primary metals	−2	−2	+8	+4	−3	−5	--------	--------
Machinery (including electrical)	+10	−1	(1)	(2)	(2)	−3	--------	--------
Transportation equipment (including motor vehicles)	−13	−4	(1)	(2)	(3)	−9	--------	--------
Stone, clay, and glass	−11	+2	−6	(3)	(3)	+7	--------	--------
Food and beverages	(2)	(2)	(2)	(2)	(2)	(2)	--------	--------
Paper	−13	0	0	+8	(1)	(1)	--------	--------
Chemical	−22	+4	+5	+9	−2	−2	--------	--------
Petroleum and coal	−4	+4	(1)	(1)	−3	(4)	--------	--------
Rubber	(4)	−4	+10	−2	−3	−11	--------	--------
Timing of investment to sales turns								
Deflated data:								
Total manufacturing	−1	−4	(1)	(2)	(3)	−5	--------	--------
Durable-goods industries, total	−4	−2	(1)	(2)	(3)	−5	--------	--------
Nondurable-goods industries, total	(2)	(2)	(2)	(2)	(2)	(2)	--------	--------
Undeflated data:								
Total manufacturing	−1	−4	(1)	(2)	(3)	−5	−14	−1
Durable-goods industries, total	−4	−2	(1)	(2)	(3)	−5	−14	−2
Nondurable-goods industries, total	(2)	(3)	(2)	(2)	(2)	(2)	(2)	(2)
Primary metals	−4	−2	+8	+5	−5	−6	--------	--------
Machinery (including electrical)	−1	−7	(1)	(2)	(3)	−8	--------	--------
Transportation equipment (including motor vehicles)	−10	−4	(1)	(2)	(3)	−11	--------	--------
Stone, clay, and glass	−11	−4	−6	(3)	(3)	+7	--------	--------
Food and beverages	(2)	(2)	(2)	(2)	(2)	(2)	--------	--------
Paper	−13	−2	(3)	+2	(1)	(1)	--------	--------
Chemical	−18	+4	+8	+8	−3	−2	--------	--------
Petroleum and coal	−4	+1	(1)	(1)	−2	(4)	--------	--------
Rubber	+1	−8	(1)	(1)	−5	−14	--------	--------

TABLE 31.—*Timing and conformity of manufacturers' goods-in-process inventory investment at output and sales turns*—Continued

B. SUMMARY OF CONFORMITY TO OUTPUT

	9 industry series		4 durable-goods industries		5 nondurable-goods industries	
	All turns	All turns except Korean	All turns	All turns except Korean	All turns	All turns except Korean
Number of comparisons	38	28	20	16	18	12
Matching inventory turns	34	25	16	13	18	12
Percentage of matching turns	90	90	80	81	100	100

[1] Inventory investment turn occurs, but there is no activity turn.
[2] No turn occurs in either activity or inventory investment.
[3] Activity turn occurs but no matching inventory investment turn.
[4] Not available.

Source: Based on material from Department of Commerce.

Timing comparisons of the comprehensive series and reference turns are shown in table 32. The total manufacturing and durables series (both deflated and undeflated) lead at all business cycle turns.

TABLE 32.—*Timing of manufacturers' goods-in-process inventory investment at reference turns*

Industry	Lead (−) or lag (+) in months							
	Business cycle		Korean cycle		Business cycles			
	Peak November 1948	Trough October 1949	Peak February 1951	Trough June 1952	Peak July 1953	Trough August 1954	Peak July 1957	Trough April 1958
Deflated data:								
Total manufacturing	−3	−2	+9	(1)	(1)	−3		
Durable-goods industries, total	−3	−2	+6	(1)	(1)	−3		
Nondurable-goods industries, total	(1)	(1)	(1)	(1)	(1)	(1)		
Undeflated data:								
Total manufacturing	−3	−2	+3	(1)	(1)	−3	−20	−2
Durable-good industries, total	−3	−2	0	(1)	(1)	−3	−20	−2
Nondurable-goods industries, total	(1)	(1)	(1)	(1)	(1)	(1)	(1)	(1)

[1] No turn in inventory investment.
Source: Based on material from Department of Commerce.

For the individual industry series, turn sequences are summarized below.

Comparisons with purchased materials investment turns

	Number	Percent
Total comparisons:		
Goods-in-process investment	35	100
Leads, 4 or more months	4	11
Rough coincidences	25	72
Leads, less than 4 months	(10)	(29)
Coincidences	(9)	(26)
Lags, less than 4 months	(6)	(17)
Lags, 4 or more months	6	17

Comparisons with finished goods investment turns

	Number	Percent
Total comparisons: Goods-in-process investment	37	100
Leads, 4 or more months	15	40
Rough coincidences	19	52
Leads, less than 3 months	(12)	(33)
Coincidences	(4)	(11)
Lags, less than 3 months	(3)	(8)
Lags, 4 or more months	3	8

A clear timing tendency is revealed: turns in goods-in-process investment occur roughly coincidently with turns in purchased-materials investment, but lead turns in finished-goods investment.

These findings are sufficiently in agreement with the measures for the other comprehensive series presented in table 35 (ch. 7) to permit a generalization as to postwar timing. Goods-in-process investment, like purchased-materials investment, will tend to lead business cycle turns. The lead may be of considerable duration.

ANALYSIS AND REVISION OF ABRAMOVITZ' THEORY

If one attempts to pass judgment on Abramovitz' theory in the light of the observed behavior of the data, the results are ambiguous. The general tendency for goods in process to roughly coincide with turns in output is consistent with Abramovitz' explanation. On the other hand, there is nothing in the theory that would lead one to expect the several very long leads and lags that occur in the industry series, or the failure of such goods in process as total nondurables and certain of the industry series to conform to the Korean cycle.

The behavior of inventory investment is even less consistent with the theory. In a comparison of investment turns in the undeflated industry series with turns in rates of change in comparable output series, of the 36 turns in the latter, timing was as follows: 6 leads (3 of which 6 or more months); 9 coincidences; 21 lags (17 of which, 6 or more months).

The leads and lags of 6 months and more would appear to be well outside the range of possible timing according to Abramovitz' theory. Especially difficult to explain is the behavior of investment in the total manufacturing and durable series after 1949. The great upward movement in inventory investment observed in these series in chart 15 lasted until the latter half of 1951, the peak occurring roughly coincidently with the trough in the rate of change in output.

I can suggest four possible explanations for this disagreement between Abramovitz' theoretical statement and the behavior of the data: (1) Errors in the data due to price movements; (2) definitional difficulties leading to a reporting of stocks other than goods in process; (3) changes in composition of goods-in-process stocks since World War II; and (4) theoretical omissions.

Little need be said regarding the first point; it has already been shown that formidable obstacles to deflation exist. While we can be confident of neither the undeflated nor the deflated data, the differences noted between the timing in the series and the timing postulated by Abramovitz cannot be attributed principally to this difficulty. Experience with the purchased-materials and finished-goods series, for which deflation is more reliable, indicate that only in a small minority of cases does deflation significantly alter the essential pattern of movements in stocks and inventory investment.

It is quite possible that in the current data goods in process are not identical with those defined by Abramovitz. We do not know for instance how much of these goods are fully fabricated items held by plants in vertically integrated organizations, goods which are in process only in the sense that they will enter into further production in another division of the organization. In a nonintegrated firm such stocks would be reported as finished goods. Although there is no way to determine the extent to which this is true, its significance is doubtful. It is only reasonable to expect integrated corporation reports to be composed of consolidated accounting records kept by member plants or divisions. Since the cost records of individual plants or divisions contain separate statements of inventories held at each stage of fabrication the consolidated report should not provide a different figure from that which would have been reported had the production units been individual firms.

The third possible reason for differences between theory and observed behavior appears to be of greater importance. Abramovitz' analysis rested on the assumption that continuous process operations were the most important in American industry, and that the behavior of goods in process within stages dominated the cyclical pattern of total goods in process. This assumption was based on his estimates of the relative amount of goods in process held by continuous, mixed, and discontinuous industries in 1939.

As shown previously, there has been a marked change in the structure of American industry since 1939; the durables, especially transportation equipment and machinery, having assumed a more prominent place. It is precisely these industries that have discontinuous production processes.[9]

Approximately 50 percent of total stocks were held by durables manufacturers at the close of 1939. Comparable figures for December 31, 1953, show durables with 58 percent of total stocks.[10]   The dis-

	Value of total stocks by production process of minor industries		
	Continuous	Discontinuous	Mixed
Nondurable goods manfacturing:			
Food and tobacco products	88	12	
Textiles and textile products	36	2	62
Leather and leather products	57	43	
Rubber products	100		
Paper and allied products	73		27
Chemicals	100		
Petroleum and coal products	100		
Durable goods manufacturing:			
Lumber and wood products	20	43	37
Stone, clay, and glass	15	38	47
Ferrous and nonferrous metals and their products (excluding machinery)	45	30	25
Machinery (including electrical)	5	62	33
Transportation equipment (including auto)	17	83	

[9] This is clearly seen in Abramovitz' estimates of the value of total stocks held by production processes on Dec. 31, 1939 (compiled from table 105, with dollar figures converted to percentages, ibid., p. 560).

[10] I derived the 1939 figure from ibid., table 105, p. 560, omitting the miscellaneous category and classifying the industries as durable or nondurable. The 1953 figure was obtained similarly using the 1953 Annual Survey of Manufactures data.

parity between the amounts of goods-in-process stocks held by the durables and nondurables categories on the two dates is even greater because the discontinuous processes, so important to the durables industries, carry a higher proportion of total stocks as goods in process than do the mixed or continuous processes. Using Abramovitz' assumptions, it is estimated that durable manufactures held 57 percent of all goods in process in 1939 and 65 percent in 1953.[11] But the latter figure, although comparable with Abramovitz', is too low. According to the census estimates (Annual Survey of Manufactures), goods in process held in 1953 by these same industries amounted to 81 percent of the total.[12]

The effect of this increased role of durables is, of course, to increase the proportion of total goods in process held by discontinuous process industrial activities. Using Abramovitz' assumptions and method, comparable estimates for 1939 and 1953 are as follows:

	1939	1953
Continuous	37.7	32
Discontinuous	36.1	46
Mixed	26.2	22

An estimate made directly from the postwar census goods-in-process data, rather than the Abramovitz method, results in a slightly higher proportion of goods-in-process stocks held by industries engaging in discontinuous processes, roughly 50 percent. The significance of this finding is clear. The increased importance of that type of goods in process most loosely tied to the rate of production could account, in part, for the disparity noted between the behavior hypothesized and that observed in the data.

Finally, it appears that Abramovitz in his theoretical discussion omitted some possible types of behavior which may be of importance. The first omission concerns the behavior of goods in process between stages. As pointed out previously, Abramovitz' treatment of the behavior of these stocks was somewhat sketchy; only surplus stocks could move in an inverted fashion, but they need not. In the main, he holds, these between-stage stocks may be expected to move fairly closely with output. I suggest that when these goods in process are standardized component parts they need not behave either in an inverted fashion or move with the rate of output, but may be treated in a manner similar to purchased materials; that is, increased in advance of actual utilization on the basis of orders received. Further, as in the case of purchased materials, it may be desirable for the manufacturer to allow these goods in process to accumulate when there is a rapidly rising backlog of orders or when a large order backlog is not being significantly reduced. Such a hypothesis is particularly helpful in explaining the long expansion in durables goods-in-process investment from 1949 to 1951.

The second omission concerns goods in process held within stages of production. Abramovitz assumes that these will be effected by

---

[11] In preparing this estimate I made use of Abramovitz' estimates of the value of each industry's total stocks held in continuous, discontinuous, and mixed type operations and converted these by using his average ratios of goods in process to total stocks for the 3 types of processes. See ibid., p. 164, for these ratios.
[12] Excluding the miscellaneous category. See footnote 10 above.

changes in the rate of output. I suggest that this need not be the
case if output is varied simply by working more or fewer days per
week or more or fewer shifts per day, without increasing or decreasing
the number of machines used.   Under such conditions the amount of
material in process at any time need not be altered.   This practice
is quite important in some industries (e.g., in the cotton broad-woven
goods industry, varying the number of days worked per week is the
principal device for varying output).   Further, it is a well-established
fact that the length of the workweek in manufacturing varies with
the business cycle.   To the extent that output is varied in this fashion,
fluctuations in the level of goods in process within stages will tend to
be muted, and the type of movement visualized by Abramovitz will
play a lesser role.

If these previously omitted cases are added to the theoretical description of goods-in-process inventory behavior and due account is
taken of the changed composition of these stocks, the composite picture
is altered substantially.   The movements of within-stage stocks become less important in determining the overall pattern because these
stocks are smaller and because they are not so completely tied to movements in the rate of change in output as was formerly supposed.
The movements of between-stage stocks, on the other hand, become
more important, for they are much larger than in prewar years.
Moreover, they are no longer so closely tied to output movements
under the revised theory, but are related in a larger measure to the
volume of incoming orders and to the levels of unfilled orders.

These revisions do not leave us with a very precise theory, but
certain conclusions may be drawn as to expected behavior.   Goods-in-
process stocks may be expected to conform closely to cyclical movements.   Expected timing of these movements is somewhat indeter-
minate, except that there would seem to be little reason to anticipate
the development of inverted tendencies.   Goods-in-process investment movements would be expected to resemble those of purchased-
materials investment, moving with a lead at both peak and trough
and thereby contributing to the early set of forces which brings about
the end of the expansion and of the contraction phases.

Such a theory goes far toward explaining the difference in behavior
of durable and nondurable goods-in-process investment.   Investment series for durables manufacturers' goods-in-process inventories,
which contain a large proportion of between-process stocks, are
relatively sensitive to business cycles; those for nondurables, which
contain a small proportion of such stocks, are relatively insensitive.

SUMMARY

Although problems of deflation render conclusions regarding goods-
in-process behavior less dependable than those for purchased materials
and finished goods, certain characteristics may be noted.   The inventory series conformed to business cycles with virtually coincident timing at four of the six reference cycle turns, and inventory investment
led all business cycle turns.   Analysis of sequence of timing among the
industry series indicates that, for both inventory and investment,
goods in process lead or turn coincidently with purchased materials
and lead finished-goods series.

Although these findings are generally consistent with Abramovitz' theory among the individual industry investment series, irregularities in timing appear which cannot be explained by his analysis.   Three factors appear to contribute to this behavior:

(1) The composition of postwar goods in process is different from that observed by Abramovitz.   Owing to the increased role of durables, there is a much larger proportion of these stocks held by industries engaging in discontinuous processes, roughly 50 percent compared with his estimate of 36 percent.

(2) Goods-in-process stocks in discontinuous-process industries are likely to be held in substantial quantities between stages.   These stocks may be expected to rise and fall in a manner similar to that of purchased materials.

(3) Goods held within stages need not fluctuate in as close conformity to changes in output as Abramovitz maintained.

7

Cyclical Behavior of Inventory and Inventory Investment Movements at the Three Stages of Fabrication: Summary

It is now possible to bring together summary statements regarding manufacturers' inventories and investment, and to note how movements at each stage of fabrication form the composite patterns of total manufacturers' inventory and inventory investment behavior.[1]

TABLE 33.—*Timing of inventories and inventory investment at business cycle turns: Summary*

A. INVENTORIES, ALL MANUFACTURERS

Business cycle turn	Lead (−) or lag (+), in months			
	Purchased materials	Finished goods	Goods in process	Total inventories
Peak, November 1948	−3.0	+7.0	−14.0	+4.0
Trough, October 1949	+6.0	+11.0	+2.0	+6.0
Korean peak, February 1951	+9.0	+14.0	(1)	(1)
Korean trough, June 1952	+4.0	+4.0	(1)	(1)
Peak, July 1953	+1.0	+8.0	0	+2.0
Trough, August 1954	+8.0	+1.0	+1.0	+1.0
Peak, July 1957	+4.0	+6.0	+2.0	+2.0
Trough, April 1958	+5.0	+8.0	+7.0	+8.0
Averages:				
Peaks	+2.8	+8.8	−4.0	+2.7
Troughs	+5.8	+6.0	+3.3	+5.0
Peaks and troughs	+4.5	+7.4	−.3	+3.8
Prewar average, peaks and troughs				+8.6

B. INVENTORIES, DURABLE AND NONDURABLE MANUFACTURERS

Business cycle turn	Lead (−) or lag (+), in months							
	Purchased materials		Finished goods		Goods in process		Total inventories	
	Durable	Nondurable	Durable	Nondurable	Durable	Nondurable	Durable	Nondurable
Peak, November 1948	−16.0	−1.0	+8.0	+6.0	−14	(1)	−14	(1)
Trough, October 1949	+4.0	+8.0	+11.0	+11.0	+4	(1)	+4	(1)
Korean peak, February 1951	+13.0	+9.0	(1)	+14.0	(1)	(1)	(1)	(1)
Korean trough, June 1952	+2.0	(1)	(1)	+10.0	(1)	(1)	(1)	(1)
Peak, July 1953	+1.0	(1)	+5.0	(1)	+1	−1.0	+2	+2.0
Trough, August 1954	+10.0	+7.0	+1.0	(1)	+1	+1.0	+9	+1.0
Peak, July 1957	−4.0	+1.0	+6.0	+6.0	+1	+6.0	+3	+1.0
Trough, April 1958	+4.0	+10.0	+9.0	+5.0	+7	+6.0	+8	+5.0
Averages, peaks and troughs	+1.8	+5.7	+6.7	+8.8	0	+3.2	+2	+3.2

[1] Timing measures mentioned in this section are presented in table 33; inventory investment movements are shown in chart 16.

TABLE 33.—*Timing of inventories and inventory investment at business cycle turns: Summary*—Continued

C. INVENTORY INVESTMENT, ALL MANUFACTURERS

Business cycle turn	Lead (−) or lag (+), in months			
	Purchased materials	Finished goods	Goods in process	Total inventory investment
Peak, November 1948	−6.0	+3.0	−3.0	−6.0
Trough, October 1949	−5.0	−2.0	−2.0	−2.0
Korean peak, February 1951	−3.0	+6.0	+9.0	+3.0
Korean trough, June 1952	+2.0	−1.0	(1)	−1.0
Peak, July 1953	−2.0	+1.0	(1)	−2.0
Trough, August 1954	−9.0	−3.0	−3.0	0
Peak, July 1957	−23.0	−14.0	−20.0	−14.0
Trough, April 1958	+1.0	+1.0	−2.0	+1.0
Averages:				
Peaks	−8.5	−1.0	−4.7	−4.8
Troughs	−2.8	−1.2	−2.3	−.5
Peaks and troughs	−5.6	−1.1	−3.5	−2.6
Prewar average, peaks and troughs				+0.2

D. INVENTORY INVESTMENT, DURABLE AND NONDURABLE MANUFACTURERS

Business cycle turn	Lead (−) or lag (+), in months							
	Purchased materials		Finished goods		Goods in process		Total inventories	
	Durable	Nondurable	Durable	Nondurable	Durable	Nondurable	Durable	Nondurable
Peak, November 1948	−6.0	−6	0	−6.0	−3	(1)	−6.0	−6.0
Trough, October 1949	−5.0	−11	−2	−2.0	−2	(1)	−2.0	+7.0
Korean peak, February 1951	−3.0	−3	+6	+6.0	+6	(1)	+6.0	+3.0
Korean trough, June 1952	−1.0	(1)	+2	−1.0	(1)	(1)	−1.0	(1)
Peak, July 1953	−2.	(1)	+1	+1.0	(1)	(1)	−2.0	(1)
Trough, August 1954	0	−6	−3	+3.0	−3	(1)	−3.0	−9.0
Peak, July 1957	−23.0	−2	−8	−14.0	−20	(1)	−20.0	−14.0
Trough, April 1958	+1.0	+4	+4	+1.0	−2	(1)	+1.0	+4.0
Averages, peaks and troughs	−4.9	−8	0	−1.5	−4	(1)	−3.4	−2.5

No matching inventory turn.

Source: Tables 8, 9, 12, 14, 21, 23, 28, and 30. Source of prewar (1919–39) averages, based on annual data: Abramovitz, "Inventories and Business Cycles," pp. 95 and 338. All 1948–54 data are deflated (1947 dollars) undeflated (book value) data are used thereafter.

CHART 16

MANUFACTURERS' INVENTORY INVESTMENT: SUMMARY

A. Total Manufacturing

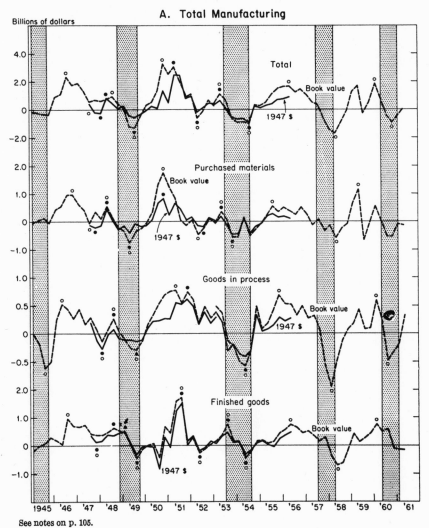

Billions of dollars

See notes on p. 105.

CHART 16—Continued

B. Durable-goods Industries

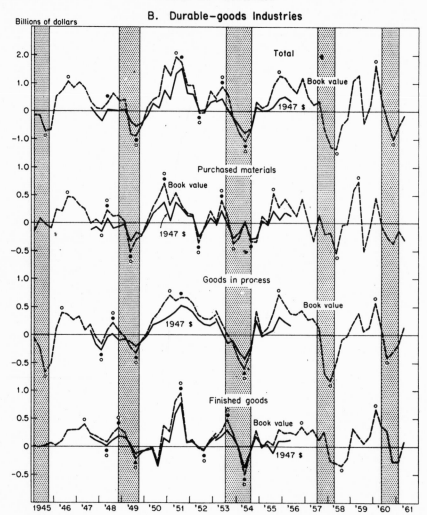

See notes on p. 105.

Chart 16—Continued

C. Nondurable-goods Industries

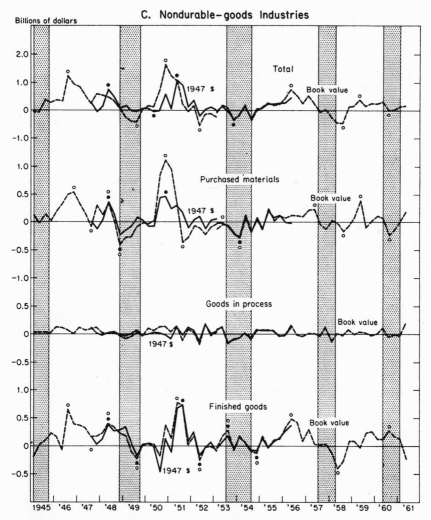

Shaded areas represent business contractions; unshaded areas, expansions.
Dots identify peaks and troughs of deflated cycles; circles, of undeflated cycles.

Source: Department of Commerce. Data deflated by the author.

PURCHASED MATERIALS

Purchased materials show a high degree of sensitivity to business cycles, particularly in the durables group. The stocks proper tend to turn roughly coincidently with business cycle peaks and to lag at business cycle troughs. But the rates of change (the investment series) show a single well-developed tendency: They lead at all turns. It is interesting to observe that the timing is very similar to that of new orders. When orders begin to turn up late in the recession, the rate of disinvestment declines. As the trough is reached and early recovery is noted, purchased-materials stocks continue to decline but at a decreasing rate. Several months after the trough, declining disinvestment changes to rising investment as the stocks turn and move up. A similar movement occurs at the peak, except that stocks proper turn relatively earlier.

The amplitude of the investment movements appears to be influenced by the level of unfilled orders. When orders are rising at a faster pace than shipments, so that the backlog of unfilled orders is growing rapidly, or when the backlog is very large and not significantly diminishing, upward movements of new orders prompt much heavier investment in purchased materials than otherwise.

FINISHED GOODS

Finished stocks are, of course, the lagging series. They lag behind business cycle turns from 1 to 11 months. Finished-goods inventory investment, however, reaches its peak or trough roughly coincidently with the business cycle peak or trough.

The relatively early timing of finished-goods investment turns is a well-established finding, based upon observation of commodity series as well as the Department of Commerce data. In the activity expansion phase, the latest occurrence of the trough in inventory investment is the quarter in which shipments spurt forward at their most rapid rate; frequently it occurs somewhat earlier. The converse is true for the peak in investment: it rarely occurs later in the activity contraction phase than the quarter during which shipments fall at their most rapid rate. Since it is a well-established characteristic of the business cycle that the highest rate of increase in activity typically occurs during early recovery, and the highest rate of decrease during the early or middle stages of recession, it may be concluded that any countercyclical movement of finished-goods investment is terminated early in each business cycle phase.

GOODS IN PROCESS

Problems of deflation render conclusions regarding goods-in-process behavior less dependable than those for purchased materials and finished goods. Several characteristics may be noted, however. The deflated inventory series conform to business cycles with virtually coincident timing at four of the six business cycle turns. Analysis of timing sequence indicates that goods in process lead or turn coincidently with purchased-materials inventory turns, and lead finished-goods turns. Goods-in-process inventory investment movements are cyclically sensitive and give evidence of being influenced by unfilled order levels. Although timing is somewhat irregular, the typical sequence is one in which these series turn roughly coincidently with turns in purchased materials, but lead turns in finished-goods investment.

TOTAL STOCKS AND INVENTORY INVESTMENT

The three components combine to form a total manufacturing inventory complex which is highly responsive to cyclical forces. During the period studied, total stocks lagged behind business cycle turns from 1 to 8 months, and total inventory investment turned coincidently or led by as much as 14 months (table 33).

Of course, the pattern of behavior for total stocks is merely an average of the component patterns, and there is actually a considerable diversity in the timing of inventory turns at each stage of fabrication. The striking feature is that inventory investment at each stage is so sensitive to cyclical forces. Throughout the analysis it has been noted that inventory investment conformed somewhat better to business cycles than did the inventory series proper. Even the finished-goods investment series lags behind the other investment series by no more than 6 months at four of the six business cycle turns, and shows almost no countercyclical tendencies.

AMPLITUDE OF INVESTMENT MOVEMENTS COMPARED

Tables 34 and 35 present relative and dollar value measures of change during movements in inventory investment for each stage of fabrication. It may be observed that changes in each type of inventory investment have contributed significantly to cyclical instability. Comparing total manufacturers' purchased materials and finished goods investment, we find that the amplitude of total change is somewhat greater for the latter in six of the seven phases. This is true for measures of change in dollars and on a relative basis. Amplitude of changes in goods-in-process investment is more variable. In the earlier phases it ranked behind purchased materials and finished goods investment, but more recently it has tended to move with greater amplitude than either.

TABLE 34.—*Amplitude of change in inventory investment cycles, by phase, 1948–58*

Industry	Peak-trough (1948–49)	Trough-peak (1949–50)	Peak-trough (1950–52)	Trough-peak (1952–53)	Peak-trough (1953–54)	Trough-peak (1954–56)	Peak-trough (1956–58)
	Total change (millions of dollars)						
Total manufacturing:							
Purchased materials	−843	+1,220	−1,017	+336	−627	+1,143	−1,136
Goods in process	−208	+753			1 −779	+1,273	−1,649
Finished goods	−835	+1,821	−1,703	+666	−790	+1,190	−1,436
Total durables manufacturing:							
Purchased materials	−415	+700	−626	+406	−513	+921	−1,089
Goods in process	−224	+734			1 −739	+1,328	−1,550
Finished goods	−315	+908	−815	+360	−668	+856	−700
Total nondurables manufacturing:							
Purchased materials	−588	+680			1 −320	+507	−415
Goods in process							
Finished goods	−561	+923	−920	+379	−278	+602	−882
	Change per month (millions of dollars)						
Total manufacturing:							
Purchased materials	−70	+68	−48	+112	−52	+54	−54
Goods in process	−15	+27			1 −52	+71	−61
Finished goods	−139	+76	−142	+55	−88	+49	−60
Total durables manufacturing:							
Purchased materials	−35	+39	−35	+34	−29	+44	−52
Goods in process	−12	+24			1 −49	+74	−57
Finished goods	−52	+38	−68		−74	+29	−33
Total nondurables manufacturing:							
Purchased materials	−98	+28			1 −36	+34	−11
Goods in process							
Finished goods	−37	+38	−102	+25	−18	+33	−37

1 To permit comparison of amplitudes of downward movements during recession of 1953–54, purchased-materials investment change in nondurable goods has been measured from 2d quarter 1953 to 1st quarter 1954; goods in process (except nondurable) change has been measured from 1st quarter 1953 to 2d quarter 1954.

Source: Based on deflated material from Department of Commerce. All 1948–54 data have been deflated (1947 dollars). Measures for the 2 most recent phases are based on undeflated (book value) data.

TABLE 35.—*Amplitude of change in inventory investment cycles, 1948–58, as percent of mean level of inventories during each phase* [1]

Industry	Peak–trough (1948–49)	Trough–peak (1949–50)	Peak–trough (1950–52)	Trough–peak (1952–53)	Peak–trough (1953–54)	Trough–peak (1954–56)	Peak–trough (1956–58)
	Total change (relative)						
Total manufacturing:							
Purchased materials	−7.15	+10.28	−7.82	+2.43	−4.57	+7.44	−7.20
Goods in process	−3.06	+9.73			²−7.65	+9.76	−11.44
Finished goods	−7.72	+15.95	−13.51	+4.92	−5.83	+6.93	−7.60
Total durables manufacturing:							
Purchased materials	−8.60	+14.94	−12.12	+7.23	−9.69	+12.72	−14.78
Goods in process	−4.85	+14.21			²−9.67	+12.83	−13.45
Finished goods	−7.35	+19.44	−15.74	+6.43	−11.23	+10.16	−7.60
Total nondurables manufacturing:							
Purchased materials	−8.27	+9.28			²−3.93	+6.38	−5.00
Goods in process							
Finished goods	−9.37	+13.55	−12.40	4.88	−3.56	+6.74	−9.00
	Change per month (relative)						
Total manufacturing:							
Purchased materials	−.60	+.57	−.37	+.81	−.38	+.35	−.34
Goods in process	−.20	+.36			²−.51	+.54	−.42
Finished goods	−1.29	+.66	−1.13	+.41	−.65	+.29	−.32
Total durables manufacturing:							
Purchased materials	−.72	+.83	−.67	+.60	−.65	+.61	−.70
Goods in process	−.40	+.59			²−.64	+.72	−.50
Finished goods	−.82	+.81	−1.31	.71	−1.25	+.34	−.36
Total nondurables manufacturing:							
Purchased materials	−1.38	+.39			²−.44	+.42	−.13
Goods in process							
Finished goods	−.62	+.56	−1.38	+.33	−.24	+.37	−.38

[1] Mean level of inventories was computed separately for each phase using average of beginning and ending level of inventories of terminal quarters of the phase.

² See note (1) to table 34.

Source: Based on deflated material from Department of Commerce.

POSTWAR AND PREWAR TIMING COMPARED

Since frequent mention has been made of Abramovitz' study, a brief comparison of his timing measures with those for the postwar period is relevant. [2]

Lagging movements in total inventories have been characteristic in the postwar period, but relative to business cycle turns they have been shorter, averaging about 4 months compared with 8 or 9 months during the previous period. In part, this earlier timing may be due to the shift in composition toward durables and goods in process, resulting in greater sensitivity and consilience with the cycle. It may also be due to a tighter control of inventories by management.

Abramovitz' estimate of short lags (about 3 months) in purchased-materials inventories is fairly consistent with postwar experience. Lags at troughs (averaging about 6 months) have been longer than at peaks (averaging about 3 months).

Abramovitz drew no conclusions regarding the timing of finished-goods inventories as a whole, but dealt with the behavior of the component classifications. It is important to observe that the largest

[2] Timing measures mentioned in this section are presented in table 33.

component (demand-oriented staples made to order), which demonstrates marked inverted characteristics, has been relatively smaller since the war, and that the positively-conforming, made-to-order category is larger as a result of the increased share of durable-goods production. Accordingly, there seems to be little doubt that lags in aggregate finished stocks have been shorter in the postwar period. They have averaged about 7 months, always turning before the end of the phase even when the phase is short.

The roughly coincident postwar behavior of goods-in-process stocks is consistent with Abramovitz' estimate, but inventory investment behaves somewhat differently.

Leads in total manufacturers' inventory investment have been characteristic in the postwar period, whereas Abramovitz calculated rough coincidences from prewar annual data. Abramovitz concluded that investment would be likely to show a substantial lag behind rates of change in output, and this has been confirmed by the postwar data. He expected that normally the business cycle peak would occur at about the same time as the inventory peak. This would be due, however, to the reciprocal effect of inventory investment on national product. He did not rule out the possibility that leads might occur.

Abramovitz expected short leads in purchased-materials investment relative to business activity, but lags relative to the rate of change in output. Postwar experience is reasonably consistent with this, although some lags behind rates of change in output were longer than could be explained by Abramovitz' theory.

As in the case of finished-goods inventories, it is not possible to compare postwar and prewar timing in finished-goods investment directly, but the evidence points to earlier turns since the war. For the postwar period as a whole, rough coincidence has been the rule. Investment in goods made to stock has moved inversely to the rate of change in output, frequently with a lead. Since turns in the rate of change have occurred rather early in expansions or contractions, investment has moved positively to output during most of the phase (i.e., lags on a positive basis, when they have occurred, have been fairly short). Investment in goods made to order, which probably moves positively, has been more important since the war because of the greater importance of durables.

Abramovitz expected long leads, in goods-in-process investment because it should turn coincidently with the rate of change in output. But short leads have been characteristic since the war, goods in process having lagged behind the rate of change in output. These goods are not tied so closely to output as Abramovitz thought.

Conclusion

It is well to note the degree to which these findings attest the value of Abramovitz' approach to the study of manufacturers' inventories. This analysis of the behavior of various component stocks, constructing the composite from knowledge so derived, has made it possible to observe the characteristic behavior of various types of inventory and, thereby, to evaluate the effects of shifts in composition. Without such a study it would have been impossible to assess the significance of declines in the relative size of finished stocks and of increases in the importance of durables, or to explain why manufacturers' stocks, which are smaller today than before the war, have played no less important a role in business cycles.

The analysis must be regarded as incomplete, however, on the grounds that the business cycle has been assumed as given. Inventory movements have been regarded as responsive to the cycle, aggravating the fluctuations, but not themselves causing either upturn or downturn. In short, the income effect of inventory investment has not been treated, nor has the possibility of a self-generating inventory cycle. These matters are the concern of the chapter which follows.

8

How Inventory Movements
Contribute to Instability

In observing the behavior of manufacturers' inventories, it has been assumed that fluctuations in general business activity are caused by forces unrelated to inventory movements, and that the latter may be regarded as dependent fluctuations, superimposed upon the business cycle.

It has been shown, however, that inventory investment movements are among the major variables in the economy. The demonstrated cyclical sensitivity of this important component of the national product raises two fundamental questions: In what manner do changes in inventory investment contribute to the cumulative forces of expansion and contraction? Is it possible that movements in inventory investment may spark the upswing and bring about the downturn, thereby constituting an underlying cause as well as an aggravating force?

Metzler's Inventory Cycle Theory

To answer these questions it is useful to examine Lloyd Metzler's theory of the inventory cycle.[1] Metzler presents his study, not as a theory of the business cycle, but as a contribution to the understanding of its nature. In the American Economic Review article in which he summarizes his theory and explains its significance, Metzler reviews several of the earlier cycle theories and points to what he considers their common property: each conceives of expansion and contraction as highly cumulative in nature and capable of being terminated only through certain limiting forces which are operative only toward the end of each phase. These older theories hold "that the economy is essentially unstable." [2]

In Metzler's alternative explanation, business cycles may be regarded as recurrent deviations from equilibrium levels of income, deviations which come about as a result of the structure of the economic system. In this view the economy is essentially stable, but any increase in demand (through, say, a change to a permanently higher level of autonomous investment) will set up oscillations around a new equilibrium.

The inventory cycle is offered as an example of such a structural cycle. It comes about as a result of the attempts of businessmen to bring inventories into a desired relationship with sales. Initially, efforts to replace or increase depleted inventories increase income and consumption, thereby pulling down the level of stocks further and causing additional increases in inventory demand, income, and con-

[1] Metzler's elaboration of the nature and significance of inventory cycles is set forth in three articles: "The Nature and Stability of Inventory Cycles," Review of Economic Statistics, August 1941, pp. 113-129; "Factors Governing the Length of Inventory Cycles," ibid., February 1947, pp. 1-15; "Business Cycles and the Modern Theory of Employment," American Economic Review, June 1946, pp. 278-291.
[2] Metzler, "Business Cycles and the Modern Theory of Employment," p. 280.

sumption. Ultimately, however, efforts to adjust stocks become more successful in spite of the derived increases in consumption, and at some point the rate of inventory accumulation reaches a peak and begins to decline. This brings a corresponding decline in income and consumption, resulting in unwanted stocks. Efforts of businessmen to reduce stocks cause further declines in income and consumption, again defeating inventory objectives. But once again inventory adjustment ultimately begins to be achieved. Disinvestment reaches its maximum and begins to diminish (i.e., there is an increase in the inventory investment series), bringing an increase in aggregate demand, and a new cycle follows.

It is essential to the argument that the interaction of the multiplier and accelerator causes the rate of change in sales to decline after a time during expansion (and rise after a time during contractions). The accelerator is defined below. The multiplier is simply the reciprocal of the marginal propensity to save. This reversal in direction of movement in the rate of change in sales brings in its wake a reversal of inventory investment and of income.[3]

In his two articles dealing with the properties of inventory cycel models, Metzler varies assumptions regarding the size of the marginal propensity to consume, the nature of expectations, and the inventory accelerator.[4] In all the models the marginal propensity to consume is equal to the average propensity to consume, and consumption is not lagged (i.e., all consumption expenditures are made from current income). On the other hand, production is lagged, in the sense that production in a given period is guided by the sales of the preceding period. In the simplest models, production for sales in period t is equal to sales in $t-1$, and businessmen attempt to maintain a constant level of stocks. But in the more complex models, the coefficient of expectations and the inventory accelerator are introduced. The coefficient of expectations is a percentage figure, applied to the change

---

[3] The argument may be stated in terms of a relatively simple model in which sales in period t are expected to be those observed in period $t-1$ and desired inventories are a constant proportion of sales:
(1) Output (Y_t) =autonomous investment (A) plus output for sale, i.e., sales of last period (S_{t-1}), plus planned inventory investment (I_t)

$$Y_t = A + S_{t-1} + I_t$$

(2) Planned inventory investment is the sum of:
    (a) Unplanned inventory disinvestment of last period (I_t') which is the difference between expected and actual sales last period. Since the expected sales last period are S_{t-2}, and the actual sales are S_{t-1},

$$I_t' = S_{t-1} - S_{t-2}$$

    (b) The increase in required stocks made necessary by the increase in sales (I_t''). Stocks required in period t equal expected sales in t times the inventory sales ratio (a). Stocks required in period $t-1$ equal expected sales in $t-1$ times a. Since I_t' would only bring stocks into line with sales in $t-2$, I_t'' must bring stocks into line with S_{t-1} (expected S_t). Therefore,

$$I_t'' = a\ (S_{t-1} - S_{t-2})$$
(c) $$I_t = I_t' + I_t'' = (S_{t-1} - S_{t-2}) + a(S_{t-1} - S_{t-2})$$
$$I_t = (1+a)(S_{t-1} - S_{t-2})$$
(3) Total output, therefore, is:

$$Y_t = A + S_{t-1} + (1+a)(S_{t-1} - S_{t-2})$$

(4) From the above, the conditions under which the movement of output is revised may be noted. In period t the change in output from the previous period is $Y_t - Y_{t-1}$

where $$Y_t = A + S_{t-1} + (1+a)(S_{t-1} - S_{t-2})$$ and
$$Y_{t-1} = A + S_{t-2} + (1+a)(S_{t-2} - S_{t-3})$$

As long as sales are rising at an increasing rate Y must rise, and at an increasing rate. But if the rate of change in sales begins to decline, $Y_t - Y_{t-1}$ will remain positive only so long as S_{t-1} exceeds S_{t-2} by more than $(1+a)$ times the difference between the rates of change in sales. If the rate of change in sales is declining, $S_{t-1} - S_{t-2}$ is becoming a smaller positive quantity while $(S_{t-1} - S_{t-2}) - (S_{t-2} - S_{t-3})$ is becoming a larger negative quantity. Given a decline in the rate of increase in sales, the sign of $Y_t - Y_{t-1}$ must, therefore, eventually become negative.
[4] Metzler, "The Nature and Stability of Inventory Cycles"; "Factors Governing the Length of Inventory Cycles." See note 1.

in sales in the current period $(S_t - S_t - 1)$, to give the expected change in the next period. The inventory accelerator is expressed as a percentage figure which, when applied to expected sales, gives the inventory objective for the next period.

Metzler concludes that the propensity to consume is a more important factor governing the length of the cycle than are the inventory accelerator and the coefficient of expectations. Expansion and contraction phases of the cycle are shown to be more prolonged the larger the propensity to consume or the larger the inventory accelerator, but less prolonged with larger values of the coefficient of expectations. The cycle can only occur for certain values of the marginal propensity to consume and the accelerator. At values below the critical limits, a disturbance merely leads to a new position of equilibrium; above the critical limits, the cycle is unstable, aggregate output moving continuously upward with wavelike fluctuations in the rate of increase.

Observations on the Validity of Metzler's Theory

That it is rarely possible to submit an economic theory to a conclusive empirical test is an all too familiar observation. Useful theory requires a high level of abstraction and the generous use of ceteris paribus assumptions. When the theorist makes use of the rigorous language of mathematics these difficulties may be multiplied, for special assumptions must be kept at a minimum, and the language permits of few ambiguities. In short, theory attempts to cut through to essential and recurrent processes, but empirical tests must be conducted in a complex and changing world, in which parameters change and essential processes are fused with accidental or irregular ones.

If Metzler's theory were to be tested it is expected that the following specific problems would be encountered:

(1) There is no means available of determining either the size or the degree of stability of the accelerator or the expectations coefficient. Moreover, only ex post facto observations can be made of the relationships between income and consumption, thus making it impossible to compute in advance the value of the marginal propensity to consume. An additional complication involving parameters is that there is no means of determining the duration of lags between the receipt and the spending of a given income dollar and, consequently, no means of determining directly the duration of a "period" as Metzler visualizes it in his model.

(2) The problem is rendered especially difficult by the fact that Metzler is concerned with inventory, rather than business cycles; his theory is directed toward understanding the process by which an economy seeks a new equilibrium. He recognizes that the business cycle is a complex phenomenon and that the establishment of a single causal relationship for any given cycle is unlikely.[5] Yet the data needed to establish or to disprove the Metzler theory bear the stamp of the additional forces present in the business cycle itself.

(3) Associated with this difficulty is the fact that Metzler does not elaborate a theory of durable-goods investment. He makes only brief reference to it, stating that his models may be readily abridged to remedy the omission by combining the induced demand for invest-

[5] Metzler, "Business Cycles and the Modern Theory of Employment," p. 282;

ment goods with the demand for consumers goods in a general "propensity to spend."

There are, however, at least three grounds for suspecting that the relationship is more complex than Metzler implies:

(*a*) Evidence indicates that the lag between the decision to invest and the investment expenditure is longer than that which he hypothesizes for the decision to consume (derived immediately from income) and consumption expenditure.[6]

(*b*) Inventory requirements arising out of changes in durables investment are likely to be smaller than those in consumption expenditures. An examination of institutional arrangements supports this view: In the marketing of producers investment goods, the channels from manufacturer to ultimate purchaser are largely direct, with no middlemen's stocks held. Moreover, it is well established that such investment goods as heavy machinery are produced principally to order, and that manufacturers' finished-goods requirements for such products are small.

(*c*) It is unlikely that durable-goods investment is derived merely from changes in income. Very likely it is influenced importantly by a number of other factors, including the existing stock of equipment, changes in technology, changes in population, changes in costs of production, and changes in availability of funds.

(4) Metzler makes simplifying assumptions regarding price movements and supply conditions. He assumes that prices remain unchanged and that supply is perfectly expansible. In fact, most prices have a degree of cyclical sensitivity, and it is reasonable to suppose that price movements influence businessmen's anticipations and inventory objectives. Moreover, supply conditions deteriorate during certain stages of the business cycle and improve during others, and these changes influence inventory objectives and the purchasing process.

Although it appears unlikely that conclusive tests of Metzler's theory can be devised, it stands as an hypothesis of major importance: (*a*) It suggests that attempts to adjust inventories may, because of income feedback, be partially self-defeating, thereby providing a cumulative force in expansion and in contraction; (*b*) it suggests a way in which movements in inventory investment may be reversed prior to reversals in aggregate demand.

Is there, then, any evidence which will permit at least a tentative judgment as to the validity of the Metzler thesis in explaining the nature of forces at work in the cyclical process? Some such evidence may be found in the behavior of consumption and saving, and in timing comparisons of turns in inventory investment with turns in rates of change in final purchases.

BEHAVIOR OF CONSUMPTION AND SAVING

During the postwar years a number of studies have been undertaken to determine the relations of consumption or saving to income and other

[6] Victor Zarnowitz has compiled series which portray both aggregate fixed investment commitments (equipment orders placed and industrial construction contracts let) and aggregate fixed investment expenditures. During the period covered by these series (1949–58) timing comparisons reveal a systematic lag between orders and expenditures ranging between 6 and 12 months, with the exception of a lag of 30 months associated with the unusual demand and supply conditions arising out of the Korean war. Victor Zarnowitz, "The Timing of Manufacturers' Orders During Business Cycles," *Business Cycle Indicators*, New York, Princeton for NBER, pp. 476–477.

variables, and to measure the stability of such relationships.[7] While, to a considerable extent the conclusions drawn from these studies remain controversial, there seems to be general agreement on at least the following:

1. The relationship between consumption and income is markedly less stable for short periods than for long.

2. Consumption is significantly related to a number of variables other than current income. These variables include liquid asset position, past income (or some concept of permanent income), and expectations regarding future income and prices.

In the years since the war consumer spending has been maintained at high levels for a number of months after each decline in aggregate activity.[8] Moreover, there is evidence that on occasions such stability existed before the war. Unpublished quarterly estimates prepared for the National Bureau of Economic Research by Harold Barger indicate that consumption increased during the recession of 1923–24 and remained virtually unchanged during the recession of 1926–27.

What are the implications of these findings? Certainly it can be held that the behavior of consumption during minor business cycle recessions (the sort which have characterized the postwar period) is distinctly different from that described by Metzler. If the marginal propensity to consume is very low (i.e., if the response of consumption to a decline in aggregate income is very small), the feedback process which is the essential element of Metzler's theory will be broken or become relatively unimportant. The expansion would terminate at the point at which inventories are brought into the desired relationship with sales. A decline in inventory investment, and thus in output, would follow; but an equilibrium adjustment of aggregate income would be readily attained, since the decline in investment would not set off a downward movement in sales.

Under such circumstances, the full extent of the observed declines in both inventory investment and inventories proper would not be explainable in terms of the Metzler process. Such declines might be due to a correction of earlier speculative overcommitment in stocks and to the downward revision of inventory objectives (i.e., a reduction in the desired inventory-to-sales ratio) arising out of changes in supply conditions. They might be due also to the adjustment of stocks to an independently determined decline in the production of durable capital goods. This latter cause would appear to be a partial explanation at best, for marked inventory disinvestment during recession is characteristic of all sectors of industry, and of wholesaling and retailing as well.

In regard to expansion periods, the findings which show consumption to be influenced by factors other than current income, and which

---

[7] Cf. Franco Modigliani, "Fluctuations in the Savings Income Ratio: A Problem in Economic Forecasting," Conference on Research in Income and Wealth, New York, NBER, 1949, vol. II, p. 379ff. Robert Rosa, "Use of the Consumption Function in Short Run Forecasting," Review of Economics and Statistics, May 1948, pp. 100–102. Robert Ferber, "A Study of Aggregate Consumption Functions," New York, NBER, Technical Paper 8, 1953, and "Accuracy of Aggregate Savings Function in Postwar Years," Review of Economics and Statistics, May 1953, pp. 144–145. Arnold Zellner, "Short Run Consumption Function," Econometrica, vol. 25, 1957, p. 565. Milton Friedman, "A Theory of the Consumption Function," Princeton for NBER, General Series 63,1957. M. J. Fanell, "The New Theories of the Consumption Function," Economic Journal, December 1959, pp. 678–696. J.S. Duesenberry, Otto Eckstein, and Gary Fromm, "A Simulation of the U.S. Economy in Recession," Econometrica, October 1960, pp. 749–809.

[8] A. F. Burns, "Progress Toward Economic Stability," American Economic Review, March 1960, pp 9–10. In speaking of postwar consumption behavior, Dr. Burns concludes that "this new role of the consumer reflects some of the developments of the postwar period * * *, particularly the greatly enhanced stability in the flow of personal income, the steady expansion in the number of income recipients, and the relative increase in the number of steady jobs. It reflects also the improvements of financial organization and other structural change which have strengthened the confidence of people * * *. Whatever may have been true of the past, it can no longer be held that consumers are passive creatures who lack the power or the habit of initiating changes in economic life." Ibid., p. 10.

demonstrate a very considerable degree of short-run instability in the consumption function, argue that Metzler's thesis is an abstraction which neglects significant relationships and provides, at best, a very imperfect description of the forces at work.

This is not to say, however, that the income effect is of no importance during expansions. The marginal propensity to consume may be unstable, but aggregate consumption usually does rise with rising incomes. Moreover, business spending also rises. Under such conditions it is to be expected that efforts to increase inventories will be self-frustrating to a degree, and the process of inventory investment may, in some measure, feed upon itself. If all planned inventory investment is not realized, then investment demand has contributed more significantly to the cumulative forces of expansion than the data show. This does not mean that these expansions could have been sustained by a Metzler-type process alone. But it is a suggestion that the demand arising out of attempted investment is probably well in excess of that which can be measured from the (realized) inventory investment data.

TIMING OF INVENTORY INVESTMENT AND RATES OF CHANGE IN FINAL PURCHASES

In Metzler's theory, not only must final purchases respond to changes in aggregate output and income, but the response must be large enough to defeat inventory objectives significantly. During the expansion phase increased final purchases, along with such inventory investment as may be realized, bear aggregate activity upward. The peak in the rate of inventory accumulation cannot be attained until the rate of increase in final purchases has begun to subside. Similarly, it is the unanticipated decline in final purchases during the contraction phase, along with realized inventory disinvestment, that carries aggregate activity downward. The highest rate of inventory liquidation cannot be attained until the rate of decrease in final purchases has begun to subside, for only then may adjustment of stocks reach a maximum.[9]

We have already had occasion (ch. 4) to observe the timing relationship between movements in rates of change in manufacturing activity and in purchased-materials investment. A similar relationship exists: (1) between rates of change in manufacturing activity (either output or sales) and investment in manufacturers' total stocks, and (2) between rates of change in activity (sales) and inventory investment for both retailers and wholesalers (chart 17, table 36). In the manufacturing series, inventory investment lags behind rates of change in activity at every comparison. In the retailing and wholesaling series, the same lag occurs in 7 out of 10, and 6 out of 8 comparisons, respectively.

---

[9] The point may be demonstrated by reference to equation 2c (see note 4), which shows that planned inventory investment is dependent on the rate of change in sales with a one-period lag. Thus total inventory investment would show a one-period lag if it depended only on planned inventory investment. Actually it also includes unplanned investment (U_t).

$$U_t = S_{t-1} - S_t = -(S_t - S_{t-1}) \tag{4}$$

and total inventory investment is:

$$I_t + U_t = (1+a)(S_{t-1} - S_{t-2}) - (S_t - S_{t-1}) \tag{5}$$

Since the second term ($S_t - S_{t-1}$) is increasing as long as the rate of growth of sales is increasing, total inventory investment is prevented from rising as fast as the rate of increase in sales during the period of acceleration. Thereafter, the offsetting effect of unplanned investment diminishes. Accordingly, the lag of investment behind the turning points in the rate of increase would, in general, be more than one period.

TABLE 36.—*Timing of selected inventory investment series to related purchase or sales series*

[Current dollars]

	Peak	Trough	Peak	Trough	Peak	Trough	Peak	Trough	Peak	Trough
Quarter-to-quarter change final purchases (less services)	Aug. 1946	Feb. 1949	Aug. 1950	Aug. 1952	Nov. 1952	Feb. 1954	Aug. 1955	Feb. 1956	Feb. 1957	Feb. 1958
Nonfarm inventory investment	-3	+9	+9	-3	0	-3	+3	(1)	(1)	0
Quarter-to-quarter change, manufacturing output (FRB)	May 1946	Feb. 1949	Aug. 1950	Aug. 1951	Nov. 1952	Nov. 1953	May 1955	Feb. 1956	Nov. 1956	Feb. 1958
Manufacturers' inventory investment (book value)	+3	+6	+3	+9	+6	+9	+12	(1)	(1)	+3
Quarter-to-quarter change, retail sales	Aug. 1946	Feb. 1949	Feb. 1951	May 1951	Nov. 1952	Aug. 1953	May 1955	Feb. 1956	Aug. 1957	Feb. 1958
Retailers' inventory investment (book value)	+3	+9	0	+12	+9	+15	+6	+6	-9	0
Quarter-to-quarter change, wholesale sales	Aug. 1946	May 1949	Aug. 1950	May 1951	Aug. 1952	Nov. 1953	Nov. 1955	Feb. 1956	(2)	Feb. 1958
Wholesalers' inventory investment (book value)	+3	0	-3	+6	+3	+9	+3	(2)	(2)	+3

Source: Based on material from Department of Commerce.

1 No matching turn.
2 No turn.

CHART 17

QUARTER-TO-QUARTER CHANGE IN FINAL PURCHASES AND SALES, AND
INVENTORY INVESTMENT, SELECTED SERIES, 1946–58

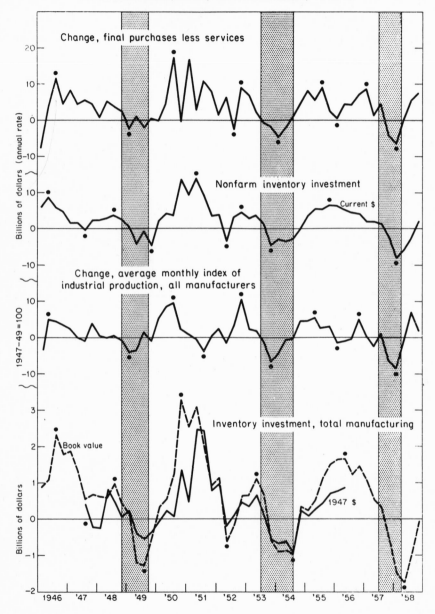

CHART 17—Continued

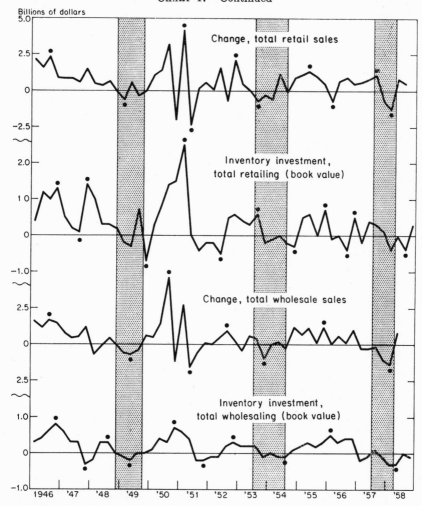

Billions of dollars

Change, total retail sales

Inventory investment,
total retailing (book value)

Change, total wholesale sales

Inventory investment,
total wholesaling (book value)

1946 '47 '48 '49 '50 '51 '52 '53 '54 '55 '56 '57 '58

Shaded areas represent business contractions; unshaded areas, expansions.
Dots identify peaks and troughs of specific cycles.

Source: All series except change in average index of manufacturers' output were compiled from Department of Commerce data.   Manufacturers' output series from Federal Reserve Board.

It should be noted, however, that there is not a completely consistent relationship between movements in the two types of series. Looking once again at the total manufacturers, total wholesalers, and total retailers data, it will be observed that there are two instances of this lack of correspondence.   The first occurs early in the postwar period, when each inventory investment series shows a second cycle following a trough in the third or fourth quarter of 1947.   There is no full-fledged corresponding cycle to be found in any of the series representing rates of change in activity, although each of these series do turn up for a single quarter at the end of 1947.   In the second instance, the manufacturing and retailing activity series trace out an "extra" cycle after forming a trough in the first quarter of 1956.   The manufacturers' inventory investment series, however, moves downward from second quarter 1956 to first quarter 1958.   The retailing investment series shows only a poorly defined and somewhat erratic cyclical movement beginning in the third quarter of 1956 and ending in the first quarter of 1958.

In the nonfarm inventory investment series, movements are found which conform in most instances to the pattern of quarter-to-quarter change in final purchases, in a manner similar to that observed between inventory investment and rates of change in activity for manufacturing, retailing and wholesaling (chart 17).[10]   During the first business cycle, inventory investment shows two distinct cycles.   The first peak occurs within 3 months of the peak in the final purchases series, but the trough and peak which follow have no counterpart in the latter series.   In the second business cycle there are once again two well-established cycles in inventory investment, but in this instance both conform to roughly similar movements in the final purchases series.   In the third business cycle, inventory investment moves in conformity to changes in final purchases during approximately the first half of the expansion.   Following the first quarter of 1956, a second cycle is noted in the final purchases series, but inventory investment moves steadily downward.

In contrast to the behavior of the manufacturing, wholesaling, and retailing series, nonfarm inventory investment does not show a well-defined tendency to lag behind rates of change in its corresponding purchases series.   Turns in the nonfarm investment series coincided with final purchase turns in two of the eight comparisons, led by one quarter in three comparisons, and lagged by one to three quarters in the remaining three comparisons.

There is no present method to reconcile statistically the consistent lagging relationship of inventory investment to rates of change in activity in the manufacturing, wholesaling, and retailing series, with the irregular timing of total nonfarm inventory investment relative to rates of change in final purchases.   It should be recognized, however, that the manufacturing and wholesaling activity series are not closely comparable to final purchases.   The former series reflect, in part, variations in inventory investment of their customers as well as production or sale of goods destined for end use, whereas the final purchases data are free of inventory investment changes.   Whatever may be the explanation of the differences, the aggregative data conform more closely to the concepts envisioned in the theory and must be given great weight.

Although these findings are inconclusive as regards the relevance of Metzler's theory, they provide the basis for a general conclusion of some importance: in spite of the lack of a well-established timing characteristic, movements in aggregate nonfarm inventory investment appear to be significantly related to movements in the rate of change in activity.   There have been two postwar instances in which this has not been true, but the overall consistency of the relationship, despite its looseness, is impressive.   There are no observations of timing

[10] The final-purchases series used in this analysis excludes consumer purchases of services.   It covers only spending for commodities, construction and Government (Government spending on services is included). It should be noted, however, that some inventory investment occurs in the service industries or in response to spending on services.

differences in nonfarm inventory investment and final purchases which are greater than 9 months.

The question arises, however, whether or not this observed conformity necessarily implies that the acceleration principle is at work. Bert G. Hickman takes the position that it does not.[11] In an analysis of the role of the acceleration principle in business cycles he shows that most of the retardation in manufacturing production and sales and in retail sales (observed above) appears to be accounted for by diffusion, i.e., by actual expansions or contractions in individual industries or retail store classifications. Such a finding leads him to conclude that "acceleration-induced inventory investment may be a comparatively unimportant initiating (as contrasted with amplifying) factor in business contractions."[12]

It is important to note that the emphasis here is on the words, "acceleration induced." His evidence does not rule out other models in which inventory investment is an initiating factor (one such model is presented later in this chapter). Moreover, until he examines the data for individual industries, his evidence against even acceleration-induced investment is indirect.

BEHAVIOR OF INVENTORY INVESTMENT UNDER CONDITIONS OF CHANGING INVENTORY OBJECTIVES

One major gap in Metzler's theory has not been examined: its failure to treat the influence of supply conditions and the ordering process on the determination of inventory behavior. In the economic world of Metzler's models there is only one stage of economic activity, and it is assumed implicitly that all sales are made for immediate delivery. Firms have no suppliers; there are no purchase orders and no backlogs of unfilled orders. The entrepreneur's output plans are guided by his anticipated sales to consumers and by his inventory objectives. The latter (except in the model in which stock objectives are held constant) are based entirely upon the level of sales anticipated in the subsequent period.

In practice, however, inventory objectives are influenced by other factors. In chapter 4 it was shown that order backlogs vary cyclically, especially in the important durables group, and that sellers' willingness to hold purchased-materials stocks is thereby affected. Moreover, these fluctuations in order backlogs are indicative of changing supply conditions which alter buyers' desired inventory target levels. Such changes in supply conditions have a well-defined cyclical pattern.[13]

Thus we find that forces operating through supply conditions act upon individual manufacturers in their roles as both buyers and sellers, causing them to attempt to adjust their stocks. These changes in inventory demand are superimposed upon cyclical changes in final demand. Moreover, they are likely to both set up price movements and to be accentuated by them. In a sense the result is a sort of

---

[11] Bert G. Hickman, "Diffusion, Acceleration, and Business Cycles," American Economic Review, September 1959, pp. 551–558.
[12] Ibid., p. 588.
[13] As indicated earlier the pattern was outlined as follows:
1. Availability of materials reaches its maximum at approximately the trough of the business cycle and begins to deteriorate with the beginning of recovery, or very shortly thereafter. Supply conditions deteriorate at an accelerating rate during early expansion and then at a diminishing rate.
2. By midexpansion, supply conditions begin to improve, although high levels of unfilled orders attest to substantial delays. Improvement may proceed at varying rates, but it is continuous throughout the latter half of the expansion.
3. In the final months of expansion and during early recession, availability improves at an accelerating rate. The maximum rate of improvement is attained by midrecession.

accelerator, but the process is quite different from that visualized in Metzler's theory.

THE OCCURRENCE OF "EXTRA" INVESTMENT CYCLES

It will be recalled that during the 1945–48 and 1949–53 expansions there were additional upward movements in inventory investment not matched by a movement in rates of change in final purchases, but that in the 1954–57 expansion there was not. Is it possible that differences in the availability of materials may provide a key to explaining inventory investment behavior on these occasions? Such evidence as does exist is indirect, but it points to supply conditions as a significant factor in determining the response of inventory investment movements to changes in final purchases during the latter half of expansion periods. In the 1945–48 expansion, the durable-goods sector adjusted quickly to immediate postwar demand. Durables unfilled orders began to decline after October 1946. The ratio of unfilled orders to sales reached a peak of 5.99 in the first quarter of 1946; by the second quarter of 1947 it had fallen to a level of 4.10, and continued to fall thereafter (see chart 7). [14] Under these conditions, there was no significant upward movement in purchased-materials investment after mid-1947. In fact, the deflated data show continuous disinvestment.

This behavior is in complete contrast to that of the nondurables sector during the same period. For the latter, the immediate postwar period was one of continued strong demand and limited capacity. Unfilled orders rose to near-peak levels in early 1947, and remained virtually unchanged throughout the remainder of the year. Unfilled-orders-to-sales ratios are not available prior to 1948 but in the first quarter of that year the ratio stood at 1.78, a level which was subsequently exceeded only in first quarter 1951. It was under these conditions of sustained high demand and short supply that nondurable purchased-materials inventory investment moved upward in a second expansion during the second half of 1947.

In the 1949–53 expansion, it was the nondurables sector that adjusted quickly to demand conditions. A flood of orders immediately followed the outbreak of the Korean war, and the unfilled-orders-to-sales series attained a peak level of 1.91 in first quarter 1951. But unfilled orders began to decline following the peak in March 1951, and by the fourth quarter of 1952 the ratio had fallen to 1.10. Thus, the initial upsurge in purchased-materials investment was short lived. Investment reached its peak in fourth quarter 1950, and there was no upward movement thereafter.

In the durables sector, demand outstripped supply during almost the entire expansion period. Unfilled orders rose until September 1952 and remained at a high level until mid-1953. The unfilled-orders-to-sales ratio reached a maximum of 7.02 in August 1952. In contrast to the nondurables, durables purchased-materials investment moved upward during the latter half of 1952 and first half of 1953.

In the 1954–57 expansion, neither durables nor nondurables showed a record rise in unfilled order backlogs. The nondurables unfilled-

[14] Absolute levels of unfilled orders to sales differ substantially between the durables and nondurables categories, the former being much higher, due to longer periods of production and a much larger percentage of business done on order. In the postwar period durables ratios have ranged between 6.8 and 2.41, nondurables between 1.8 and 0.85. It is the relative movements in these ratios, not their absolute levels, which are significant.

orders-to-sales ratio reached a peak at 1.11 in the fourth quarter of 1955 and fell continuously thereafter. Unfilled orders rose for a longer period in the durables sector, but the levels of order backlogs never reached the peak of the preceding expansion. In third quarter 1956, the peak ratio of 4.43 was attained.

In the same period, total manufacturers' purchased-materials investment failed to respond to the sharp upward movement in rates of change in final purchases. Unfortunately, there are no deflated data subsequent to mid-1956, and the behavior of the durable and nondurable categories cannot be ascertained with certainty. In the undeflated data the peak in durables purchased-materials investment was reached in third quarter 1955, and there was no second cycle thereafter. The nondurables undeflated series shows a gentle rise to a peak in second quarter 1957. The inventory investment movement had but little amplitude, however, and it is possible that deflated data would show no significant movement.

To summarize: the first two postwar expansion periods were characterized by double cycles in total manufacturers' purchased-materials inventory investment. In contrast, there was no second movement in the 1954–57 expansion, in spite of the well-defined upturn in rates of change of final purchases in 1956. The two "extra" cycles were not generalized throughout the manufacturing sector, but are traceable to the nondurables group in the first instance and to the durables group in the second. These movements occurred only under conditions of relatively high levels of unfilled orders.

There is evidence here that general availability of materials influences the behavior of inventory investment in the later stages of expansion, when the upward movement in final purchases continues because certain types of final expenditures still rise; under conditions of "tight" supply, there may be a resurgence of inventory investment, whereas under conditions of ready availability there will not.

This is by no means a solid finding. I am not able to establish the precise relationship between supply and inventory investment. Moreover, I generalize from the behavior of purchased materials to that of total nonfarm inventory investment. Nevertheless, the observed behavior is interesting. It suggests the hypothesis that after the initial surge in inventory investment, the relative availability of materials will determine whether or not it may once again become a source of strength during the expansion.

THE RELATIVE IMPORTANCE OF CHANGES IN INVESTMENT DURING RECESSION

In chapter 2, it was pointed out that movements in inventory investment were greater, relative to changes in national product, during early than during later expansion, and were greatest during recession. These observations may readily be interpreted in the light of observed supply conditions. Shifts in the vendor-performance and purchasing-policy series are most abrupt during the first half of expansion phases and during contractions (chart 9). Inspection of these data indicates that changes in supply conditions affect the initial stages of expansion and contraction about equally, but the expansions having been much longer, the effect is weakened during the latter part of these phases. In addition, inventory movements are larger relative to change in national product during recession because final purchases, particularly consumption, remain relatively stable in this phase but rise during expansion.   The interesting point is that inventory investment can show such sharp declines during recessions under conditions of relatively stable consumption.

It would appear that these declines are due in part to the abrupt shifts in purchasing policy already noted.   When purchase based on requirements extending well into the future is changing abruptly to purchase based on immediate needs, it seems likely that firms are cutting inventory objectives drastically and attempting to trim stocks.   The observed behavior of vendor-performance and purchasing-policy series provide evidence to support this thesis.   Thus, in Metzler's terminology, there occurs a sharp increase in the accelerator (i.e., an increase in the amount of inventories to be liquidated for a given decline in sales or output) resulting in a sharper inventory disinvestment than would otherwise occur under conditions of relatively slight declines in final purchases.

Factors Contributing to Turning Points

The present section is concerned with the manner in which inventory investment may contribute to business cycle turning points.

In early expansion, as sales rise, purchase orders also rise sharply. Two reasons for this rise in orders have already been discussed: (a) The firm places orders to meet rising sales requirements; and (b) the firm places orders to increase the volume of stocks on hand.   A third reason may be added: (c) The firm may place orders simply to increase its order commitments on the supplier's books.   At a time when delivery periods are being extended, the purchaser will realize that his order may be desirable, not only to build up his stocks, but also to provide him with additional protection against the possibility of price increases or against being "uncovered" at some future date.   Thus the purchasing firm looks not only to its stock on hand or in transit from supplier in assessing the degree to which it is protected; it looks also to its "goods on order."   It is this "total ownership position" along with sales requirements which guides purchasing policy.[15]

Throughout the buying movement, firms increasingly place orders in excess of their requirements in order to provide themselves with this kind of protection.   At some point the ownership position approaches a "satisfactory" condition (given existing anticipations as to sales, prices, and vendor performance) and orders tend to recede toward a level which covers sales alone.   It is highly likely that such a decline will contribute to the termination of the expansion.

It is conceivable, of course, that sales will continue to increase; additional purchase orders to cover sales requirements and, perhaps, to keep the ratio of stocks and orders to sales at a satisfactory level, may be enough to keep total orders rising.   But the increase in demand would need to be quite sharp; presumably it would stem from some vigorous new source, such as a shift in the propensity to consume or a sharp increase in investment spending.

On the other hand, if something were to cause delivery periods to shorten, or anticipations of vendor performance to improve, the in-

---

[15] I am indebted to Ruth Mack for introducing me to this concept and stressing its importance. See Ruth P. Mack and Victor Zarnowitz, "Cause and Consequence of Change in Retailers' Buying," American Economic Review, March 1958, pp. 27ff.

ventory objective and the desired ratio of ownership to sales would
be reduced. Under these conditions, it would be highly probable
that orders would fall. Such changes are easily visualized: delivery
conditions might improve as a result of expansion of capacity as
cyclical expansion goes on. Or, as has already been suggested, a
decline in the current rate of deterioration of vendor performance
may affect anticipations favorably.

Given the initial downturn in [orders and sales, the decline in
purchasing orders proceeds during recession under the combined im-
petus of forces paralleling those noted during expansion: (*a*) there is
a decline in sales requirements, (*b*) the firm reduces orders in order
to reduce the volume of stocks, and (*c*) the improvement in vendor
performance, leads to a reduction in the desired ratio of outstanding
orders to sales. As recession deepens, purchasing policy shifts very
sharply, and within a relatively short period of time a majority of
firms are purchasing on a short-range basis. When this occurs, inventory policy is no longer influenced significantly by considerations
of delays in delivery. The target level for stocks is then related
principally to anticipated sales requirements.

At this point it is to be expected that forces (*b*) and (*c*) are no longer
operative and that inventory objectives will no longer decline. Orders
must turn up unless the decline in final sales alone is sufficient to
decrease them further. If the only reason for the decline in total
sales and output has been the attempt to achieve the goals mentioned
under (*b*) and (*c*) (that is, if final sales were constant), then the level
of orders and of activity may be expected to rise. This seems to
approximate what has occurred during postwar recessions. Consumption expenditures have been relatively insensitive to declines in national income, and Government expenditures have tended to be stable
or to rise. As a result, the postwar recessions have been characterized
by an early upturn in inventory investment. Of course, if final purchases were sensitive to declines in income, in the manner assumed
by Metzler, the decline in inventory investment would set up a
cumulative process and the trough would be reached under conditions
described at the beginning of this chapter.

This discussion of the impact of changing supply conditions has
been stated in terms of manufacturers' purchased-materials inventory
policy alone. Chapter 6 indicates that the analysis can probably be
extended to certain types of goods in process, since these stocks, when
held between stages, behave similarly to purchased materials (see
chart 16). The behavior of finished goods must be explained in
somewhat different terms, but we have seen that investment in these
stocks does not lag behind that of purchased materials and goods in
process by many months (ch. 7, table 33, chart 16). No confident
statement regarding retailers' and wholesalers' stocks can be made,
since this study has dealt with them only in passing. On an a priori
basis, however, the analysis would appear to be applicable, for dis-
tributors, to the extent that they purchase from manufacturers, have
as much reason to respond to changing supply conditions as do
manufacturers' purchasing agents.

Conclusions

It is now possible to bring together certain observations made in this chapter and to draw conclusions regarding their usefulness in explaining cyclical fluctuations. For this task it is convenient to arrange the various points according to the light they shed upon the two questions posed previously. How do changes in inventory investment contribute to the cumulative forces of business cycle expansion and contraction? Do movements in inventory investment spark the upswing and bring about the downturn, thereby constituting an underlying cause of business cycles as well as an aggravating force?

There is no doubt that inventory fluctuations contribute to the cumulative movements which constitute business cycles. Both the prewar and postwar data show clearly that changes in the rate of realized inventory accumulation are an important source of increase in demand during the greater part of expansions, and are a principal source of decline in demand during contractions. (See ch. 2.) Moreover, it is probable that the contribution is greater than may be observed in these data, since they show only realized inventory investment. One of the great contributions made by Metzler is his conclusion that adjustments in inventory contribute more to instability than may be observed, because they set up increases or decreases in final purchases which, in part, defeat the attempted adjustments. It would appear, however, that this income effect has been more important in expansions than contractions.

Another source of instability has been traced to the interaction between availability of materials and purchasing policy. An important reason for the cumulative force developed by buying movements is that purchasing policy alters with any increase in activity: The volume of orders rises not only to provide for sales, but to provide for inventories and to increase the time-range of advance purchasing. Increased demand gives rise to a deterioration of supply conditions which in turn, causes firms to raise their inventory objectives and their commitment to suppliers. The process occurs in reverse during the contraction phase.

This interaction alone could not long sustain a buying movement or a curtailment phase, but coupled to an income effect, speculative tendencies, or effect on plant and equipment investment (particularly through expectations) the result is a mechanism capable of generating very powerful cumulative forces. It is fortunate that the process has within it the means of its own termination within a relatively short period of time, and that the income feedback effect is limited during recession. Otherwise, business cycles would be much more severe than we have known them to be in recent times.

Turning points in planned inventory investment must be regarded as reversals in demand. Ceteris paribus, when firms cease to attempt to accumulate stocks at as high a rate as previously, their purchases from suppliers decline; when firms cease to attempt to reduce stocks at as fast a rate as previously, their purchases increase.

According to Metzler, the explanation of turning points in the business cycle lies in this process.[16] Turns in inventory investment

---

[16] For the purposes of his analysis, Metzler treats the business cycle as an inventory cycle. He fully realizes, of course, the complexity of business cycle relationships.

occur after rates of change in activity have reached a peak or trough, thereby permitting accumulation or liquidation of stocks to proceed at a rate more closely approximating the desired level.

Timing comparisons of turns in nonfarm inventory investment and final purchases show that, on a number of occasions, investment has turned earlier than would be expected in Metzler's theory. Under existing institutional arrangements, however, there is another way in which inventory investment turns can come about. Management considers not only stocks on hand when examining its inventory position, but also its outstanding purchase orders. As expansion proceeds, the quantity of goods on hand and on order increases. Ultimately, management must consider itself sufficiently protected and, other things being equal, the volume of orders which it places with suppliers will decline.

The observation that inventory investment has led all three postwar business cycle peaks and two of the three business cycle troughs lends support to the argument that turns in inventory investment play a role in sparking the upturn from recession and in halting the process of expansion. During expansion, continued increases in fixed investment and consumption expenditures seem characteristic of the modern business cycle, but the inventory requirements traceable to such expenditures are not likely to be large.

It is my conclusion that these observations are useful in explaining both the cumulative forces of expansion and contraction and the processes by which these phases may be terminated. This is not to deny the complexity of the forces which are combined in the business cycle. Evidence abounds that there are other contributory processes at work, some of which are also capable of causing cyclical reversals. But this, in turn, does not detract from the proposition that the processes which surround the accumulation and liquidation of inventories also contribute significantly to an explanation of cyclical fluctuations.

In a period such as the years since the war, when the underlying forces of growth have been strong and the recessions interrupting the general rise in national output have been only a year or less in duration, the inventory investment mechanism, as modified above, appears as a highly likely candidate for explaining turning points and, in part, the cumulative character of the business cycle.

Appendix A
Sources and Processing of Data

The principal data studied are Department of Commerce end-of-month estimates of the book value of manufacturers stocks.[1] Series for total inventories covered the 3 comprehensive groupings (total manufacturing, durable-goods industries, nondurable-goods industries) and 16 industry groups. Stage-of-fabrication series covered the comprehensive groupings - and nine industry groups. All data were deflated by the author for the period 1947–56. Only material for the comprehensive groupings were studied for the period after 1956. These more recent data were not deflated. Prior to dating turns in the inventory series, the end-of-month figures were centered by use of a 2-month moving average.

These data comprised the principal source for the analysis in chapters 3 through 7. In addition, chapters 2 and 3 make use of Department of Commerce inventory data for total nonfarm, total manufacturing, and durable-goods industries, deflated (in 1954 dollars) by the Department for purposes of computing the inventory investment component of gross national product. These figures cover the period 1947 to date and are roughly comparable to those deflated by the author; they differ only in that coverage and procedures used in deflation were not identical.

Finally, activity (shipments or output) and finished-goods inventory data for 25 commodities were analyzed in chapter 5. These figures, shown in table 21, required seasonal adjustment only.

DEFLATION PROCEDURE

The approach used in deflating the book value series was as follows:
1. In constructing deflators the Bureau of Labor Statistics Wholesale Price Indexes were used. No deflation was attempted before 1947 since the Wholesale Price Indexes were revised in that year.

---

[1] The Department of Commerce book value series were as follows:

Total-stocks series	*Stage-of-fabrication series*
Total manufacturers	Total manufacturers.
Durable-goods manufacturers	Durable-goods manufacturers.
Nondurable-goods manufacturers	Nondurable-goods manufacturers.
Primary metals	Primary metals.
Fabricated metals	
Electrical machinery	Total machinery.
Machinery, excluding electrical	
Motor vehicles and parts	Total transportation equipment.
Transportation equipment, excluding motor vehicles	
Stone, clay, and glass products	Stone, clay, and glass products.
Food and kindred products	Food and beverages.
Textile mill products	
Apparel	
Leather and leather products	
Paper products	Paper product
Chemical products	Chemical prod ts.
Printing and publishing	
Petroleum and coal products	Petroleum and al products.
Rubber products	Rubber produc .

128

2. Inventories were deflated separately for each stage of fabrication in both the durables and nondurables classifications. The more aggregative series (i.e., total manufacturers, durable-goods and nondurable-goods industries; total purchased materials, total goods in process, total finished goods) were secured by adding the appropriate deflated components.

Purchased-materials and finished-goods deflators were built up from deflators constructed separately for each industry. In combining these, the weights assigned were based on the proportions of the stage-of-fabrication inventory held by the various industries according to census data.[2] (See table A–1 for industry weights.) The goods-in-process deflators were constructed by averaging the purchased-materials and finished-goods deflators.

3. Purchased-materials industry deflators were constructed by examining materials inputs to each industry as revealed by the Bureau of Labor Statistics interindustry study for the year 1947, selecting and weighing price indexes accordingly. Code numbers and weights of the price indexes chosen are presented in table A–2. Finished-goods industry deflators were constructed by examining the composition of finished stocks within each industry according to the 1947 Census of Manufactures and selecting and weighing the price indexes accordingly. Code numbers and weights of the price indexes are shown in table A–2.

4. Prior to combining the industry deflators the months covered by the turnover period[3] were averaged for each industry. Thus, if the turnover period were 3 months, the adjusted industry deflator for the month of March would be secured by averaging the deflators in the months of January, February, and March.

5. There were difficulties in making allowance for the LIFO component of stocks and for the fact that certain companies make cost or market adjustments at the end of fiscal periods. In general, the procedure used was to remove, monthly or quarterly, a fixed LIFO component and deflate the remainder, adding the LIFO component to the deflated portion to secure the final deflated stock value. The value of the LIFO component was taken from published estimates by Daly in the Survey of Current Business (July 1953, p. 17). No cost or market adjustments could be made in monthly series, but year-end deflations were checked with comparable National Income Division deflations for which cost of market adjustments had been made.

6. The total stocks series for 16 individual industries, which are discussed in chapter 3, were deflated in a somewhat different manner; deflators were constructed as described above but with assumptions of a fixed composition of total stock by stage of fabrication.

[2] Finished-goods weights were based upon the composition of finished goods according to the 1947 Census of Manufactures. Purchased-materials weights were derived from 1953 Annual Survey of Manufacturers' material.
[3] A turnover period is a period of time during which the stocks held as of a given date are presumed to have been accumulated. Information concerning the duration of these periods for the several industries was secured from the Department of Commerce.

TABLE A–1.—*Weights and turnover periods assigned to industry deflators*

DURABLE-GOODS INDUSTRIES

Industry	Turnover period (in months)	Weights	
		Purchased materials	Finished goods
Primary metals	4	20.6	15.3
Fabricated metal products	4	16.7	14.4
Total machinery	6	29.2	41.0
Total transportation	4	21.2	10.3
Lumber products	4	} 8.1 {	9.5
Furniture and fixtures	4		3.0
Stone, clay, and glass	4	4.2	6.5

NONDURABLE-GOODS INDUSTRIES

Industry	Turnover period (in months)	Purchased materials	Finished goods
Food and beverage	3	22.7	41.0
Tobacco products	6 (3) [1]	13.6	9.9
Textile mill products	4	12.2	8.0
Apparel	4	8.8	9.4
Leather products	4	2.9	2.5
Paper	3	9.8	2.6
Chemicals and allied products	4	19.8	13.7
Petroleum and coal products	3	6.8	9.6
Rubber and rubber products	4	3.4	3.3

[1] Figure enclosed by parenthesis relates to finished-goods turnover period; other figure relates to purchased materials turnover period only.

TABLE A-2.—*Index numbers and weights used in constructing industry deflators*

DURABLE-GOODS INDUSTRIES

Industry	Purchased materials		Finished goods	
	Index numbers	Weight	Index numbers	Weight
Primary metals	10-11	6	10-14	59
	05-2	10	10-15	11
	10-13	27	10-22	9
	10-12	8	10-24	9
	10-14	29	10-25	12
	10-23	4		
	10-22	13		
	10-24	3		
Fabricated metals products	10-14	85	10-4	26
			10-6	26
	10-25	15	10-7	21
			10-8	27
Total machinery	06-21	3	11-7	17
	06-73	2	12-5	8
	08	5	11	63
	10-14	25	12-4	12
	10-15	24		
	10-2	26		
	10-81	8		
	10-82	7		
Total transportation equipment	03	4	11-8	68
	07-2	8	10-4	9
	08	6	11-54	10
	10-14	32	11-7	13
	10-15	26		
	10-2	9		
	10-4	5		
	10-82	10		
Stone, clay, and glass products	09-3	13	13-1	8
	13-1	18	12-63	20
	13-2	24	13-4	13
	13-4	14	12-61	7
	13-7	31	13-3	18
			13-7	27
			13-2	7
Lumber and lumber products, furniture and fixtures	08	100	08	76
			12-1	24

NONDURABLE-GOODS INDUSTRIES

Industry	Purchased materials		Finished goods	
	Index numbers	Weight	Index numbers	Weight
Food and beverages	01-3	9	02-2	20
			02-3	5
	01-52	5	02-4	24
	01-1	14	02-1	8
	01-2	47	02-5	10
	02-5	14	14-4	25
	02-71	11	02-8	8
Tobacco	01-82	100	14-1	100
Textile mill products	01-4	78	03-1	48
			03-2	30
	03-31	22	03-3	22
	03-12	40		
Apparel	03-24	38	03-5	100
	03-33	22		
			04-3	65
Leather and products	04-2	100	04-4	35
Paper and allied products	09-1	94	09-3	34
	09-2	6	09-5	22
			09-4	44
Chemicals and allied products	06	25	06-1	27
	06-3	4	06-3	17
	06-4	18	06-71	9
			06-4	14
	06-7	5	06-21	14
	06-22	5	06-7	14
	01-73	28	06-5	5
	05-56	5		
	05-20	5		
	09-7	5		
Petroleum and coal products	05-56	65	(1)	95
	05-12	35	05-2	5
Rubber products	07-1	71	07-2	61
	03-12-76	29	07-3	39

[1] 05-5 (weight 100) minus 05-56 (weight 18) divided by 82.

Appendix B — Inventory Data

[Billions of dollars, seasonally adjusted]

	January	February	March	April	May	June	July	August	September	October	November	December
	Total inventories (book value)											
1946	18.21	18.90	19.27	19.61	19.96	20.37	21.36	22.11	22.69	23.73	24.19	24.46
1947	25.28	25.31	26.33	26.95	27.39	27.64	27.80	28.17	28.19	28.37	28.72	28.87
1948	29.02	29.16	29.48	29.64	29.99	30.27	30.67	30.98	31.26	31.51	31.66	31.69
1949	31.91	32.08	31.85	31.50	31.17	30.63	30.19	29.82	29.34	29.02	28.74	28.86
1950	28.96	29.02	29.19	29.30	29.52	29.75	29.81	30.12	31.02	31.95	33.38	34.31
1951	35.30	35.94	36.87	38.17	39.08	39.94	40.78	41.58	41.91	42.30	42.58	42.82
1952	43.53	43.76	43.93	43.88	43.73	43.32	42.93	43.13	43.15	43.30	43.46	43.80
1953	43.96											
1953 [1]	43.93	44.00	44.25	44.56	45.04	45.35	45.54	46.06	46.05	45.85	45.76	45.43
1954	45.21	44.88	44.53	44.07	43.77	43.65	43.14	42.88	42.65	42.98	43.18	42.98
1955	43.15	43.14	43.22	43.24	43.54	43.73	44.08	44.77	44.86	45.79	45.92	46.36
1956	46.80	47.56	47.98	48.65	49.32	49.62	50.04	50.38	50.84	51.75	52.21	52.30
1957	52.43	52.92	53.33	53.66	53.91	53.85	53.85	54.09	54.20	54.17	54.10	53.52
1958	52.91	52.44	52.01	51.49	50.90	50.25	49.78	49.42	49.30	49.34	49.30	49.18
1959	49.49	49.92	50.45	51.05	51.60	52.14	52.24	52.12	51.89	51.52	51.62	52.43
1960	53.31	53.90	54.34	54.66	54.95	55.10	54.90	54.98	54.71	54.38	54.01	53.74
1961	53.67	53.60	53.31	53.88	53.37	53.36	53.58					
	Total inventories (1947 dollars)											
1947				27.32	27.69	28.02	28.24	28.54	28.43	28.27	28.30	28.21
1948	27.86	27.82	27.97	28.18	28.50	28.78	29.05	29.10	29.27	29.28	29.26	29.33
1949	29.52	29.69	29.56	29.45	29.30	29.15	29.05	28.84	28.60	28.36	28.09	28.24
1950	28.21	28.19	28.17	28.19	28.27	28.42	28.23	28.12	28.50	28.88	29.59	29.87
1951	29.96	29.99	30.35	31.18	31.94	32.82	33.84	34.70	35.25	35.76	35.92	36.04
1952	36.53	36.83	37.00	37.04	36.94	36.79	36.75	36.85	36.89	37.01	37.06	37.35
1953	37.44											
1953 [1]	37.50	37.56	37.69	37.88	38.17	38.33	38.30	38.55	38.38	38.14	38.05	37.80
1954	37.65	37.37	37.11	36.78	36.56	36.50	36.08	35.81	35.57	35.97	35.97	35.80
1955	35.92	35.84	35.90	35.83	36.06	36.19	36.29	36.71	36.60	37.11	37.08	37.31
1956	37.53	37.95	38.09	38.42	38.79	38.96						
	Purchased materials (book value)											
1946	8.10	8.28	8.53	8.77	8.86	9.07	9.47	9.83	10.04	10.44	10.72	11.00
1947	11.23	11.46	11.62	11.79	11.97	12.02	11.91	11.96	11.95	11.96	12.17	12.28
1948	12.18	12.28	12.37	12.48	12.62	12.92	13.04	13.02	13.06	13.01	12.89	12.77
1949	12.88	12.84	12.46	12.22	12.00	11.72	11.51	11.43	11.36	11.17	11.07	11.08
1950	11.01	11.05	11.04	11.04	11.18	11.35	11.66	12.07	12.69	13.21	13.88	14.48
1951	14.91	15.26	15.71	16.15	16.28	16.55	16.72	16.79	16.56	16.76	16.59	16.42
1952	16.56	16.57	16.47	16.34	16.26	16.00	15.86	15.76	15.77	15.79	15.83	15.87
1953	15.74											
1953 [1]	15.76	15.66	15.71	15.80	16.09	16.07	16.14	16.27	16.14	15.91	15.83	15.55
1954	15.54	15.25	15.01	15.05	15.08	15.17	15.05	14.84	14.68	14.53	14.60	14.38
1955	14.50	14.41	14.36	14.40	14.59	14.61	14.81	15.08	15.17	15.53	15.50	15.54
1956	15.70	15.92	16.05	16.21	16.44	16.45	16.57	16.59	16.68	17.08	17.20	17.20
1957	17.24	17.42	17.45	17.26	17.34	17.33	17.36	17.42	17.43	17.56	17.49	17.09
1958	17.14	17.10	16.93	16.75	16.57	16.36	16.21	16.15	16.14	16.37	16.23	16.07
1959	16.27	16.47	16.74	17.03	17.37	17.88	17.90	17.70	17.26	17.00	17.04	17.24
1960	17.63	17.75	17.81	17.90	17.93	17.82	17.68	17.58	17.31	17.12	16.83	16.80
1961	16.77	16.69	16.70	16.69	16.75	16.57	16.68					
	Purchased materials (1947 dollars)											
1947				11.95	12.12	12.21	12.16	12.18	12.08	11.93	11.96	11.88
1948	11.62	11.64	11.76	11.86	12.01	12.20	12.29	12.23	12.25	12.18	12.04	11.95
1949	12.04	12.02	11.78	11.65	11.53	11.38	11.32	11.32	11.30	11.15	11.08	11.11
1950	11.05	11.02	10.98	10.95	10.99	11.06	11.19	11.39	11.74	11.96	12.30	12.56
1951	12.62	12.63	12.82	13.13	13.24	13.49	13.72	13.94	13.91	14.17	14.10	13.94
1952	14.04	14.09	14.09	14.09	14.09	13.93	13.82	13.74	13.73	13.72	13.79	13.87
1953	13.80											
1953 [1]	13.83	13.77	13.81	13.85	14.06	14.00	14.02	14.04	13.88	13.65	13.60	13.39
1954	13.40	13.13	12.93	12.95	12.97	13.04	12.94	12.74	12.58	12.47	12.55	12.39
1955	12.46	12.36	12.31	12.32	12.50	12.51	12.61	12.80	12.81	13.05	13.00	12.98
1956	13.08	13.16	13.18	13.19	13.32	13.29						

[1] Data revised January 1953.

132

TABLE B–1.—*Total manufacturing, inventories*—Continued

[Billions of dollars, seasonally adjusted]

	Janu- ary	Feb- ruary	March	April	May	June	July	Au- gust	Sep- tem- ber	Octo- ber	No- vem- ber	De- cem- ber
					Goods-in-process (book value)							
1946	5.22	5.22	5.27	5.34	5.59	5.78	5.96	6.05	6.21	6.27	6.34	6.46
1947	6.64	6.76	6.90	7.00	7.02	7.06	7.12	7.31	7.34	7.33	7.43	7.43
1948	7.33	7.30	7.28	7.30	7.32	7.36	7.42	7.58	7.62	7.69	7.73	7.65
1949	7.61	7.60	7.54	7.44	7.37	7.27	7.25	7.09	6.97	6.89	6.80	6.82
1950	6.87	6.90	6.97	7.05	7.16	7.32	7.48	7.63	7.84	8.05	8.30	8.54
1951	8.82	9.01	9.29	9.63	9.83	10.05	10.19	10.30	10.60	10.79	11.14	11.34
1952	11.57	11.80	11.94	12.01	12.10	12.13	12.22	12.49	12.60	12.77	12.67	12.86
1953	12.92											
1953 [1]	2.96	13.19	13.37	13.54	13.58	13.73	13.71	13.83	13.59	13.39	13.37	13.38
1954	13.16	13.05	12.88	12.69	12.52	12.29	12.02	12.08	11.97	12.24	12.47	12.45
1955	12.44	12.44	12.54	12.52	12.62	12.72	12.88	13.16	13.16	13.55	13.75	13.85
1956	13.96	14.17	14.38	14.65	14.90	14.89	15.00	15.09	15.23	15.60	15.86	15.73
1957	15.76	15.86	16.01	16.37	16.39	16.31	16.40	16.52	16.39	16.21	16.13	15.79
1958	15.39	15.08	14.83	14.66	14.53	14.35	14.25	14.24	14.24	14.21	14.22	14.32
1959	14.38	14.38	14.50	14.70	14.83	14.93	15.03	14.99	15.01	14.88	14.85	15.11
1960	15.31	15.52	15.69	15.73	15.82	15.95	15.79	15.77	15.48	15.35	15.26	15.14
1961	15.15	15.69	14.95	15.00	15.10	15.28	15.35					
					Goods-in-process (1947 dollars)							
1947				7.18	7.17	7.20	7.25	7.41	7.38	7.31	7.31	7.24
1948	7.10	7.02	6.96	6.95	6.95	6.94	6.96	7.04	7.01	7.02	7.01	6.92
1949	6.86	6.85	6.80	6.74	6.73	6.70	6.74	6.64	6.56	6.49	6.41	6.44
1950	6.48	6.49	6.52	6.57	6.65	6.74	6.83	6.89	6.97	7.04	7.15	7.22
1951	7.31	7.34	7.48	7.70	7.84	8.03	8.15	8.28	8.54	8.72	9.00	9.16
1952	9.34	9.52	9.63	9.68	9.76	9.79	9.90	10.09	10.18	10.31	10.21	10.34
1953	10.42											
1953 [1]	10.44	10.62	10.73	10.85	10.85	10.94	10.85	10.87	10.63	10.45	10.42	10.43
1954	10.27	10.19	10.06	9.83	9.83	9.65	9.42	9.44	9.33	9.52	9.70	9.66
1955	9.66	9.64	9.69	9.66	9.72	9.78	9.84	10.02	9.93	10.12	10.21	10.22
1956	10.25	10.36	10.44	10.59	10.72	10.71						
					Finished goods (book value)							
1946	5.28	5.49	5.50	5.48	5.51	5.52	5.83	6.16	6.46	6.94	7.08	7.14
1947	7.48	7.66	7.81	8.06	8.31	8.52	8.72	8.85	8.93	9.07	9.12	9.28
1948	9.43	9.51	9.65	9.80	10.01	10.13	10.34	10.44	10.74	10.84	10.98	11.26
1949	11.38	11.57	11.68	11.71	11.66	11.64	11.47	11.33	11.18	11.12	10.97	11.02
1950	10.99	10.99	11.03	11.03	11.03	11.08	10.72	10.50	10.65	10.85	11.25	11.31
1951	11.40	11.56	11.74	12.16	12.77	13.33	14.09	14.70	15.04	15.03	14.96	15.05
1952	15.25	15.30	15.38	15.36	15.17	15.12	15.06	15.07	15.02	14.99	15.04	15.08
1953	15.18											
1953 [1]	15.20	15.15	15.16	15.23	15.37	15.55	15.69	15.96	16.32	16.55	16.56	16.49
1954	16.50	16.58	16.64	16.32	16.16	16.18	16.07	15.96	16.01	16.21	16.10	16.16
1955	16.21	16.29	16.32	16.32	16.33	16.40	16.39	16.52	16.53	16.71	16.68	16.97
1956	17.14	17.47	17.56	17.79	17.98	18.29	18.47	18.70	18.93	19.08	19.15	19.37
1957	19.44	19.64	19.87	20.04	20.18	20.21	20.29	20.26	20.35	20.33	20.25	20.64
1958	20.38	20.26	20.24	20.08	19.80	19.54	19.32	19.04	18.92	18.76	18.85	18.80
1959	18.84	19.06	19.21	19.38	19.40	19.33	19.30	19.43	19.62	19.64	19.73	20.07
1960	20.37	20.63	20.84	21.03	21.20	21.33	21.43	21.64	21.92	21.91	21.91	21.81
1961	21.75	21.82	21.67	21.69	21.52	21.51	21.55					
					Finished goods (1947 dollars)							
1947		9.13	9.16	9.25	8.19	8.40	8.62	8.83	8.95	8.97	9.04	9.04	9.09
1948	9.13	9.16	9.25	9.36	9.55	9.64	9.80	9.83	10.02	10.09	10.21	10.47
1949	10.62	10.82	10.98	11.05	11.04	11.07	10.99	10.88	10.74	10.73	10.60	10.69
1950	10.68	10.68	10.67	10.66	10.64	10.62	10.20	9.84	9.80	9.88	10.14	10.09
1951	10.03	10.02	10.04	10.35	10.85	11.30	11.97	12.49	12.80	12.87	12.82	12.94
1952	13.14	13.22	13.28	13.28	13.09	13.08	13.04	13.02	12.99	12.99	13.06	13.14
1953	13.22											
1953 [1]	13.23	13.17	13.15	13.17	13.25	13.39	13.44	13.64	13.87	14.03	14.03	13.98
1954	13.99	14.06	14.12	13.88	13.76	13.81	13.72	13.62	13.66	13.92	13.73	13.76
1955	13.80	13.84	13.90	13.85	13.84	13.90	13.83	13.89	13.86	13.95	13.87	14.10
1956	14.20	14.43	14.48	14.65	14.75	14.96						

[1] Data revised January 1953.

Source: Department of Commerce; deflations by the author.

TABLE B–2.—*Durable-goods industries, total inventories*

[Billions of dollars, seasonally adjusted]

	January	February	March	April	May	June	July	August	September	October	November	December
Total inventories (book value)												
1946	8.55	8.99	9.29	9.52	9.72	10.06	10.40	10.77	11.15	11.49	11.76	12.00
1947	12.47	12.76	13.06	13.32	13.62	13.87	14.00	14.18	14.19	14.33	14.34	14.30
1948	14.27	14.29	14.39	14.46	14.53	14.69	14.92	15.16	15.35	15.50	15.71	15.74
1949	16.01	16.23	16.16	15.97	15.70	15.35	15.11	14.80	14.47	14.16	13.89	13.97
1950	13.95	14.05	14.13	14.20	14.34	14.57	14.65	14.77	15.12	15.53	16.29	16.78
1951	17.31	17.71	18.10	18.70	19.38	20.08	20.70	21.38	21.84	22.19	22.51	22.81
1952	23.32	23.57	23.76	23.87	24.00	23.70	23.30	23.55	23.65	23.89	23.98	24.41
1953	24.61											
1953 ¹	24.55	24.66	24.97	25.24	25.61	25.88	26.09	26.48	26.49	26.44	26.41	26.24
1954	26.00	25.72	25.48	24.99	24.70	24.41	23.97	23.86	23.74	23.90	24.04	24.08
1955	24.08	24.08	24.20	24.16	24.32	24.43	24.74	25.23	25.38	26.09	26.23	26.66
1956	26.91	27.45	27.87	28.28	28.74	28.76	29.00	29.12	29.45	30.23	30.65	30.66
1957	30.63	30.96	31.18	31.46	31.57	31.44	31.70	31.74	31.82	31.75	31.51	31.15
1958	30.62	30.27	29.86	29.42	28.98	28.53	28.31	28.07	28.05	27.93	27.88	27.82
1959	28.11	28.41	28.92	29.36	29.73	30.23	30.35	30.14	29.82	29.25	29.35	30.08
1960	30.76	31.26	31.77	31.92	32.07	32.23	32.05	32.08	31.84	31.43	31.07	30.86
1961	30.76	30.65	30.30	30.15	30.15	30.20	30.41					
Total inventories (1947 dollars)												
1947				13.72	13.94	14.12	14.23	14.32	14.24	14.26	14.19	14.10
1948	13.92	13.82	13.74	13.72	13.73	13.80	13.86	13.84	13.83	13.79	13.80	13.84
1949	13.94	14.01	13.90	13.80	13.68	13.52	13.41	13.23	13.00	12.79	12.53	12.59
1950	12.46	12.45	12.46	12.49	12.61	12.76	12.75	12.74	12.88	13.10	13.49	13.66
1951	13.79	13.93	14.10	14.45	14.90	15.48	16.06	16.63	17.02	17.34	17.53	17.71
1952	17.98	18.17	18.31	18.37	18.42	18.32	18.21	18.34	18.38	18.49	18.47	18.72
1953	18.79											
1953 ¹	18.83	18.90	19.10	19.26	19.47	19.57	19.59	19.74	19.66	19.58	19.56	19.45
1954	19.28	19.09	18.94	18.58	18.38	18.14	17.78	17.67	17.53	17.60	17.67	17.69
1955	17.65	17.62	17.71	17.59	17.66	17.74	17.80	18.00	17.92	18.22	18.20	18.38
1956	18.45	18.73	18.92	19.09	19.34	19.31						
Goods-in-process (book value)												
1946	3.56	3.58	3.64	3.71	3.87	4.04	4.18	4.30	4.40	4.44	4.56	4.66
1947	4.83	4.92	4.98	5.04	5.07	5.07	5.10	5.22	5.24	5.24	5.26	5.21
1948	5.15	5.07	5.05	5.07	5.07	5.12	5.17	5.27	5.33	5.38	5.41	5.40
1949	5.37	5.38	5.37	5.31	5.24	5.14	5.10	4.95	4.83	4.78	4.70	4.72
1950	4.69	4.72	4.75	4.82	4.93	5.03	5.12	5.24	5.43	5.58	5.80	5.99
1951	6.33	6.49	6.70	6.95	7.12	7.31	7.54	7.72	7.98	8.19	8.46	8.63
1952	8.82	9.05	9.19	9.32	9.47	9.55	9.58	9.76	9.84	9.95	9.88	10.12
1953	10.15											
1953 ¹	10.22	10.36	10.60	10.69	10.72	10.83	10.87	11.01	10.85	10.68	10.71	10.73
1954	10.55	10.44	10.28	10.02	9.88	9.68	9.47	9.51	9.43	9.64	9.79	9.84
1955	9.76	9.76	9.86	9.84	9.91	9.98	10.13	10.32	10.37	10.75	10.92	11.09
1956	11.18	11.37	11.62	11.84	12.06	11.98	12.06	12.16	12.34	12.65	12.92	12.78
1957	12.76	12.89	13.04	13.42	13.44	13.33	13.50	13.55	13.45	13.24	13.14	12.73
1958	12.40	12.11	11.90	11.76	11.61	11.41	11.34	11.28	11.32	11.26	11.27	11.31
1959	11.38	11.37	11.51	11.67	11.81	11.89	11.92	11.92	11.91	11.95	11.78	12.08
1960	12.26	12.47	12.66	12.63	12.70	12.80	12.63	12.60	12.39	12.25	12.12	12.06
1961	12.07	12.05	11.90	11.87	11.91	12.03	12.06					
Goods-in-process (1947 dollars)												
1947				5.22	5.21	5.19	5.21	5.28	5.26	5.21	5.18	5.10
1948	5.00	4.89	4.83	4.82	4.78	4.80	4.81	4.84	4.84	4.82	4.82	4.72
1949	4.66	4.66	4.64	4.60	4.58	4.53	4.53	4.42	4.32	4.28	4.22	4.23
1950	4.19	4.20	4.21	4.25	4.34	4.39	4.44	4.50	4.60	4.68	4.79	4.87
1951	5.06	5.11	5.22	5.38	5.49	5.64	5.82	5.97	6.17	6.33	6.54	6.66
1952	6.80	6.98	7.08	7.17	7.29	7.36	7.40	7.52	7.56	7.62	7.55	7.73
1953	7.74											
1953 ¹	7.79	7.90	8.06	8.11	8.10	8.15	8.12	8.16	8.00	7.86	7.88	7.90
1954	7.77	7.69	7.59	7.40	7.31	7.15	6.98	6.99	6.91	7.04	7.13	7.16
1955	7.09	7.07	7.14	7.10	7.13	7.16	7.21	7.29	7.25	7.43	7.50	7.56
1956	7.59	7.68	7.80	7.92	8.04	7.96						

¹ Data revised January 1953.

TABLE B-2.—*Durable-goods industries, total inventories*—Continued

[Billions of dollars, seasonally adjusted]

	Janu-ary	Feb-ruary	March	April	May	June	July	Au-gust	Sep-tem-ber	Octo-ber	No-vem-ber	De-cem-ber
	Purchased materials (book value)											
1946	3.25	3.29	3.44	3.54	3.57	3.65	3.80	3.94	4.12	4.31	4.46	4.57
1947	4.65	4.81	4.89	4.93	5.07	5.14	5.18	5.20	5.13	5.16	5.14	5.19
1948	5.13	5.16	5.17	5.22	5.28	5.40	5.46	5.47	5.52	5.57	5.66	5.65
1949	5.83	5.84	5.68	5.56	5.38	5.16	5.00	4.93	4.86	4.72	4.60	4.62
1950	4.58	4.62	4.64	4.70	4.80	4.93	5.06	5.20	5.39	5.54	5.82	6.10
1951	6.15	6.27	6.41	6.55	6.70	6.94	7.09	7.20	7.25	7.39	7.42	7.42
1952	7.51	7.56	7.57	7.52	7.41	7.21	7.05	7.09	7.14	7.25	7.29	7.35
1953	7.30											
1953 [1]	7.29	7.23	7.26	7.39	7.63	7.67	7.72	7.92	7.79	7.68	7.62	7.41
1954	7.38	7.25	7.14	7.12	7.13	7.17	7.00	6.89	6.83	6.66	6.65	6.49
1955	6.64	6.62	6.60	6.61	6.64	6.61	6.82	7.02	7.15	7.38	7.33	7.42
1956	7.52	7.71	7.85	8.05	8.13	8.13	8.25	8.17	8.25	8.50	8.63	8.66
1957	8.64	8.72	8.71	8.60	8.49	8.37	8.39	8.38	8.51	8.61	8.57	8.31
1958	8.35	8.29	8.12	7.98	7.76	7.58	7.46	7.44	7.54	7.71	7.64	7.52
1959	7.71	7.84	8.11	8.34	8.52	8.86	8.90	8.74	8.35	8.05	8.11	8.30
1960	8.60	8.67	8.75	8.81	8.80	8.69	8.63	8.56	8.42	8.26	8.05	8.05
1961	8.03	8.01	7.91	7.81	7.78	7.60	7.73					
	Purchased materials (1947 dollars)											
1947				5.10	5.23	5.28	5.30	5.28	5.16	5.13	5.05	5.08
1948	4.98	4.97	4.93	4.92	4.94	5.02	5.05	4.96	4.92	4.88	4.89	4.86
1949	4.97	4.98	4.84	4.76	4.65	4.51	4.42	4.39	4.35	4.23	4.12	4.12
1950	4.07	4.08	4.08	4.11	4.17	4.25	4.33	4.40	4.50	4.57	4.74	4.88
1951	4.84	4.86	4.91	5.00	5.10	5.28	5.40	5.49	5.54	5.64	5.66	5.66
1952	5.73	5.76	5.77	5.72	5.65	5.52	5.41	5.42	5.43	5.48	5.49	5.53
1953	5.49											
1953 [1]	5.48	5.43	5.44	5.52	5.67	5.66	5.65	5.74	5.62	5.52	5.48	5.34
1954	5.33	5.24	5.17	5.16	5.17	5.19	5.05	4.96	4.90	4.76	4.74	4.63
1955	4.72	4.70	4.68	4.66	4.67	4.64	4.74	4.82	4.85	4.94	4.88	4.91
1956	4.94	5.04	5.10	5.20	5.24	5.23						
	Finished goods (book value)											
1946	1.74	2.12	2.21	2.27	2.28	2.37	2.42	2.53	2.63	2.74	2.74	2.77
1947	2.99	3.03	3.19	3.30	3.42	3.58	3.67	3.73	3.81	3.94	4.02	4.00
1948	4.04	4.08	4.13	4.16	4.21	4.20	4.25	4.34	4.44	4.53	4.63	4.77
1949	4.86	4.96	5.02	5.04	5.04	5.04	4.99	4.92	4.82	4.75	4.65	4.70
1950	4.65	4.62	4.64	4.61	4.58	4.64	4.50	4.37	4.34	4.50	4.70	4.70
1951	4.75	4.89	4.96	5.12	5.44	5.76	6.14	6.55	6.72	6.78	6.73	6.80
1952	6.89	6.88	6.92	6.93	6.95	6.89	6.84	6.83	6.82	6.84	6.89	6.92
1953	7.04											
1953 [1]	7.05	7.06	7.10	7.16	7.27	7.38	7.49	7.55	7.85	8.07	8.09	8.10
1954	8.06	8.03	8.07	7.85	7.70	7.56	7.50	7.47	7.48	7.60	7.60	7.75
1955	7.68	7.70	7.73	7.71	7.76	7.83	7.79	7.89	7.85	7.97	7.99	8.16
1956	8.20	8.36	8.40	8.39	8.54	8.65	8.69	8.78	8.87	9.08	9.10	9.22
1957	9.23	9.35	9.43	9.45	9.64	9.73	9.81	9.79	9.86	9.90	9.80	10.11
1958	9.88	9.86	9.84	9.69	9.61	9.54	9.52	9.35	9.20	8.96	8.98	8.99
1959	9.01	9.19	9.30	9.35	9.40	9.47	9.53	9.49	9.52	9.42	9.45	9.71
1960	9.90	10.12	10.36	10.49	10.58	10.74	10.79	10.93	11.03	10.92	10.90	10.76
1961	10.65	10.59	10.49	10.47	10.47	10.57	10.62					
	Finished goods (1947 dollars)											
1947				3.40	3.50	3.65	3.72	3.76	3.82	3.92	3.96	3.92
1948	3.94	3.95	3.98	3.98	4.01	3.98	4.00	4.04	4.09	4.12	4.16	4.26
1949	4.31	4.38	4.42	4.43	4.45	4.48	4.46	4.41	4.33	4.27	4.19	4.24
1950	4.20	4.17	4.18	4.13	4.10	4.13	3.98	3.84	3.77	3.86	3.97	3.91
1951	3.89	3.96	3.98	4.07	4.31	4.56	4.85	5.18	5.32	5.37	5.33	5.38
1952	5.45	5.43	5.46	5.47	5.48	5.44	5.41	5.40	5.39	5.40	5.43	5.46
1953	5.55											
1953 [1]	5.56	5.56	5.59	5.63	5.70	5.76	5.82	5.84	6.05	6.20	6.20	6.21
1954	6.18	6.16	6.19	6.02	5.91	5.80	5.76	5.72	5.72	5.80	5.79	5.90
1955	5.84	5.85	5.90	5.83	5.86	5.94	5.84	5.89	5.81	5.85	5.82	5.91
1956	5.92	6.01	6.01	5.98	6.06	6.12						

[1] Data revised January 1953.

Source: Department of Commerce; deflations by the author.

TABLE B–3.—*Nondurable-goods industries, total inventories*

[Billions of dollars, seasonally adjusted]

	January	February	March	April	May	June	July	August	September	October	November	December
Total inventories (book value)												
1946	9.66	9.91	9.98	10.09	10.25	10.30	10.96	11.34	11.54	12.24	12.43	12.46
1947	12.81	13.05	13.28	13.63	13.78	13.78	13.81	14.00	14.00	14.04	14.38	14.58
1948	14.75	14.87	15.09	15.19	15.46	15.58	15.75	15.82	15.92	16.01	15.95	15.96
1949	15.90	15.85	15.69	15.54	15.46	15.28	15.08	15.02	14.87	14.87	14.85	14.89
1950	15.00	14.97	15.06	15.10	15.17	15.18	15.16	15.36	15.89	16.42	17.08	17.53
1951	18.00	18.23	18.77	19.47	19.69	19.86	20.08	20.20	20.07	20.12	20.07	20.01
1952	20.21	20.19	20.18	20.01	19.73	19.62	19.63	19.58	19.50	19.41	19.48	19.39
1953	19.34											
1953 [1]	19.38	19.34	19.28	19.32	19.43	19.47	19.45	19.58	19.55	19.42	19.35	19.19
1954	19.21	19.16	19.05	19.08	19.06	19.24	19.17	19.01	18.92	19.08	19.14	18.90
1955	19.08	19.06	19.02	19.09	19.22	19.30	19.34	19.54	19.49	19.69	19.69	19.70
1956	19.89	20.11	20.12	20.37	20.58	20.86	21.03	21.26	21.39	21.52	21.56	21.64
1957	21.80	21.96	22.15	22.20	22.34	22.42	22.40	22.46	22.35	22.35	22.36	22.37
1958	22.29	22.18	22.14	22.06	21.92	21.72	21.47	21.36	21.25	21.40	21.42	21.36
1959	21.38	21.51	21.53	21.69	21.86	21.91	21.89	21.97	22.08	22.27	22.28	22.34
1960	22.55	22.64	22.57	22.73	22.88	22.87	22.85	22.90	22.87	22.95	22.93	22.88
1961	22.91	22.95	23.01	23.22	23.22	23.16	23.17					
Total inventories (1947 dollars)												
1947				13.60	13.75	13.91	14.01	14.22	14.19	14.02	14.11	14.11
1948	13.93	14.00	14.23	14.46	14.77	14.99	15.19	15.26	15.45	15.49	15.46	15.50
1949	15.58	15.68	15.66	15.65	15.62	15.64	15.64	15.61	15.60	15.58	15.56	15.65
1950	15.75	15.74	15.71	15.70	15.66	15.65	15.48	15.39	15.63	15.78	16.10	16.21
1951	16.17	16.06	16.25	16.73	17.04	17.34	17.78	18.07	18.23	18.41	18.39	18.33
1952	18.55	18.66	18.69	18.67	18.52	18.48	18.54	18.50	18.51	18.52	18.60	18.63
1953	18.66											
1953 [1]	18.67	18.67	18.59	18.62	18.70	18.76	18.71	18.80	18.71	18.56	18.49	18.36
1954	18.38	18.38	18.17	18.20	18.18	18.36	18.29	18.14	18.04	18.31	18.30	18.11
1955	18.26	18.22	18.19	18.24	18.40	18.46	18.49	18.71	18.68	18.90	18.89	18.92
1956	19.08	19.22	19.17	19.33	19.46	19.65						
Purchased materials (book value)												
1946	4.85	4.98	5.09	5.20	5.31	5.42	5.68	5.89	5.92	6.13	6.26	6.44
1947	6.59	6.65	6.74	6.85	6.92	6.88	6.74	6.74	6.80	6.78	7.03	7.09
1948	7.05	7.10	7.21	7.27	7.38	7.52	7.58	7.54	7.52	7.40	7.21	7.12
1949	7.06	7.00	6.84	6.72	6.66	6.56	6.51	6.48	6.47	6.42	6.44	6.45
1950	6.43	6.42	6.42	6.40	6.42	6.44	6.58	6.84	7.27	7.62	8.01	8.38
1951	8.74	8.99	9.33	9.66	9.64	9.65	9.62	9.57	9.27	9.30	9.12	8.99
1952	9.03	9.02	8.93	8.90	8.89	8.82	8.78	8.67	8.60	8.49	8.52	8.51
1953	8.43											
1953 [1]	8.47	8.42	8.45	8.40	8.46	8.40	8.42	8.35	8.35	8.23	8.22	8.14
1954	8.16	8.00	7.88	7.93	7.95	8.00	8.06	7.95	7.84	7.88	7.96	7.89
1955	7.86	7.79	7.76	7.79	7.95	8.00	7.99	8.07	8.02	8.15	8.17	8.12
1956	8.18	8.20	8.20	8.16	8.31	8.32	8.32	8.42	8.44	8.58	8.57	8.53
1957	8.60	8.70	8.74	8.66	8.85	8.96	8.97	9.02	8.92	8.95	8.92	8.79
1958	8.80	8.81	8.81	8.77	8.80	8.78	8.75	8.71	8.61	8.65	8.59	8.55
1959	8.55	8.63	8.63	8.69	8.85	9.02	9.00	8.95	8.92	8.95	8.93	8.95
1960	9.02	9.08	9.06	9.09	9.13	9.13	9.05	9.02	8.89	8.85	8.78	8.75
1961	8.74	8.68	8.78	8.88	8.97	8.97	8.96					
Purchased materials (1947 dollars)												
1947				6.84	6.89	6.93	6.86	6.90	6.93	6.80	6.90	6.80
1948	6.64	6.67	6.83	6.95	7.07	7.18	7.25	7.27	7.33	7.29	7.15	7.09
1949	7.07	7.04	6.94	6.89	6.88	6.87	6.90	6.93	6.96	6.92	6.96	6.99
1950	6.97	6.94	6.90	6.84	6.82	6.81	6.86	6.99	7.23	7.39	7.56	7.68
1951	7.78	7.77	7.91	8.13	8.15	8.21	8.32	8.45	8.37	8.52	8.44	8.27
1952	8.31	8.33	8.32	8.36	8.44	8.42	8.41	8.32	8.30	8.24	8.30	8.34
1953	8.31											
1953 [1]	8.35	8.33	8.37	8.33	8.40	8.34	8.37	8.30	8.26	8.14	8.12	8.05
1954	8.07	7.88	7.76	7.79	7.80	7.85	7.89	7.78	7.68	7.71	7.80	7.76
1955	7.74	7.66	7.63	7.66	7.83	7.87	7.87	7.98	7.96	8.11	8.12	8.08
1956	8.13	8.12	8.08	7.99	8.08	8.07						

[1] Data revised January 1953.

TABLE B–3.—*Nondurable-goods industries, total inventories*—Continued

[Billions of dollars, seasonally adjusted]

	January	February	March	April	May	June	July	August	September	October	November	December
	Goods-in-prccess (book value)											
1946	1.67	1.63	1.63	1.63	1.72	1.75	1.78	1.75	1.81	1.82	1.77	1.81
1947	1.82	1.84	1.92	1.96	1.96	2.00	2.02	2.10	2.09	2.10	2.16	2.21
1948	2.19	2.24	2.23	2.23	2.26	2.24	2.24	2.30	2.28	2.31	2.32	2.25
1949	2.24	2.22	2.16	2.12	2.12	2.12	2.15	2.14	2.14	2.12	2.10	2.11
1950	2.19	2.18	2.22	2.23	2.22	2.28	2.35	2.39	2.41	2.46	2.50	2.55
1951	2.49	2.52	2.59	2.67	2.70	2.73	2.64	2.58	2.62	2.61	2.68	2.72
1952	2.76	2.75	2.75	2.68	2.63	2.57	2.65	2.72	2.76	2.83	2.79	2.73
1953	2.78											
1953 [1]	2.75	2.83	2.77	2.84	2.86	2.90	2.84	2.82	2.74	2.71	2.66	2.65
1954	2.61	2.61	2.59	2.67	2.65	2.62	2.56	2.57	2.54	2.60	2.68	2.60
1955	2.68	2.68	2.67	2.68	2.71	2.74	2.75	2.85	2.80	2.80	2.83	2.76
1956	2.78	2.80	2.76	2.81	2.83	2.91	2.93	2.93	2.90	2.95	2.94	2.96
1957	3.00	2.97	2.97	2.95	2.95	2.98	2.94	2.97	2.94	2.96	3.00	3.06
1958	2.99	2.97	2.94	2.90	2.92	2.94	2.91	2.96	2.92	2.95	2.96	3.00
1959	3.00	3.01	3.00	3.03	3.02	3.04	3.11	3.08	3.06	3.09	3.07	3.03
1960	3.05	3.05	3.03	3.10	3.13	3.14	3.17	3.17	3.09	3.10	3.14	3.08
1961	3.07	3.04	3.05	3.12	3.20	3.25	3.29					
	Goods-in-process (1947 dollars)											
1947				1.97	1.96	2.01	2.05	2.13	2.12	2.10	2.13	2.14
1948	2.09	2.13	2.12	2.14	2.16	2.14	2.15	2.20	2.19	2.23	2.25	2.19
1949	2.20	2.19	2.16	2.14	2.15	2.17	2.21	2.21	2.23	2.20	2.19	2.21
1950	2.29	2.29	2.31	2.32	2.30	2.35	2.39	2.39	2.36	2.37	2.36	2.36
1951	2.26	2.23	2.26	2.32	2.35	2.39	2.34	2.31	2.38	2.39	2.46	2.50
1952	2.54	2.54	2.55	2.50	2.47	2.42	2.50	2.57	2.61	2.69	2.66	2.62
1953	2.68											
1953 [1]	2.65	2.73	2.67	2.74	2.75	2.79	2.73	2.71	2.62	2.59	2.54	2.54
1954	2.50	2.49	2.48	2.55	2.52	2.50	2.44	2.46	2.42	2.48	2.56	2.50
1955	2.57	2.56	2.56	2.57	2.59	2.62	2.63	2.73	2.68	2.69	2.72	2.66
1956	2.66	2.68	2.63	2.67	2.68	2.75						
	Finished goods (book value)											
1946	3.18	3.32	3.29	3.25	3.26	3.21	3.43	3.65	3.87	4.24	4.34	4.26
1947	4.44	4.56	4.62	4.76	4.89	4.95	5.06	5.13	5.11	5.13	5.14	5.28
1948	5.38	5.42	5.52	5.63	5.78	5.92	6.08	6.09	6.27	6.30	6.37	6.49
1949	6.54	6.62	6.67	6.67	6.60	6.57	6.47	6.40	6.34	6.38	6.32	6.34
1950	6.37	6.40	6.40	6.44	6.45	6.43	6.23	6.11	6.26	6.34	6.56	6.64
1951	6.68	6.71	6.78	7.04	7.34	7.55	7.94	8.12	8.27	8.27	8.25	8.29
1952	8.39	8.45	8.47	8.44	8.22	8.22	8.21	8.20	8.19	8.16	8.18	8.18
1953	8.15											
1953 [1]	8.15	8.09	8.06	8.07	8.10	8.18	8.19	8.40	8.46	8.48	8.47	8.40
1954	8.44	8.55	8.58	8.48	8.46	8.62	8.·56	8.49	8.53	8.61	8.50	8.41
1955	8.53	8.58	8.59	8.61	8.57	8.57	8.60	8.63	8.68	8.74	8.69	8.82
1956	8.93	9.10	9.16	9.40	9.44	9.63	9.78	9.91	10.06	9.99	10.05	10.15
1957	10.21	10.29	10.44	10.59	10.54	10.47	10.48	10.46	10.49	10.44	10.44	10.52
1958	10.50	10.40	10.40	10.40	10.39	10.19	10.00	9.80	9.69	9.72	9.80	9.81
1959	9.83	9.87	'9.90	9.97	10.00	9.86	9.78	9.94	10.10	10.22	10.28	10.36
1960	10.48	10.51	10.48	10.54	10.62	10.60	10.63	10.71	10.89	11.00	11.01	11.05
1961	11.10	11.23	11.18	11.22	11.05	10.94	10.93					
	Finished goods (1947 dollars)											
1947				4.79	4.90	4.97	5.10	5.19	5.14	5.12	5.07	5.17
1948	5.20	5.20	5.28	5.38	5.54	5.66	5.80	5.78	5.93	5.97	6.06	6.21
1949	6.31	6.45	6.56	6.62	6.59	6.60	6.53	6.47	6.42	6.45	6.40	6.45
1950	6.48	6.51	6.50	6.54	6.54	6.49	6.22	6.00	6.03	6.02	6.17	6.18
1951	6.13	6.06	6.07	6.28	6.54	6.74	7.11	7.31	7.48	7.50	7.50	7.56
1952	7.70	7.79	7.82	7.81	7.62	7.64	7.62	7.61	7.60	7.59	7.63	7.67
1953	7.67											
1953 [1]	7.67	7.61	7.56	7.54	7.55	7.63	7.62	7.80	7.82	7.83	7.83	7.77
1954	7.80	7.90	7.94	7.86	7.85	8.01	7.96	7.90	7.94	8.12	7.94	7.86
1955	7.96	7.99	8.00	8.02	7.98	7.96	7.99	8.01	8.05	8.10	8.05	8.19
1956	8.28	8.42	8.46	8.67	8.69	8.84						

[1] Data revised, January 1953.

Source: Department of Commerce; deflations by the author.

TABLE B-4.—*Nonfarm inventory investment*

[Billions of dollars, seasonally adjusted at annual rates]

	Total nonfarm								Total manufacturing							
	Current dollars				1954 dollars				Current dollars				1954 dollars			
	I	II	III	IV	I	II	III	IV	I	II	III	IV	I	II	III	IV
1947	+1.5	+1.5	−0.3	+2.4	+1.4	+1.8	−0.3	+2.9	+1.0	−0.1	+0.9	0	+0.9	0	+1.2	−0.1
1948	+2.3	+2.9	+3.9	+2.8	+1.9	+3.1	+4.1	+3.0	+1.2	+2.2	+2.1	+.7	−.5	+2.3	+2.2	+1.8
1949	+.6	−4.1	−.6	−4.7	+.4	−4.6	−.8	−5.4	+1.5	−2.7	−2.6	−2.2	+1.2	−3.0	−3.1	+6.6
1950	+2.2	+4.2	+3.8	+13.8	+2.4	+4.8	+4.1	+14.5	+4.7	+.9	+.7	+6.5	+1.6	+1.2	+.9	+6.6
1951	+9.3	+14.0	+9.1	+3.8	+9.2	+13.7	+9.2	+3.9	+6.0	+11.1	+11.2	+4.4	+4.7	+10.8	+11.2	+4.1
1952	+4.0	−3.3	+3.4	+4.7	+4.0	−3.3	+3.3	+4.7	+2.5	+1.4	+1.8	+2.0	+6.0	−1.3	−3.2	+2.1
1953	+4.0	+4.0	+1.5	−4.3	+3.2	+4.1	+1.5	−4.1	−3.8	+2.9	+1.5	+2.2	−3.7	+3.0	+3.2	−2.1
1954	−2.8	−3.2	−2.8	+.7	−2.6	−3.4	−2.7	+.7	+.8	−3.9	−3.3	+.6	+4.8	−4.1	−1.8	+.6
1955	+6.0	+5.7	+5.5	+4.1	+3.9	+5.8	+5.4	+6.9	+5.0	+2.4	+3.2	+3.8	+1.9	+2.5	+1.5	+3.7
1956	+6.5	+5.2	+4.4	+4.1	+6.4	+5.0	+4.3	+3.9	+3.6	+4.8	+2.8	+2.4	+4.8	+4.6	+.4	+2.2
1957	−.5	+2.0	+1.5	+2.6	+1.8	+1.7	+1.3	−2.0	−3.6	+5.3	−.4	−3.0	+1.4	+4.4	−1.8	+1.6
1958	+6.9	−5.5	−2.5	+2.3	−5.5	−4.3	−2.1	+2.4	+4.8	+5.8	−2.0	+1.1	−2.9	−4.5	−.5	+3.7
1959	+10.8	+11.6	+.7	+5.5	+9.9	+10.3	+1.0	+5.1	+7.6	+2.0	+.4	+4.0	+4.2	+5.0	+1.8	+3.2
1960	−4.3	+5.1	+2.0	−2.2	−3.5	+4.7	+2.0	−1.3	−.3		+.4	−3.5	+6.9	+1.7	+.5	+2.6
1961													−.1		+.4	

	Durable-goods manufacturing								Nondurable-goods manufacturing							
	Current dollars				1954 dollars				Current dollars				1954 dollars			
	I	II	III	IV	I	II	III	IV	I	II	III	IV	I	II	III	IV
1947	-0.5	+0.6	+1.2	-0.7	-0.7	+0.7	+1.5	-0.9	+1.5	-0.7	-0.3	+0.7	+1.6	-0.7	-0.3	+0.8
1948	-1.2	0	+.3	+.1	-1.6	0	+.4	+.2	+1.2	+2.3	+1.8	+.6	+1.1	+2.3	+1.8	+.6
1949	+.7	-2.1	-2.1	-1.8	+.7	-2.4	-2.8	-2.1	+1.5	-.6	-.4	-.5	+1.5	-.6	-.2	-.5
1950	-.1	+1.6	+1.1	+3.6	-.1	+1.6	+1.2	+3.9	+.6	-.4	-.4	+3.0	+.7	-.5	-.4	+2.9
1951	+3.3	+6.8	+7.6	+3.3	+3.4	+7.1	+8.2	+3.5	+1.5	+4.3	+3.3	-1.1	+1.2	+3.7	+3.0	+.3
1952	+4.1	-.2	+.2	+1.9	+4.3	-.2	+.6	+1.8	+1.8	-1.2	+.2	+.2	+.8	-1.1	-.2	+.3
1953	+2.3	+2.5	+1.7	-1.9	+2.4	+2.6	+1.7	-1.8	+.2	+.4	-.7	-.3	+.2	+.4	-.7	+1.4
1954	-3.2	-4.0	-2.5	+.3	-3.1	-4.1	-2.5	+.3	-.6	0	+1.9	+1.3	-.6	0	+1.3	+.2
1955	+4.3	+1.6	+1.9	+2.5	+3.8	+1.6	+1.8	+2.3	+1.5	+1.5	-.5	0	+1.4	+1.5	-.5	0
1956	+4.0	+3.3	+.9	+2.1	+1.0	+3.1	+.8	+1.9	+.4	-.4	+1.1	+1.2	+.3	-.4	+1.1	+1.6
1957	+1.2	+.9	0	-2.9	+3.8	+.8	0	-2.6	+.3	-1.1	+.3	+1.6	+1.5	-1.0	+1.1	+.4
1958	-3.9	-4.2	-1.5	0	+1.0	-3.5	-1.3	0	+1.3	+1.0	+1.1	+1.6	+1.3	+1.6	+.3	
1959	+3.8	+4.8	-.7	+2.0	-3.3	+4.0	-.6	+1.7	+1.5	+.6	+.3	+.4				
1960	+6.2	+1.3	+.1	+3.8	+3.2	+1.1	+.1	-3.0	+1.4							
1961	-1.6				+5.4											

Source: Department of Commerce, National Income Division.

TABLE B–5.—*Inventory investment: Summary*

[Millions of dollars, seasonally adjusted]

A. TOTAL INVESTMENT

TOTAL MANUFACTURING

	Book value				1947 dollars			
	I	II	III	IV	I	II	III	IV
1946	+880	+1,097	+2,319	+1,771				
1947	+1,877	+1,310	+543	+687			+400	-219
1948	+608	+790	+992	+429	-245	+813	+490	+61
1949	+161	-1,221	-1,295	-478	+229	-409	-548	-362
1950	+328	+559	+1,271	+3,296	-73	+246	+88	+1,366
1951	+2,556	+3,070	+1,971	+904	+478	+2,467	+2,439	+784
1952	+1,117	-607	-171	+645	+960	-204	+100	+456
1953	+232				+417			
1953 [1]	+450	+1,104	+694	-616	+352	+638	+50	-571
1954	-900	-881	-999	+334	-693	-611	-929	+228
1955	+230	+514	+1,133	+1,502	+98	+295	+408	+708
1956	+1,620	+1,641	+1,217	+1,453	+781	+866		
1957	+1,039	+519	+313	-646				
1958	-1,511	-1,763	-950	-117				
1959	+1,275	+1,684	-246	+538				
1960	+1,910	+760	-390	-970				
1961	-430	+40						

DURABLE-GOODS INDUSTRIES

	Book value				1947 dollars			
	I	II	III	IV	I	II	III	IV
1946	+520	+777	+1,087	+846				
1947	+1,058	+813	+323	+107			+124	-138
1948	+90	+306	+654	+389	-363	+57	+30	+9
1949	+424	-813	-879	-495	+65	-383	-516	-410
1950	+156	+438	+557	+1,655	-128	+302	+113	+778
1951	+1,316	+1,981	+1,767	+962	+446	+1,373	+1,548	+685
1952	+951	-55	-51	+761	+604	+7	+62	+338
1953	+454				+403			
1953 [1]	+561	+907	+613	-249	+368	+473	+94	-215
1954	-759	-1,079	-671	+349	-507	-799	-616	+159
1955	+113	+229	+949	+1,289	+24	+26	+181	+466
1956	+1,204	+892	+691	+1,209	+533	+392		
1957	+525	+253	+382	-672				
1958	-1,284	-1,336	-480	-233				
1959	+1,110	+1,302	-410	+263				
1960	+1,690	+460	-390	-980				
1961	-560	-130						

NONDURABLE-GOODS INDUSTRIES

	Book value				1947 dollars			
	I	II	III	IV	I	II	III	IV
1946	+360	+320	+1,232	+925				
1947	+819	+497	+220	+580			+285	-81
1948	+518	+484	+338	+40	+118	+756	+460	+52
1949	-263	-408	-416	+17	+164	-26	-32	+48
1950	+172	+121	+714	+1,641	+55	-56	-25	+588
1951	+1,240	+1,089	+204	-58	+32	+1,094	+891	+99
1952	+166	-552	-120	-116	+356	-211	+38	+118
1953	-223				+14			
1953 [1]	-111	+197	+81	-367	-16	+165	-44	-356
1954	-141	+198	-328	-15	-186	+188	-313	+69
1955	+117	+285	+184	+213	+74	+269	+227	+242
1956	+416	+749	+526	+244	+248	+474		
1957	+514	+266	-69	+26				
1958	-227	-427	-470	+116				
1959	+165	+382	+164	+265				
1960	+230	+300	0	+10				
1961	+130	+170						

[1] Data revised January 1953.

TABLE B-5.—*Inventory investment: Summary*—Continued

[Millions of dollars, seasonally adjusted]

B. PURCHASED-MATERIALS INVESTMENT

TOTAL MANUFACTURING

	Book value				1947 dollars			
	I	II	III	IV	I	II	III	IV
1946	+425	+542	+968	+969				
1947	+613	+407	−78	+329			−122	−204
1948	+95	+553	+135	−286	−122	+442	+46	−296
1949	−308	−749	−361	−277	−166	−401	−80	−189
1950	−43	+315	+1,344	+1,785	−138	+81	+681	+819
1951	+1,231	+841	+14	−142	+207	+667	+418	+28
1952	+49	−469	−232	+97	+150	−156	−198	+138
1953	−40				+40			
1953 [1]	−60	+356	+72	−585	−70	+195	−121	−489
1954	−542	+161	−497	−298	−466	+116	−464	−193
1955	−19	+252	+558	+368	−80	+205	+297	+175
1956	+516	+396	+232	+515	+195	+113		
1957	+258	−120	+93	−333				
1958	−161	−578	−212	−70				
1959	+670	+1,140	−620	−20				
1960	+570	+10	−510	−510				
1961	−100	−130						

DURABLE-GOODS INDUSTRIES

	Book value				1947 dollars			
	I	II	III	IV	I	II	III	IV
1946	+245	+210	+465	+454				
1947	+320	+249	−4	+58			−123	−73
1948	−20	+229	+119	+134	−153	+87	−97	−63
1949	+27	−525	−301	−236	−16	−328	−166	−223
1950	+26	+284	+462	+706	−47	+171	+257	+372
1951	+309	+538	+307	+173	+35	+367	+256	+130
1952	+150	−364	−65	+206	+105	−254	−83	+96
1953	+20				−12			
1953 [1]	−20	+404	+124	−380	−40	+222	−45	−276
1954	−278	+35	−338	−344	−173	+24	−291	−274
1955	+115	+9	+541	+265	+47	−36	+215	+53
1956	+434	+276	+118	+418	+196	+123		
1957	+49	−343	+143	−205				
1958	−184	−548	−40	−20				
1959	+590	+750	−510	−50				
1960	+450	−60	−270	−370				
1961	−140	−310						

NONDURABLE-GOODS INDUSTRIES

	Book value				1947 dollars			
	I	II	III	IV	I	II	III	IV
1946	+184	+331	+498	+522				
1947	+305	+137	−84	+291			+1	−131
1948	+125	+309	+3	−409	+31	+355	+143	−233
1949	−278	−273	−92	−23	−150	−73	+86	+34
1950	−31	+27	+827	+1,107	−91	−90	+424	+447
1951	+947	+320	−372	−282	+232	+300	+162	−102
1952	−59	−111	−219	−92	+45	+98	−115	+42
1953	−39				+52			
1953 [1]	−122	−48	−52	−205	−30	−27	−76	−213
1954	−264	+126	−159	+46	−293	+92	−173	+81
1955	−134	+243	+17	+103	−127	+241	+82	+122
1956	+82	+120	+114	+97	−1	−10		
1957	+209	+223	−50	−128				
1958	+23	−30	−172	−60				
1959	+80	+390	−100	+30				
1960	+110	+60	−240	−140				
1961	+30	+190						

[1] Data revised January 1953.

TABLE B–5.—*Inventory investment: Summary*—Continued

[Millions of dollars, seasonally adjusted]

C. GOODS-IN-PROCESS INVESTMENT

TOTAL MANUFACTURING

	Book value				1947 dollars			
	I	II	III	IV	I	II	III	IV
1946	+234	+510	+430	+252				
1947	+436	+156	+285	+86			+187	−140
1948	−150	+85	+257	+32	−285	−14	+68	−96
1949	−117	−267	−298	−146	−112	−106	−140	−118
1950	+149	+345	+527	+691	+85	+218	+225	+258
1951	+752	+764	+543	+741	+254	+548	+518	+613
1952	+604	+186	+469	+261	+477	+152	+388	+169
1953	+388				+294			
1953 [1]	+486	+858	−141	−207	+362	+204	−309	−193
1954	−508	−583	−327	+481	−370	−417	−312	+323
1955	+88	+187	+442	+690	+35	+88	+151	+289
1956	+521	+514	+344	+498	+216	+270		
1957	+276	+306	+77	−600				
1958	−959	−480	−116	+80				
1959	+180	+430	+80	+100				
1960	+580	+260	−470	−340				
1961	−190	+330						

DURABLE-GOODS INDUSTRIES

	Book value				1947 dollars			
	I	II	III	IV	I	II	III	IV
1946	+100	+399	+360	+254				
1947	+325	+85	+177	−37			+75	−165
1948	−157	+72	+212	+72	−263	−36	+20	−97
1949	−35	−225	−317	−112	−80	−112	−204	−99
1950	+36	+276	+400	+566	−15	+179	+215	+262
1951	+705	+614	+662	+654	+348	+423	+530	+495
1952	+564	+355	+291	+285	+418	+282	+198	+167
1953	+353				+239			
1953 [1]	+431	+229	+12	−113	+298	+84	−147	−104
1954	−449	−608	−250	+416	−309	−441	−237	+251
1955	+20	+121	+384	+720	−26	+27	+88	+315
1956	+528	+361	+357	+441	+239	+156		
1957	+264	+294	+116	−724				
1958	−830	−489	−90	−10				
1959	+200	+380	+60	+130				
1960	+580	+140	−410	−330				
1961	−160	+130						

NONDURABLE-GOODS INDUSTRIES

	Book value				1947 dollars			
	I	II	III	IV	I	II	III	IV
1946	+128	+120	+62	+5				
1947	+109	+74	+98	+119			+112	+25
1948	+18	+13	+41	−38	−22	+22	+48	+1
1949	−82	−47	+27	−32	−32	+6	+64	−19
1950	+105	+62	+133	+136	0	+39	+10	−4
1951	+40	+143	−109	+95	−94	+125	−12	+118
1952	+34	−181	+190	−34	+59	−130	+190	+2
1953	+46				+55			
1953 [1]	+55	+129	−153	−94	+64	+120	−162	−89
1954	−59	+25	−79	+65	−61	+24	−75	+72
1955	+68	+66	+58	−30	+61	+61	+63	−26
1956	−7	+153	−13	−43	−23	+114		
1957	+12	+12	−39	+124				
1958	−129	+9	−26	+80				
1959	0	+40	+20	−30				
1960	0	+110	−50	−10				
1961	−30	+200						

[1] Data revised January 1953.

TABLE B-5.—*Inventory investment: Summary*—Continued

[Millions of dollars, seasonally adjusted]

D. FINISHED GOODS INVESTMENT

TOTAL MANUFACTURING

	Book value				1947 dollars			
	I	II	III	IV	I	II	III	IV
1946	+178	+18	+937	+686	--------	--------	--------	--------
1947	+663	+717	+402	+359	--------	--------	+344	+125
1948	+365	+480	+606	+526	+162	+385	+376	+453
1949	+421	−48	−451	−160	+507	+98	−328	−55
1950	+3	+57	−437	+664	−20	−53	−818	+289
1951	+426	+1,590	+1,708	+16	−43	+1,252	+1,503	+143
1952	+331	−259	−100	+52	+333	−200	−90	+149
1953	+184	--------	--------	--------	+83	--------	--------	--------
1953 [1]	+106	+390	+763	+176	+60	+239	+480	+111
1954	+150	−459	−175	+151	+143	−310	−153	+98
1955	+161	+75	+133	+444	+143	+2	−40	+244
1956	+583	+731	+641	+440	+370	+483	--------	--------
1957	+505	+333	+143	+287	--------	--------	--------	--------
1958	−391	−705	−622	−120	--------	--------	--------	--------
1959	+410	+120	+290	+450	--------	--------	--------	--------
1960	+770	+490	+590	−110	--------	--------	--------	--------
1961	−140	−160	--------	--------	--------	--------	--------	--------

DURABLE-GOODS INDUSTRIES

	Book value				1947 dollars			
	I	II	III	IV	I	II	III	IV
1946	+16	+97	+282	+294	--------	--------	--------	--------
1947	+299	+396	+229	+190	--------	--------	+172	+100
1948	+125	+75	+243	+325	+53	+6	+107	+169
1949	+251	+16	−221	−117	+161	+57	−146	−88
1950	−54	−7	−299	+365	−66	−48	−359	+144
1951	+262	+799	+955	+85	+63	+583	+762	+60
1952	+115	−29	−74	+109	+81	−21	−53	+75
1953	+237	--------	--------	--------	+176	--------	--------	--------
1953 [1]	+150	+274	+477	+244	+110	+167	+286	+165
1954	−32	−506	−85	+277	−25	−382	−88	+182
1955	−22	+99	+24	+304	+3	+35	−122	+98
1956	+242	+255	+216	+350	+98	+113	--------	--------
1957	+212	+302	+123	+257	--------	--------	--------	--------
1958	−270	−299	−350	−210	--------	--------	--------	--------
1959	+310	+170	+50	+190	--------	--------	--------	--------
1960	+650	+380	+290	−270	--------	--------	--------	--------
1961	−270	+80	--------	--------	--------	--------	--------	--------

NONDURABLE-GOODS INDUSTRIES

	Book value				1947 dollars			
	I	II	III	IV	I	II	III	IV
1946	+162	−79	+655	+392	--------	--------	--------	--------
1947	+364	+321	+166	+173	--------	--------	+172	+25
1948	+239	+397	+346	+226	+109	+379	+269	+284
1949	+177	−96	−232	+3	+346	+41	−182	+33
1950	+52	+33	−173	+378	+46	−5	−459	+145
1951	+142	+776	+720	+19	−106	+669	+741	+83
1952	+182	−255	−31	−10	+252	−179	−37	+74
1953	−90	--------	--------	--------	−93	--------	--------	--------
1953 [1]	−44	+166	+286	−68	−50	+72	+194	−54
1954	+182	+47	−90	−126	+168	+72	−65	−84
1955	+183	−24	+109	+140	+140	−33	+82	+146
1956	+341	+476	+425	+90	+272	+370	--------	--------
1957	+293	+31	+20	+30	--------	--------	--------	--------
1958	−121	−406	−272	+90	--------	--------	--------	--------
1959	+90	−40	+240	+260	--------	--------	--------	--------
1960	+120	+120	+290	+160	--------	--------	--------	--------
1961	+130	−240	--------	--------	--------	--------	--------	--------

[1] Data revised, January 1953.

Source: Department of Commerce; deflations by the author.

Index

Abramovitz, Moses, 1, 4, 6n, 7n, 15n, 26n, 27n, 61n, 62n, 63n, 64n, 73n, 79n
estimates of:
  finished goods, 25-26, 61-65, 71-73, 79, 83, 108-109
  goods in process, 25-26, 85-86, 95-99, 109
  inventories, 2, 17, 19-20, 110
  inventory investment, 9, 15, 109
  manufacturers stock to output ratios, 15
  purchased materials, 3, 25-28, 27n, 30, 40-41, 58, 108-109

Barger, Harold, 115
Burns, A. F., 115n

Consumption, relation of, to cycles, 114-115
Continuous and discontinuous process operations in industry, 4, 96-97, 99

Deflation procedure, 128-131
Duesenberry, J. S., 115n
Durable goods, *see* comprehensive series for each stage of fabrication

Eckstein, Otto, 115n

Fanell, M. J., 115n
Ferber, Robert, 115n
Final purchases, 7-10, 116-123, 127
Finished goods inventories, 1
composition of, 61-64
comprehensive series for, 2, 25-26, 133, 135, 137
  timing comparisons in, 3, 66-69, 101-106

Finished goods inventories, (cont.)
demand-dominated, 61-64
industry series of, timing comparisons for, 65-66, 68-69, 95
made to order goods, 61-63, 83
made to stock goods, 61, 63-64, 83
perishables, 61-63
staples, 61-63
staples, made to stock, 3, 64, 69-76, 83
  timing comparisons for, 3, 64-66
supply-dominated, 61-64
Finished goods inventory investment:
comprehensive series for, 143
  cyclical amplitude in, 82-83, 107-108
  timing comparisons for, 3, 79-82, 101-106
industry series of, 80, 82-83
staples, made to stock, 70-71, 74-76, 83
timing of, to rates of change in activity, 71-74, 76-78
Friedman, Milton, 115n
Fromm, Gary, 115n

Korean war:
influence of, on investment and accumulation, 11-12, 46, 55
subcycle reference turns of, 20, 29, 33, 38, 80, 81n, 95
Kuznets, Simon, 6n, 7n, 9n, 15

Mack, Ruth, 20n, 54n, 124n
Manufacturers' inventory investment, *see* Inventory investment, manufacturers'

144